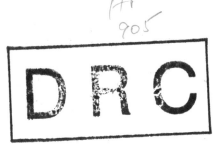

WOMEN AS PRODUCERS AND CONSUMERS OF TOURISM IN DEVELOPING REGIONS

WOMEN AS PRODUCERS AND CONSUMERS OF TOURISM IN DEVELOPING REGIONS

Edited by Yorghos Apostolopoulos,
Sevil Sönmez, and Dallen J. Timothy

Foreword by Linda K. Richter

PRAEGER

Westport, Connecticut
London

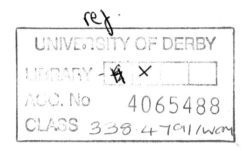
Library of Congress Cataloging-in-Publication Data

Women as producers and consumers of tourism in developing regions / edited by Yorghos
Apostolopoulos, Sevil Sönmez, and Dallen J. Timothy ; foreword by Linda K. Richter.
    p.   cm.
    Includes bibliographical references and index.
    ISBN 0–275–96397–7 (alk. paper)
    1. Tourism—Developing countries. 2. Women travelers—Developing countries. 3.
Women—Employment—Developing countries. 4. Women in development—Developing
countries. I. Apostolopoulos, Yorghos. II. Sönmez, Sevil F. III. Timothy, Dallen J.
G155.D44W64 2001
338.4′79104—dc21   00–052861

British Library Cataloguing in Publication Data is available.

Library of Congress Catalog Card Number: 00–052861
ISBN: 0–275–96397–7

First published in 2001

Praeger Publishers, 88 Post Road West, Westport, CT 06881
An imprint of Greenwood Publishing Group, Inc.
www.praeger.com

Printed in the United States of America

The paper used in this book complies with the
Permanent Paper Standard issued by the National
Information Standards Organization (Z39.48–1984).

10 9 8 7 6 5 4 3 2

Contents

Tables

Foreword

Linda K. Richter

Readers of this fine volume are in for a treat. It is an excellent introduction to the outpouring of new research examining women's tourism roles in developing countries. It also points out how much we don't know about those relationships in the context of particular political systems and regions. The studies include not only the descriptive situation and development theories, but also specific case studies of strategies and policies. These may serve as examples to insure more participation in and control of tourism by women as both producers and consumers.

Given the fact that tourism is the world's largest industry and women make up more than half the globe's people, it is striking that scholarly studies of tourism in general are largely drawn from the last quarter century. Academic research on the linkages between gender and tourism are of even more recent vintage, largely from the last decade. Nearly thirty years ago Valene Smith wrote of American woman as the "tastemakers" of tourism, choosing family destinations and planning tourism activities. Since then, market research has explored gendered decision making, but only rarely and recently have women's lives been evaluated in terms of tourism.

This volume illustrates how much more complex and multifaceted those impacts have been—and we're only beginning to assess the effects in most societies, as these authors acknowledge. While travel writing has chronicled the adventures of women tourists, the overall tone has been their "exceptionalist" experiences in moving beyond the expectations of society, including those of their publishers and biographers! The few women travel consumers were highlighted; the women in gendered societies that hosted them at home or abroad were rarely acknowledged. Such travelers were scarcely representative of their gender, race, or class but their examples do suggest the eagerness of those who could to move out of the gendered boxes in which they were often put.

The engaging and diverse group of authors range widely in their consideration of this topic. They cover most of the developing world. Their methodologies vary from the theoretical to comparative, mountain tourism study to a variety of case studies. Focused on developing nations, it is not surprising that they find much more evidence for the role women play as producers and service providers in the tourist economy than as consumers.

Few citizens in developing nations beyond the elite travel for religious purposes. Indeed, only 7 percent of the world ever travels internationally. As one author put it in the context of Central and Eastern Europe, "a dollar curtain has replaced the Iron Curtain." Poverty and lack of foreign exchange impacts those in all developing countries. In most such nations, women's tourism activities as producers or even tourists are built around an extension of their gendered family roles.

A strength of this collection is that while it includes regional contexts, the authors are not content only to generalize, but rather offer culture-specific analyses that probe the similarities and differences in women's opportunities and constraints as a consequence of tourism. Especially useful, given the dearth of research on women and tourism, this volume includes some provocative and creative speculation about the applicability of development and feminist theories to the exploration of women as producers and consumers of tourism.

As a political scientist, I was struck by the rapid and varied transitions that impacted women as a consequence of the move away from communist-style regimes in Eastern and Central Europe, from military regimes in Latin America, from decolonization in the Caribbean and South Pacific, and toward structural market reform in Southeast Asia.

In each of these regions women's tourism roles reflect familial patterns that are based on the decline of agriculture and the search for employment in the city—by the men in Africa and Eastern Europe, and disproportionately by the women in Latin America. In the Middle East, South Pacific, or in rural mountain regions, gender dictates tourism activities, albeit in the context of the extended family.

This book details how far we've come and suggests how far we need to go in coming to an understanding of women as producers and consumers of tourism. It also refines variables like sex tourism that have been applied to everything from sexual slavery, to prostitution, to consensual albeit transient "romance."

Finally, the book includes numerous examples of how tourism and nongovernmental organizations, international aid, and donor nations are beginning to develop policies that make a difference in the lives of some women tourism producers. Some are premised on the Grameen Bank model of microloans pioneered in Bangladesh. For people interested in the empowerment of women in developing societies, this book provides some needed optimism for tourism's potential contribution to that process.

Preface

The inspiration for this book came from our common interest in tourism's role in the socioeconomic development of developing regions. Our involvement with other tourism projects focusing on the Mediterranean, Indonesia, and the Caribbean, fueled by our strong interest in the role of women in tourism development and their dual (often informal) roles as tourism producers and consumers, heightened our interest in such an endeavor. Our engagement in the foregoing projects brought to the fore such issues as sustainable development, socioeconomic inequality, marginalization of people, gendered development, prostitution and tourism, restructuring and globalization, tourist migration, and public health, to mention a few, which stimulated our initial ideas even further. We then felt confident that the time was ripe for a collective book that would unite a multidisciplinary group of scholars, educators, and international experts in the task of discussing women's roles as tourism producers and consumers in developing regions.

We strongly believe that if tourism development is to be successful in developing areas, the governments of those regions must actively facilitate the expansion of women's roles in such development in an institutional and systematic rather than an opportunistic and accidental manner. The association between economic, cultural, political, and gender issues must be thoroughly understood—hence the need for the diverse backgrounds of the contributors. By its nature, a comparative approach (although long overdue) has inherent theoretical and conceptual dangers because it focuses on diverse regions such as Africa, the Caribbean, Latin America, the Middle East, Southeast Asia, the South Pacific, and the former communist European countries. Despite inevitable flaws or omissions, as this volume constitutes the first comprehensive effort to examine the role of women as tourism producers and consumers in developing regions, it is our hope that it will be the catalyst to fill this gap in the comparative development literature.

The book, in over two years from inception to publication, has triumphed over numerous difficulties and has undergone a number of phases. This volume is the fruit of the collective effort of all individuals and organizations involved. It was a great challenge to locate, commission, and coordinate high-caliber international scholars in gender, development, and tourism. The review and revision process became a highly enjoyable task, due not only to the excellence of their work and their expertise in the topic, but also to their cooperation and patience.

We would like to thank the contributors to the volume for their superb work and dedication, and Linda K. Richter for her kind foreword. We are grateful to Janet Soper and Mary Fran Draisker for their invaluable assistance with the production and editing of this volume. We thank Alan Sturmer for his support of the book from its idea stage and for being instrumental in Greenwood's acceptance of the proposal. Last but certainly not least, we wish to express our deep appreciation to Hilary Claggett, senior editor at Greenwood, for her encouragement, guidance, patience, creativity, and endless support throughout the project.

Part I

PERSPECTIVES ON GENDER,
TOURISM, AND DEVELOPMENT

1

Working Producers, Leisured Consumers: Women's Experiences in Developing Regions

Yorghos Apostolopoulos and Sevil Sönmez

TOURISM IN DEVELOPING REGIONS

As one of the oldest commercial enterprises, tourism has become the world's largest industry, surpassing both international oil and arms sales. The current prominence of tourism in the global marketplace has been largely the result of post–World War II affluence and increased leisure among the populations of the Western world, advances in relevant technologies, and a marked decline in the relative cost of travel. The growth and confluence of mutually beneficial industries (i.e., airlines, tour operators, travel agents, hotel chains)—acting in conjunction with receptive governments—have produced a vast array of touristic opportunities for the contemporary traveler, as well as the promise of lucrative investment for developing regions. As they restructure and attempt to diversify their economies, developing areas of the world, such as Africa, the Caribbean, Latin America, the Middle East, Southeast Asia, the South Pacific, and the former communist European countries, have been particularly eager to reap the foreign exchange, investment, income, and employment dividends that tourism promises. The appeal of fast returns from international mass tourism is especially tempting for developing countries, which are often characterized by low GDPs, weak economies, low socioeconomic indicators, inadequate employment opportunities, and insufficient resources (Mowforth and Munt 1997). Tourism, perceived as both less demanding in terms of infrastructural start-up requirements and as a "clean" industry, has become one of national and local governments' favorite tools for developing economically depressed regions. Consequently, the "exotic" holiday spent in less-traveled parts of the world has become the vacation of choice within the conventional mass tourist market.

Today, many developing regions that have been transformed into popular mass tourist destinations enjoy flourishing tourism sectors. Moreover, in those locations particularly constrained by extreme resource scarcity and few viable alternatives (i.e., the insular Caribbean or the South Pacific), development has become coterminous with tourism dependence (Apostolopoulos and Gayle 2001). In fact, in the Caribbean, South Pacific, and Southeast Asia, tourism has undergone significant "maturity" and already represents a major portion of export receipts (Hall 1994; Apostolopoulos and Gayle 2001). At the other end of the spectrum, in many areas of the diverse and vast regions of Latin America, the Middle East, Africa, and the former communist world in Europe, which have relatively underdeveloped tourist markets, tourism has either recently started to spearhead the economic base or is still in the early stages of development (World Tourism Organization 2000). With close geographic and long-term commercial access to the lucrative origin and investment markets of the developed world, visitor densities in these seven regions have risen significantly (albeit, in a very polarized manner) as a result of a tripartite policy of aggressive promotion, aid-financed infrastructure, and foreign capital attracted by generous tax breaks—and the prospects are even more optimistic (World Tourism Organization 2000).

After long periods of entrenched tourism policy and subsequent growth, the results in most developing regions are mixed (Mowforth and Munt 1997). Rising levels of visitors have burdened infrastructures, caused intense crowding, increased pollution, and utility breakdowns, and have produced marked alterations in fragile marine and terrestrial ecosystems (Apostolopoulos and Gayle 2001). Pristine amenities have been irreversibly damaged by hotel and marina construction and heavy cruise-ship traffic, particularly along delicate coastlines where large-scale infrastructural projects and resorts have been sited (Ioannides, Apostolopoulos, and Sönmez 2001). Added to a host of other economic distortions (e.g., inflation, dualistic development, foreign exchange leakages), tourism has allegedly caused widespread cultural losses and commoditization, demonstration effects, disruptive occupation shifts, and population displacement and substitutions that threaten the traditional cultural genius of several locations in the developing regions (Brohman 1996). The growing overdependence of developing regions on the tourism sector, as well as the aforementioned (often unforeseen) intrusions, have challenged the long-term viability of contemporary mass tourism in developing economies and spawned the search for more compatible and sustainable forms of tourism development.

PRODUCTION AND CONSUMPTION OF TOURISM: GENDERED EXPERIENCES

The sociocultural and economic divide between the tourist and the tourism worker, especially in the context of developing economies, is particularly acute. Not only do the two groups often hold sharply differing mores and behavioral standards, but these differences become more pronounced when inequalities of income and class are factored into the scenario. The tourism sector is characterized by further divisions between hosts (working producers) and guests (leisured con-sumers), and between the workers themselves, especially along the lines of gender and race. "Women are involved differently than men in both the production and consumption of tourism and so they are likely to be impacted differently" (Cukier, Norris, and Wall 1996, 250). Women, especially in developing regions, are further likely to experience tourism differently due to their positions in their respective sociocultural and socioeconomic environments.

The growing feminist scholarship in tourism (Aitchison 1996; Craik 1997; Davidson 1996; Deem 1992; Kinnaird and Hall 1994, 1996; Norris and Wall 1994; Richter 1994; Small 1999; Swain 1995) examines tourism from a gender-power relationship standpoint, placing women in the roles of tourism producers (employees in the tourist industry), tourism consumers (tourists), and residents of the receiving regions who are not directly involved in tourism. It has been argued that women are exploited by global capitalism's patriarchal drive and that tourism producers and consumers alike live in a gendered world where specific gendered contexts cause different tourism impacts (Enloe 1989). "Gender underlies political relations and power allocations in the household, community, and societal levels; is expressed in motivations, desires, traditions and perceptions; and is therefore a factor in all tourism development and underdevelopment" (Swain 1995, 251). Such divisions are significant not only for the operation of tourism but also for the relative incomes, status, and power of those involved in it. Therefore, following the lead of the literature on gender and development, it is important to examine tourism as a tool of economic development from a gender perspective (Swain 1995). A better understanding is needed about whether tourism enhances or diminishes women's status and whether it has different consequences for social and domestic lives of women compared to those of men. Tourism involves processes that are constructed out of "complex and varied social realities and relations that are often hierarchical and unequal" (Kinnaird, Kothari, and Hall 1994, 6). As a result, there are visible differences in how women and men are involved in the production and consumption of tourism. Just as particular stereotypes and hierarchies shape tourism in those societies where modernization and global capitalism converge with religion, culture, and history, gendered realities influence tourism marketing, travelers' motives, and the actions of the host community (Swain 1995). The gender discussion of the present book emanates from the perspective on gender as defined by the expression of masculine and feminine ideologies and societally and culturally constructed identities and their interplay with socially structured relationships involving power between the sexes, divisions of labor and leisure, and sexuality (Kempadoo 1999; Momsen and Kinnaird 1995; Swain 1995).

Along with other positive influences, proponents of tourism often attribute to the industry the power to integrate various underprivileged subgroups into the mainstream economy through tourism employment. Low-skilled tourism jobs, in particular, are often viewed as good work opportunities for women and ethnic minorities (Jafari 1973). Champions of tourism also believe that such economic development will lead to an "improved status and standard of living for women as they learn new skills, develop their human capital, and take increasing advantage of new wage opportunities" (Elliott 1977, cited in Levy and Lerch 1991, 70). In turn, this type of development is expected to have a positive impact on women's economic, social, and political participation in society (Levy and Lerch 1991), just as improvements in women's lives are assumed to be by-products of overall national development (Duley and Diduk 1986). Conversely, critics of tourism argue that while locals may benefit at first, tourism ultimately reinforces traditional class structures because tourism employment reflects the existing social stratification (de Kadt 1979, cited in Levy and Lerch 1991), and suggest that "women's status in particular may be eroded rather than enhanced by development" (Boserup 1970, cited in Levy and Lerch 1991, 70). While employment in multinational organizations may sometimes give women access to above-average wages and better working conditions, such employment is "often accompanied by exploitation in a labor market based on patriarchal labor relations" (Lim 1983, cited in Levy and Lerch 1991, 70). For women, tourism employment is often compared to a pyramid, with many working in seasonal, part-time, lower-skilled, and lower-paying jobs at the bottom and few in well-paid, skilled, and managerial positions at the top (Jordan 1997; Richter 1994). Even in developed nations, women often work as flight attendants, chambermaids, cooks, servers, and commercial sex workers, positions that often parallel their social roles as caregivers and societally accepted feminine characteristics. In the developing regions, where women's social roles are hierarchically lower and they often work as low-paid domestics, service employees, handicraft producers, and prostitutes, women's economic contribution becomes peripheral to the mainstream, as men are favored to assume the better jobs (Tiano 1987; Ward 1984). In this framework, as capitalist development enhances men's position relative to women's (Fernandez-Kelly 1986), women may experience increasing dependence on men for their livelihood (Tiano 1987). As an example, in her study of social change on the West Indian island of Curaçao, Abraham-VanDerMark (1983) found that as women's work changed from agriculture to manufacturing to service (including tourism), their social position evolved from one of relative autonomy to one of greater dependency on men because of job insecurity and men's control of the workplace. Viewed from this perspective, tourism as a factor in economic development may be another example of international dependency for both men and women (Kousis 1996), "but for women it may mean double jeopardy—additional dependence on men as well as on the multinationals" (Levy and Lerch 1991, 70–71).

Challenges women face in developing regions—not only as working producers but also as leisured consumers—are likely to far exceed those of their counterparts in the more developed nations. Even though the travel behavior of women reflects their respective societal norms and values, cultural or religious restrictions pertaining to their societal roles and socioeconomic limitations are likely to determine their travel abilities and style. From the Roman Empire to the eighteenth century European grand tour to the rise of modern mass tourism, travel for pleasure and adventure has been profoundly gendered. The role of women as leisured consumers has been determined by traditional gender distinctions, promoting the image of men as travelers and women as hostesses (Leontidou 1994). Especially since "being feminine has been defined as sticking close to home" (Enloe 1989, 21) in so many societies, women travelers have historically battled societal restrictions, disapproval, and tarnished reputations. Nevertheless, Victorian female travelers ventured to foreign lands in the eighteenth and nineteenth centuries undaunted by societal perceptions of them as "eccentric," leaving behind an important legacy of courage and daring by chronicling their experiences. Spirited women, who continued to travel into the twentieth century in search of identity, paved the way for social acceptance of women's travel. Today, female travelers—originating primarily from developed nations and socioeconomic classes with discretionary time and money—comprise significant percentages of overall business and leisure travelers and enjoy unparalleled freedoms compared with earlier generations of women. Travel provides the opportunity for women to achieve self-realization and to expand their societal roles to encompass new gender identities (Pruitt and Lafont 1995). Socioeconomic constraints as well as societal barriers prevent the majority of women in developing regions from traveling. In fact, as examples in the following chapters illustrate, for the majority of women in most developing societies, pleasure travel remains a remote possibility and one that leaves little room for self-expression or self-determination, even at the dawn of the twenty-first century.

THEMES AND ORGANIZATION OF THE BOOK

There are few areas in the world where travel and tourism have so extensively affected policy making, employment, culture, natural resources, and the balance of payments as in the developing regions of the Caribbean, South Pacific, and Southeast Asia. However, the dynamics and prospects of tourism development in Latin America, the Middle East, Africa, and the former communist world are beginning to mirror that of the aforementioned regions. Therefore, it becomes imperative that the tourism industries of developing nations and their immense effect on women's roles as both working producers and leisured consumers of tourism be evaluated and critically examined.

In contrast to the rich literature on women and development, the international English literature on the role of women and tourism is limited. There are several books on gender issues in developing areas, but only three edited volumes are currently available that concentrate specifically on women and tourism: *Sun, Sex, and Gold* (Kempadoo 1999), *Gender, Work and Tourism* (Sinclair 1997), and *Tourism: A Gender Analysis* (Kinnaird and Hall 1994). The most recent, Kempadoo's volume, examines Caribbean women's role in sex tourism from perspectives of globalization, race, and human rights. Sinclair's book links theoretical literature on gender and work with actual examples of women's role in tourism employment in the United Kingdom, Northern Cyprus, Bali, Mexico, the Philippines, and Japan, and also examines representations of women in tourism brochures. Kinnaird and Hall's volume presents case studies of gender and tourism employment in Southwest England, the Republic of Ireland, Greece, the Caribbean, Western Samoa, and Southeast Asia, and also touches upon women travelers. In addition, the special issue of *Annals of Tourism Research* (Swain 1995) devoted to gender and tourism represents an important contribution to the topic and includes a variety of insightful articles and research notes on women's role in tourism employment, women's tourism cooperatives, representations of women in tourism marketing, and commercial sex tourism. Finally, there are a small number of individual chapters and journal articles that focus on gender and tourism.

This volume is intended to set the stage for filling a significant literature gap by initiating a comparative examination of developing regions in order to provide a comprehensive picture of the role of women as both users and suppliers of tourism services in these regions by integrating the relatively unrelated literatures on tourism, development, and gender. The book delves into the identification and analysis of recent tourism trends in the foregoing developing regions, provides a wide-ranging synthesis of the nature and effects of gender structuring in tourism and the progress made in women's role as tourism producers, examines how women of developing regions as well as women guests consume tourism, and provides a discussion on the policy changes needed for confronting inequalities and achieving an equitable treatment of women in the tourism sectors of developing regions. In addition, efforts were made to provide chapters that go beyond mere description of the significant issues pertinent to women in these regions to provide critical analyses of the dynamics, effects, marketing, and management of tourism development in these areas. In doing so, it is hoped that this book will be utilized for its potential contribution not only to debates over development in the discussed regions, but also to dialogue on tourism and gender relations in the global context. The text should also serve as a catalyst for further research and scholarship on women and tourism in these seven broad developing regions and their respective countries, as well as in other areas of the world. The eleven chapters contained within are original works written specifically for this anthology, comprising an interdisciplinary volume from the perspectives of sociology, geography, anthropology, political science, economics, management, international relations, tourism studies, and women's studies.

The book is divided into four interdependent parts. Part I, Perspectives on Gender, Tourism, and Development, includes two chapters and provides an overview of tourism development in developing regions, women's roles within as both leisured consumers and as working producers, and gender theories. Part II, Women in the Mature Tourist Destinations, includes three chapters and focuses on the unique features of women in the mature tourist destinations of the Caribbean, the South Pacific, and Southeast Asia. Part III, Women in the Less Developed Tourist Destinations, includes four chapters and focuses on how women use and supply tourism services in Latin America, Africa, the Middle East, and the former communist world. Finally, Part IV, Women and Tourism: New Directions, includes two chapters and presents various policy recommendations and a range of conceptual models for the study of tourism and gender issues.

This first chapter presents an overview of tourism in developing regions, especially with regard to their characteristics and need for tourism, as well as the impacts of tourism and women's roles. In the second chapter, Gibson points to the paucity of attention gender issues have received in tourism studies. She synthesizes recent literature, which has reversed the trend and adopted a gender analysis of tourism, and examines these works from a theoretical perspective. Gibson's synthesis concentrates on the three areas of gendered tourists, gendered hosts, and tourism as gendered construction. A discussion of gendered tourists and preferred travel styles and patterns incorporates the relevance of, among other things, cultural and societal environments, social class, employment status, family life-cycle stage, age, lifestyle characteristics, and safety. The work opportunities and career trajectories of women tourism producers or gendered hosts are most influenced by the sexual division of labor, the traditional social practices determining gender roles, and societal and cultural norms and values. The chapter concludes with an analysis of the gendered construction of tourism, focusing on gendered and sexualized representations in tourism marketing.

In Chapter 3, Cohen examines Caribbean women as tourism producers with a heavy emphasis on the British Virgin Islands (BVI). The author begins the chapter with an overview of tourism in the Caribbean and of tourism development in the BVI. Even though the growth in Caribbean tourism has generally resulted in infrastructural developments and increases in national incomes, local participation in the industry's profits is limited and vast sectors of the region's tourist industry are controlled by foreign interests. Caribbean women's participation in tourism has been shaped largely by their societal roles. Those traditionally involved in craft work or market activity move into the tourist economy as vendors or producers of tourist crafts. Women also run guesthouses or own and operate small restaurants; the majority of women, however, hold low-paying, low-skilled positions. The author refers to the link between tourism development and BVI nationalism and women's role in both as producers of cultural products, events, and ideals. Cohen also explores the ideology of sexual difference underlying BVI representations and links between such representations as a place of erotic attraction; Western female tourists who travel to the Caribbean in search of romance and sexual encounters with local men are discussed to illustrate. The chapter concludes with an appraisal of the ways in which the discourse of heterosexual desire eroticizes and commoditizes the natural beauty of the BVI for Western consumption. It is interesting to note that from Cohen's case study,

BVI women emerge more economically and politically empowered than their sisters elsewhere, in their positions as high government officials, educators, and top tourism administrators. The BVI represents almost a contradiction considering the socioeconomic development levels of the majority of the Caribbean and societal roles of women.

Kindon, in the fourth chapter, makes observations about women's role in tourism in Southeast Asia, with special attention to the Philippines, Indonesia, and Thailand. Kindon brings into the discussion the maturity of Southeastern Asia as a destination region, while accepting that member countries are at differing stages of the tourism development cycle. Within the construction of maturity, women predominate in the informal economic sectors or as unpaid labor in family enterprises, reaffirming traditional cultural values, while men are more active participants in the formal sector. As for the relatively small percentage of women working in the formal sector, they generally form the majority of low-level, low-skilled workers. Kindon addresses the position of women in the commercial sex industry of Southeast Asia as deviant tourism production. While women's relatively high status in Southeastern Asia is considered a strength of regional cultural diversity, there is a greater degree of gender equality at the local level than at the national level, where struggles to create more uniform gender images are emerging. Women in the region are faced with the challenge of reworking cultural meanings associated with femininity and masculinity. Kindon suggests recalibrating the concept of destination maturity in order to renegotiate women's roles in acceptable society.

In Chapter 5, with a special focus on Melanesia and Polynesia, Berno and Jones examine women's role in tourism in the South Pacific. They contrast stereotypical representations of women in tourism marketing efforts, often scantily clad and passive, with their actual tourism roles. Since the early days of exploration and colonization in the region, the romantization of women by outsiders and domestication by locals have created and reinforced the "exotic otherness" of women. As a result, women are viewed in the unidimensional role of service provider with an implicit suggestion that the view of service can be extended to the fulfillment of sexual fantasies. The authors imply that the potential for South Pacific women to diversify their current economic activities in order to improve their living standards can be seriously challenged by the region's inability to address power relations between the genders that can limit women's opportunities and the inability to deal with strong collective social structures inherent in the region to ensure an equitable distribution of tourism benefits. Recommendations are made to accelerate effort at the policy, planning, and management levels as a means of verification, so that impacts of tourism development can be monitored from a gender perspective.

In Chapter 6, Sönmez examines the position of women in economic development in the Middle Eastern, North African, and Arabian Peninsula countries. More specifically, women's roles as tourism producers and consumers in Middle Eastern society are discussed within the framework of Islam and regional culture. Although Islam affords women numerous rights and privileges, it often becomes the reason for the repression and often oppression of the region's women, when in fact the primary explanation is rooted in a predominantly patriarchal Middle Eastern society that blatantly misinterprets the religion's dictates. Aside from a few exceptions and despite a diverse cultural mosaic, in the majority of the Middle East women play limited roles in economic and political spheres. Traditional norms and values not only severely restrict women's travel behaviors to those including "purposeful" travel, religious travel, and travel with family or acceptable companions, they influence the employment choices they are able to make. The service nature of tourism employment and the unavoidable contact with strangers further limits the types of jobs women are able to accept. As Middle Eastern countries face the threat of being marginalized in the era of globalization and as Islamic fundamentalism sweeps across the region's countries, the full economic and political empowerment of women becomes a more distant reality.

The intersection of gender and tourism in Latin America is explored in Chapter 7, with a special focus on Brazil, Venezuela, Mexico, and Peru, while comparisons are made between Latin America and the Caribbean. Casellas and Holcomb's discussion of the different economic impacts of tourism for men and women as well as their gendered roles is placed in the context of conventional gender roles and recent economic trends in Latin America. The authors' examination of tourism marketing materials targeting tourists in North America and Spain reveal stereotypical depictions of local women in colorful native dress, in the company of other women or children, in a market, or making handicrafts—images often distant from regional women's real lives. Further, the authors explore connections between perspectives of ecotourism—one of Latin America's fastest growing tourism segments—and *ecofeminism*. Both claim harmony with nature and support of indigenous peoples. The authors suggest that ecotourism is more a "feminist" concept than mass tourism. The chapter concludes with a discussion of the possibilities for the tourist industry to have significant repercussions on Latin American women's lives in the coming years.

In Chapter 8, Dieke explores the involvement of African women in the tourism sector in the context of Africa's socioeconomic development problems and recent economic trends. African women's full potential is inhibited by various gender disparities resulting from the consequences of educational, institutional, legal, and other societal structures, including access to capital. Such imbalances are reflected not only in the maintenance of women's traditional roles of childbearing but also as discrimination in the workplace. Tourism has been recognized as a major economic force in Africa's development, although it has not properly utilized the resource of women. The industry has the potential to provide African women with employment opportunities, even if mostly in the informal sectors of souvenir stores and craft production. Such opportunities can provide women with greater degrees of autonomy and independence. Dieke argues that women's position in African society cannot be changed without transforming existing gender relations. Further, he suggests that tourism development in Africa would benefit greatly from a sustained program aimed at eliminating the major barriers to realizing women's full potential, including the development of national policies and strategies to ensure equal work and equal terms for males and females.

Women's participation in the tourism industries of the former communist societies of Central and Eastern Europe is discussed in Chapter 9. Hall provides a wide range of evidence to suggest that women in the post-communist states of Central and Eastern Europe are disadvantaged in their roles of tourism producers and consumers compared with men. This is primarily attributed to the removal of status equality and social-welfare provisions, which existed to support women in employment under communism. In addition, foreign ownership of tourism businesses that demonstrate little regard for the social welfare of employees of either gender is credited with creating problems of employment gender inequalities. Hall suggests that the gender-role polarization in tourism consumption is demonstrated by the different roles of men and women: men travel, drive, and are in control and women undertake the repetitive domestic chores of tending to children, cooking, and cleaning. Further, Hall draws attention to challenges faced by tourism consumers as a result of the paradox of post-socialist freedoms and individuals' financial restrictions. Finally, the chapter argues that if Central and Eastern Europe's economic and social potential are to be realized, certain measures need to be taken to improve women's employment status, including improved methods for collecting data pertaining to women's issues, encouragement of women's entrepreneurial activity, and assertiveness and leadership training for women.

In Chapter 10, Walker, Valaoras, Gurung, and Godde examine women producers and consumers in the context of small-scale mountain tourism, with special emphasis on Nepal, Mexico, and Greece. Regionally, mountains constitute a significant portion of the world's developing regions. Despite many resources they provide, locals' access to health, education, and information is limited due to isolation. The isolation has also restricted development and helped to maintain cultural norms, increasing their attraction to tourists. The authors suggest that women in mountain villages have long been engaged in tourism that overlaps with their domestic responsibilities; they cook meals, provide hospitality, and are often responsible for the care of tourists. In Nepal, while clear gender roles and division of labor dictate daily life, social class often determines types of tourism-related jobs. Women from the lower castes do cooking and cleaning for trekkers, while those from upper castes run lodges and teashops. The second and third case studies illustrate women's establishment of cooperatives to pool resources and distribute economic benefits: Mexican women's cooperatives have included restaurants and nurseries and Greek women's cooperatives have been linked to agrotourism. The chapter includes a discussion of the constraints and opportunities for integrating women in mountain tourism production and concludes with recommendations for policy, practice, and research in the same area.

In the final chapter, Timothy provides an overview of the issues and problems discussed throughout the text and examines wide-ranging implications of the gender and tourism nexus, particularly in the areas of women and employment, women as product, and women as travelers in the less-developed world. He also draws attention to some of the nascent themes and concepts discussed explicitly and implicitly in the text that merit additional research attention.

EPILOGUE

Since the end of World War II, tourism has been a powerful motor for global integration and, even more than other forms of investment, it has symbolized a country's entrance into the world community. This is even more true for developing regions, as the foreign-owned mines, plantations, military outposts, or bases of the past have been replaced by tourism, which represents the drawing of "remote" societies into the global arena in less unequal terms than before (Enloe 1989). When the government of a developing nation decides to rely on tourism, this implies that it has made the decision to be internationally compliant, which means (among other things) that it will meet the expectations of incoming guests. Despite tourism's often questionable role in sustained growth for local societies, European, North American, and Japanese bankers along with tourism officials of developing regions have become avid tourism boosters. The international politics of debt and the international pursuit of pleasure have become tightly knotted together as we enter the twenty-first century (Apostolopoulos and Gayle 2001).

Since tourism is as much ideology as physical movement (Enloe 1989) within the current development context, the foregoing set of presumptions about masculinity, femininity, education, employment, and pleasure in developing regions is not surprising. In developing regions, women's roles in the tourism sector do not differ radically from those in other economic sectors (e.g., industry, agriculture), in that they comprise distinctively feminized segments that are predominantly in the lower end of the occupational hierarchy (in terms of both status and earnings). At the other end of the spectrum, and contrary to the industrialized regions (with very few exceptions), experiences of female tourism consumers range from that of limited domestic or international travel to that of complete isolation in the household as a result of power, religion, and development levels in their respective regions. Women and men in developing regions involve themselves in tourism in diverse and unequal ways as a clear consequence of individual, societal, cultural, and global influences—all of which are gendered.

REFERENCES

Abraham-VanDerMark, E. (1983). The impact of industrialization on women: A Caribbean case. In *Women, Men and the International Division of Labor*, edited by J. Nash and M. P. Fernandez-Kelly. Albany: State University of New York Press.

Aitchison, C. (1996). Gendered tourist spaces and places: The masculinisation and militarisation of Scotland's heritage. *Leisure Studies Association Newsletter* 45: 16–23.

Apostolopoulos, Y., and D. J. Gayle. (2001). *Tourism, Sustainable Development, and Natural Resource Management: Experiences of Caribbean, Pacific, and Mediterranean Islands*. Westport, Conn.: Praeger.

Boserup, E. (1970). *Women's Role in Economic Development*. New York: St. Martin's Press.

Brohman, J. (1996). New directions in tourism for Third World development. *Annals of Tourism Research* 23: 48–70.

Craik, J. (1997). The culture of tourism. In *Tourism Cultures: Transformations of Travel and Theory*, edited by C. Rojek and J. Urry. London: Routledge.

Cukier, J., J. Norris, and G. Wall. (1996). The involvement of women in the tourism industry of Bali, Indonesia. *Journal of Development Studies* 33 (2): 248–270.

Davidson, P. (1996). The holiday and work experiences of women with young children. *Leisure Studies* 15: 89–103.

Deem, R. (1992). The sociology of gender and leisure in Britain—Past progress and future prospects. *Loisir et Société/Society and Leisure* 15 (1): 21–37.

de Kadt, E. (1979). *Tourism: Passport to Development?* New York: Oxford University Press.

Duley, M. I., and S. Diduk. (1986). Women, colonialism, and development. In *The Cross-Cultural Study of Women: A Comprehensive Guide*, edited by M. Duley and M. Edwards. New York: Feminist Press.

Elliott, C. (1977). Theories of development: An assessment. *Signs: Journal of Women in Culture and Society* 3: 1–8.

Enloe, C. (1989). *Bananas, Beaches, and Bases: Making Feminist Sense of International Politics*. Berkeley and Los Angeles: University of California Press.

Fernandez-Kelly, M. P. (1986). Introduction. In *Women's Work, Development and the Division of Labor by Gender*, edited by E. Leacock and H. Safa. South Hadley, Mass.: Bergin & Garvey.

Hall, C. M. (1994). Gender and economic interest in tourism prostitution: The nature, development and implications of sex tourism in South-East Asia. In *Tourism: A Gender Analysis*, edited by V. Kinnaird and D. Hall. Chichester: Wiley.

Ioannides, D., Y. Apostolopoulos, and S. Sönmez. (2001). *Mediterranean Islands and Sustainable Tourism Development: Practices, Management, and Policies*. London: Continuum.

Jafari, J. (1973). Role of tourism on socio-economic transformation of developing countries. Master's thesis. Cornell University, Ithaca, New York.

Jordan, F. (1997). An occupational hazard? Sex segregation in tourism employment. *Tourism Management* 18: 525–534.

Kempadoo, K., ed. (1999). *Sun, Sex, and Gold: Tourism and Sex Work in the Caribbean*. New York: Rowman & Littlefield.

Kinnaird, V., and D. Hall. (1996). Understanding tourism processes: A gender-aware framework. *Tourism Management* 17 (2): 95–102.

Kinnaird, V., and D. Hall, eds. (1994). *Tourism: A Gender Analysis*. Chichester: Wiley.

Kinnaird, V., U. Kothari, and D. Hall. (1994). Tourism: Gender perspectives. In *Tourism: A Gender Analysis*, edited by V. Kinnaird and D. Hall. Chichester: Wiley.

Kousis, M. (1996). Tourism and the family in a rural Cretan community. In *The Sociology of Tourism*, edited by Y. Apostolopoulos, S. Leivadi, and A. Yiannakis. London: Routledge.

Leontidou, L. (1994). Gender dimensions of tourism sub-cultures and restructuring. In *Tourism: A Gender Analysis*, edited by V. Kinnaird and D. Hall. Chichester: Wiley.

Levy, D. E., and P. B. Lerch. (1991). Tourism as a factor in development: Implications for gender and work in Barbados. *Gender and Society* 5 (1): 67–85.

Lim, L.Y.C. (1983). Capitalism, imperialism and patriarchy: The dilemma of Third World women workers in multinational factories. In *Women, Men and the International Division of Labor*, edited by J. Nash and M. P. Fernandez-Kelly. Albany: State University of New York Press.

Momsen, J., and V. Kinnaird, eds. (1995). *Different Places, Different Voices: Gender and Development in Africa, Asia, and Latin America*. London: Routledge.

Mowforth, M., and I. Munt. (1997). *Tourism and Sustainability*. London: Routledge.

Norris, J., and G. Wall. (1994). Gender and tourism. In *Progress in Tourism, Recreation and Hospitality Management*, edited by C. P. Cooper and A. Lockwood. Chichester: Wiley.

Pruitt, D., and S. LaFont. (1995). For love and money: Romance tourism in Jamaica. *Annals of Tourism Research* 22: 422–440.

Richter, L. (1994). Exploring the political role of gender in tourism research. In *Global Tourism in the Next Decade*, edited by W. F. Theobald. Oxford: Butterworth Heinemann.

Sinclair, M. T., ed. (1997). *Gender, Work and Tourism*. London: Routledge.

Small, J. (1999). Memory-work: A method for researching women's tourist experiences. *Tourism Management* 20 (1): 25–35.

Swain, M. B. (1995). Gender in tourism. *Annals of Tourism Research* 22: 247–266.

Tiano, S. (1987). Gender, work, and world capitalism: Third World women's role in development. In *Analyzing Gender: A Handbook of Social Science Research*, edited by B. Hess and M. Ferree. Newbury Park, Calif.: Sage.

Ward, K. (1984). *Women in the World System: Its Impact on Status and Fertility*. Westport, Conn.: Praeger.

World Tourism Organization. (2000). Tourism statistics. 6 April. Available <http://www.world-tourism.org>.

2

Gender in Tourism: Theoretical Perspectives

Heather J. Gibson

According to the World Tourism Organization (WTO), tourism is the world's largest growth industry. The WTO predicts that by 2010 international arrivals will number 1 billion. In the last decade alone, global spending on tourism has doubled, with the most current figures calculated at $444.7 billion in 1998. France continues to rank as the world's top destination, followed by the United States (World Tourism Organization 1997). However, as tourists are becoming more experienced and sophisticated, an increasing number are seeking to visit places that are "new and different." As this trend continues, the number of tourists visiting the developing world is growing. Visits to the Caribbean, Latin America, the South Pacific, the Middle East, Southeast Asia, and Africa are becoming more common.

The growth in visitors from First World to Third World brings a unique blend of sociocultural impacts on both the tourism producers (hosts) and the tourism consumers (guests), that are not found to the same degree in the First World tourism regions. The cultural differentiation between First and Third World countries is more pronounced. The differences in values and beliefs, appropriate modes of dress and behavior, and the status of women can lead to conflict between hosts and guests. The economic inequalities between tourism producers and consumers is very evident in developing countries. In some cases tourists may not expect the adverse poverty endemic in many developing nations, others may feel uncomfortable with their "wealth" compared to that of the locals, and the hosts may feel some resentment toward tourists because of these apparent inequities in economic standing. In some countries the cultural differences and economic disparities are further complicated by the legacy of colonialism. Conflict may also arise due to race, religion, and gender issues. Concern over the sociocultural impacts of tourism in developing nations has been analyzed by a number of scholars (Britton 1996; Crick 1989); however, until recently a gender focus has been absent from much of this work. Indeed, in tourism studies as a whole, gender has been conspicuously absent, which is particularly curious, as many women are employed in the tourism industry and women comprise a large portion of the traveling public.

In the 1990s four notable works tried to redress the issue of the invisibility of women in tourism studies: Norris and Wall's (1994) "Gender and Tourism"; Kinnaird and Hall's (1994) "Conclusion: The Way Forward"; a special edition of the *Annals of Tourism Research* edited by Swain (1995); and Sinclair's (1997a) *Gender, Work and Tourism*. In addition to these four collections, various studies that have adopted a gender analysis of tourism can be found in the literature. The purpose of this chapter will be to review as much of this work as possible, to pay special attention to the theoretical framework of these studies, and to suggest ways in which we can contribute to the body of knowledge on tourism and gender as we start a new millennium. Swain suggests that Kinnaird and Hall "left the way open for a needed infusion of gender theory in tourism studies" (p. 252). Thus, taking a lead from Kinnaird and Hall, this chapter will be broken into three sections: (1) gendered tourists (tourism consumers), (2) gendered hosts (tourism producers), and (3) tourism as gendered construction (tourism marketing and objects).

This chapter also draws upon research in leisure studies. "The broader field of leisure studies, of which tourism can be considered a part, has begun to incorporate a feminist perspective" (Norris and Wall 1994, 58). Norris and Wall go on to write that gender differences in tourism consumption have become more commonplace in tourism studies; however, the differences are not explained. They advocate the adoption of a feminist perspective in future tourism research, where gender is a central part of the study. Henderson (1994), writing about gender-based research in leisure studies, notes that gender scholarship has gone through five phases: (1) invisible (womanless), (2) compensatory ("add women and stir"), (3) dichotomous differences (sex differences), (4) feminist (women-centered), and (5) gender. Swain (1995) observes that tourism studies have taken the same route. I would add that, at the moment, tourism studies appear to be stuck somewhere between dichotomous differences research and gender scholarship.

So what is gender scholarship or a gender-aware framework and why is it necessary for the study of tourism? Kinnaird and Hall (1996) explain that "the activities and processes involved in tourism development are constructed out of gendered societies. Consequently, the masculine and feminine identities articulated by both host and guest societies are important components of the types of tourism taking place" (p. 95). Swain (1995) taking a lead from Henderson (1994) in using a gender perspective, suggests that "researchers may study only one or both sexes together, theorizing how behaviors and roles are given gendered meanings, how labor is divided to express gender and gendered differences symbolically, and how social structures incorporate gender values and convey gender advantages in hierarchical relationships" (p. 253). So how do we define a tourist and tourism? In my own work, following the lead of Cohen (1974) and Smith (1989), I have adopted the definition of a tourist as a leisured traveler, although in examining tourism producers this conceptualization becomes problematic. Norris and Wall (1994) also raise this issue. While leisure research has applications to tourism behavior as a specialized form of leisure, they argue that it has limited use for analyzing women as workers in the tourism industry. This is certainly true on one level; however, the same criticism can be levied at leisure studies in their examination of workers in leisure services. I concur with Aitchison and Jordan (1998), who advocate theorizing about gender in leisure and tourism management using concepts from gender studies, feminist studies, cultural geography, and women-in-management studies. Thus, this chapter will draw upon some of the more recent theoretical discussions in leisure studies and suggest ways in which they may be applied to a gender analysis of tourism. While at the same time, this chapter heeds Norris and Wall's warning that we should guard against an overreliance on feminist-based research in leisure studies, as tourism has some unique qualities that may not be found in everyday leisure, such as the "notion of departure" from what is routine (Urry 1990).

GENDERED TOURISTS

Butler (1995) observes that when gendered guest–host interactions are investigated, attention is commonly given to the women as the hosts rather than the guests. In the context of the developing world, when we talk about women as guests in a country we are commonly referring to white middle-class female tourists. As Butler writes, "They are the women who have the time, money and desire to embark upon a journey that takes them away from familiar surroundings" (p. 488). Immediately, the complexities of the analysis become apparent. To understand the experiences of gendered tourists in the developing world, it is not sufficient to concentrate on gender alone, but to adopt a pluralist perspective that acknowledges the interaction between gender, class, race, and nationality that will influence the experiences of the female tourist.

Some of the earliest accounts of women tourists in the less-developed world are found in the travelogues of the eighteenth- and nineteenth-century female adventurers. Robinson (1990) writes that all of these women traveled not only "across seas from the familiar to the strange land, but across the boundaries of convention and traditional feminine restraints" (p. ix). She goes on to say an "overwhelming spirit of adventure" fired these women's enthusiasm for travel (p. 35). Women such as Mary Kingsley, Isabella Bird, and Gertrude Bell left their middle-class homes and undertook arduous journeys (Birkett 1989). Nonetheless, while on the one hand these women's accounts are examples of going against social convention and their travels can be construed as resistance and independence (Butler 1995), on the other hand Enloe (1989) asks to what extent these solo women travelers have left us with a number of contradictions. In fact, as Hall and Kinnaird (1994) suggest, we must not lose sight of the fact that these women were from a privileged class and, as Birkett points out, they represented imperialism and may have actually reinforced colonialism through their contact with the hosts on their travels. However, as Enloe proffers, women travelers have always had to resist the ideology that it is not socially acceptable for women to travel by themselves, and we should not merely think of these women as privileged. Even now, as these stories have regained popularity in the late twentieth century, Hall and Kinnaird observe that publishers appear "almost incredulous that women would wish to and could survive without a man" (p. 190). Thus, it appears that gender should be a central focus in understanding tourist preference, although as Urry (1990) points out, we need to address the interconnection of gender, generation, ethnicity, and class in determining tourist preferences. Work that has incorporated some of these dimensions into the investigation of tourist preferences has adopted a life-span perspective to understand women's travel patterns, with varying degrees of theoretical interpretation.

One of the earliest empirical investigations on women's travel examined the travel patterns of working women versus nonworking women during different stages of the life cycle (Bartos 1982). Bartos divided the life cycle into four segments: (1) husband, no children, (2) no husband, no children, (3) husband and children, and (4) children, no husband. Once you overcome the heterosexist assumptions and the sexist language in this paper, her findings not surprisingly show that single and childless women take more overseas trips, that the presence of young children in a family is a strong deterrent to travel, and that working women travel more frequently than nonworking women. She concludes that there is "no question that working women are far more valuable to the travel market than nonworking women" (p. 8). At no point in this article is there any attempt to explain why these patterns occur and to acknowledge the fact that "nonworking women" are in fact working and may be constrained in their travel choices by a number of factors, including finances, child-care responsibilities, and even motivation. Similarly, Hawes (1988) focusing on women in middle and late adulthood (fifty years and above) also adopted a marketing focus. Using psychographics, he distinguished three travel-related lifestyle profiles for women aged fifty and above. These were the women travelers who tended to be experienced; the laid-back tourists who sought quiet, relaxing vacations; and the dreamer who did not travel, but experienced the thrills of travel vicariously. In identifying these different types of female traveler, however, Hawes did not ground his work in any particular theory that may have explained why women in middle and later life exhibit these three travel preferences. Although his work did dispel some of the stereotypes of older women as inactive and vulnerable, he found that many of the women that traveled in the study were active, adventurous, and not necessarily interested in rest and relaxation.

Anderson and Littrell (1995, 1996) grounded their studies of women's souvenir-purchasing patterns in Levinson's model of the adult-life course (Levinson, Darrow, Klein, Levinson, and McKee 1978). The authors also investigated the contribution of two gender ideologies, liberal and cultural, and the concept of authenticity to explain souvenir-purchasing patterns among women in early and middle adulthood (Anderson and Littrell 1995). In face-to-face interviews all of the women felt that travel enhanced the quality of their lives and that purchasing special souvenirs was a meaningful part of their travels. The authors concluded that the two extreme gender ideologies did not explain the souvenir-purchasing patterns of these women, but life stage and travel-career stage appeared to be linked to travel styles and patterns, although travel preferences proves to be a complex phenomenon (Anderson and Littrell 1996). This work shows that some theories may not always be appropriate to understanding certain behaviors, or they may not be used to their full interpretative capabilities. For example, Levinson's framework appeared to be used to categorize the women into a life stage without really addressing the sociopsychological tasks that may face women and may help to explain their travel preferences and souvenir-buying patterns.

Studies that made more extensive use of Levinson's theory of the adult-life course to understand travel choice or tourist-role preference for both men and women were conducted by Gibson and Yiannakis (Gibson 1989, 1994, 1996; Gibson and Yiannakis 1993; Yiannakis and Gibson 1988, 1992). Working with four different samples of men and women over a ten-year period, Gibson and Yiannakis found that tourist-role preference not only appears to be linked to life stage, but a gender analysis revealed that men and women vary in their preference for different styles of travel at various stages in the life course. These differences may be explained by the fact that women may differ in the timing and the way in which they deal with the sociopsychological tasks facing them at different times in the life course (Levinson 1996). Moreover, a woman's position in society arising out of the interconnection of gender, class, race, and age may encourage or discourage certain behaviors. While this work was in a sense at the gender differences stage in tourism scholarship, it provided empirical evidence that men and women do have different preferences in travel styles and that life stage appears to be one factor that can explain these choices, drawing upon a theoretical model. In more recent women-centered work with Jordan, Gibson (Gibson and Jordan 1998b) found that among solo women travelers from the United States and the United Kingdom, life stage and life transition underlie not only choice of travel style, but sometimes provide the impetus to travel solo. Indeed, if we are to reach the gender-scholarship stage in tourism research, we need to adopt a feminist perspective to aid our understanding of the experiences of the woman traveler. Furthermore, work in leisure studies that is grounded in the new cultural geography that incorporates a gender perspective may offer insights into the experiences of the female tourist that have previously been uncharted.

Cultural geography is the recognition that space is socially constructed and is not an empty stage on which actors perform (Mowl and Towner 1995). In recent years the notion of the flâneur has been used in conjunction with the modern tourist (Urry 1990). A flâneur was originally conceived in the mid-nineteenth century to describe the act of strolling around the new modern cities, observing without being observed. As Massey (1994) notes in her treatise on space and social relations, a flâneur is a male role: "Flâneurs observed others; they were not observed themselves" (p. 234). The reason for this, as Wolff (1985) explains, is that women can never stroll around in public places without being the object of attention or "the gaze," and so the notion of a flâneuse is impossible. The conceptualization of the use of space is obviously relevant to tourism studies, as the very act of touring and sightseeing involves the use and consumption of space. But the notion that the use of space is gendered and not equal is particularly valuable in any analysis of women tourists. This perspective is particularly relevant when women travel alone and when they travel in cultures distant from their own, where they may encounter different views of the social position of women.

Whenever women travel, whether it is in their own town or on vacation, Valentine (1989) argues that they fear violence from men and this will influence their perception and use of public space. Even in familiar surroundings, Valentine found that women adopt strategies to maintain their safety. One of the most predominant strategies was avoiding "perceived dangerous places at dangerous times" (e.g., at night). Because of these strategies, women's use of public space is restricted both geographically and temporally and, as Valentine suggests, this deters women from being independent and thereby perpetuates patriarchy. This "geography of fear" is one of the reasons why a woman cannot be a flâneuse, as she cannot use public space in the same way as a man. Women's use of space will also vary according to class, age, race, and disability. Gibson and Jordan (1998a, 1998b) found that while on the road, solo women travelers use a number of strategies to keep them safe, including choice of accommodations, modes of transportation, and the construction of mental maps of their surroundings in terms of potential danger and time of day. But despite this geography of fear, these women report that the advantages of solo travel outweigh the negatives. Deem (1996b), in a study of women who took city-based domestic vacations, also found that women perceive the "urban landscape" differently from men and that age, social class, and ethnicity will influence this perception. Deem proffers the question that may help us untangle the bizarre behaviors that frequently occur while on vacation: Does being on holiday motivate people to take risks that they would not normally take? Perhaps the answer to this lies in Turner's (1974) notion of liminoid, whereupon individuals transfer into a space where the social strictures of their everyday lives are suspended (e.g., Lett 1983; Graburn 1989).

Wearing and Wearing (1996) offer an alternative conception of tourism as not an escape from the everyday or the profane (Graburn 1989), but as an escape to a space that fosters interaction and self-development. They critique the mainstream, male-oriented tourism theories that focus on a subject–object relationship between host and guest. Wearing and Wearing adopt an interactionist perspective to proffer the idea that tourism should be conceptualized as a dynamic set of social relations and meanings for the people who interact in the tourism space. As such, drawing upon Grosz's (1995) work, Wearing and Wearing suggest that the tourist destination acts as a "chora" (Plato's space between being and becoming) and the tourist as a "choraster." Thus, the focus has moved from the idea of the tourist as observer, or flâneur,

to the tourist as interacting with the host peoples as choraster. Therefore, "rather than being the object of the stroller's gaze, the concept of
'chora' suggests a space to be occupied and given meaning by the
people who made use of the space" (Wearing and Wearing 1996, 233).
Wearing and Wearing suggest that by conceptualizing a tourist destination as a space, tourism becomes an ongoing process of meaningful
interaction, rather than merely an activity. The feminization of the
destination as a dynamic space rather than a static place also allows
for a redefinition in the use of the space for women. Instead of accepting the male-defined uses of the tourism space, women would be able
to construct their own meanings and use the space as they see fit for
their own self-development, and to interact with the hosts as active
subjectivities rather than as objects of the gaze.

Certainly, the concept of a female tourist as a choraster rather than a
flâneuse appears to resolve some of the academic debate over the ap-
propriateness of the idea of a tourist as an outside observer. But more
important, the idea of a tourist as a choraster appears to more accurately reflect the experiences of women travelers. As Squire (1994)
noted, female visitors to Beatrix Potter's Hill Top Farm construct meanings of the place centered around notions of childhood, family life,
and nostalgia. Gibson and Jordan (1998a, 1998b) found that meeting
"people on the road" and interacting with the local people was an
important part of the experiences of solo women travelers. Moreover,
as suggested by Wearing and Wearing (1996), these solo women travelers viewed their travels as spaces for self-development, independence, and empowerment, rather like the Victorian women travelers
(Robinson 1990). The concepts of space, use of space, and flâneur versus choraster seem to hold some of the keys to understanding female-
tourist experiences. The recognition that women interact differently
with space and other people may help explain why some of the earlier
studies on gender differences in tourist motivations found that men
and women consistently differed in their vacation preferences (e.g.,
McGehee, Loker-Murphy, and Uysal 1996). These theoretical constructs
may also be useful in the analysis of host and guest interactions.

Another variant on the conception of space that may aid our understanding is Foucault's (1984) concept of "hereotopias," or spaces outside of everyday life that allow the individual to resist the dominant
discourse (Wearing 1998). This theoretical perspective might answer
the question posed at the start of this section: Why did so many Victorian women leave the security of their middle-class homes and undertake precarious journeys (Birkett 1989), and, given the geography of
fear, why do they continue to do so in increasing numbers to less developed destinations? These spaces may offer women opportunities
for resistance and liberation. Indeed, Wearing (1998) suggests that lei-

sure travel may be a "heterotopia," in which women may "rewrite the script of what it is to be a woman" (p. 148). However, not all pleasure travel may be construed as a heterotopia by women. As Deem (1996a) and Davidson (1996) found, family vacations can be a continuation of routine in another environment for mothers with young children. Conceivably, women traveling as tourists (i.e., touring around and experiencing the local culture) rather than as vacationers may be more likely to view travel as a space for resistance. This was exemplified by an experienced woman traveler in Gibson and Jordan's (1998b) study. She explained that travel "gives you a sense of independence and you feel powerful . . . you find yourself. You can do so many things and you say 'God, I did this by myself!' and you feel so powerful and so independent and it's a great feeling!" Likewise, Creighton (1995) found that for Japanese female tourists, trips to women-centered silk cultivation and weaving workshops offered them a chance to redefine their gender identity and to resist the hegemonic control pervasive in Japanese society.

The concepts of space and resistance do not negate the power of social structure in shaping women's lives. Indeed, with regard to understanding the dynamics of tourism in the developing world, the macro structures are an integral part of the analysis. However, the idea of agency is also valuable. More and more women are traveling to far-flung destinations in the world. To understand their experiences, their motivations, and their interactions with the host cultures, a perspective that recognizes structure and agency needs to be adopted. Women are not "squashed ants" (Wearing and Wearing 1988); even in the most constrictive environments they engage in acts of resistance. Nonetheless, as Rosaldo (1980) points out, "We will never understand the lives that women lead without relating them to men" (p. 396). As most vacation travel is still predominantly couple or small-group centered, future work into the gendered nature of tourists might well investigate the dynamics between members of a travel group to understand the true nature of the travel experience and also to attain the stage of gender scholarship in tourism studies. Indeed, Swain (1995) points out that tourism research has failed to incorporate the "personal voice of the subject" (p. 259). Interviewing tourists about their experiences may be one way to understand the meaning of travel in people's lives. Moreover, the interaction of women tourists with women guests in the developing world cannot negate the influence of social structure and women's position in relation to men. Even in Creighton's (1995) study, while on the one hand craft vacations provided a site of resistance for middle-class Japanese women, on the other hand the very acts of silk cultivation and weaving were a form of gendered domination for another generation of Japanese women.

GENDERED HOSTS

Kinnaird, Kothari, and Hall (1994) write that "for hosts the issues of employment opportunity and the control of wage employment creation are gendered" (p. 13). The types of work available in the tourism industry are frequently based on the sexual division of labor. Moreover, they go on to point out that "in many developing countries where tourists are white and those serving tourists are black, the nature of the service may be interpreted as servility—neocolonialism" (p. 17). Richter (1994) notes that the world over, women fill the jobs at the bottom of the tourism hierarchy. Jobs such as chambermaids, laundresses, and waitresses are characterized by low pay, low job security, and powerlessness. Kinnaird and Hall (1996, 96) suggest that any analysis of the gendered nature of employment in tourism needs to address the following: (1) differences in the quality and type of work available, (2) differential access of women to employment opportunities, (3) seasonal fluctuations in employment, and (4) existing and new gendered divisions of labor.

Norris and Wall (1994) denote that much of the earlier work in the gendered nature of women as tourism producers has adopted a development perspective. The development school of thought works from a liberal-feminist perspective and supports the view that women's integration in the development process will enhance their role in the public sphere of society. The limitation of this perspective is that it does not recognize the fact that women are already part of the public sphere, but their contributions are frequently invisible. One contributing factor to women's invisibility, as Kinnaird and Hall (1994) point out, is that opportunities for employment in tourism are imbued with the traditional social practices shaping men and women's roles. In a study of tourism development in Barbados, Levy and Lerch (1991) found that women's jobs in tourism resembled their domestic roles. The authors found significant gender differentiation in job security and longevity, income, job training, and job satisfaction. Men were also more likely to be unionized than women. Nonetheless, Levy and Lerch argue that while tourism employment may provide limited opportunities for women, the work is less arduous than their traditional agricultural jobs. Monk and Alexander (1986), in a study of Margarita Island in the Caribbean, also traced the change from subsistence agriculture to a tourism-based economy. Margarita hoped to attract international tourism; instead, the island became a popular domestic-tourism destination. As a result, unlike Barbados, many of the inhabitants of Margarita were not directly involved in tourism despite the government's hope for a large-scale tourism industry, although Monk and Alexander did find that tourism had altered the traditional structure of society. Like

Levy and Lerch, Monk and Alexander found that jobs were segregated on the basis of gender. Men tended to work in construction or transportation, while women did a number of "odd jobs" in addition to their domestic responsibilities. On the whole, women had not found employment in hotels, shops, or tourism-related craft production; many of these jobs were filled by women from outside the island. Also, as agriculture declined the women had lost much of their home-based production of food processing and crafts. Thus, it appears that for many of the inhabitants of Margarita, tourism development has not been economically beneficial, and in some ways it has taken traditional production roles away from women. The case studies of Barbados and Margarita show gender differentiation in employment and also class-based stratification. One of the problems of a development perspective is that it does not recognize class distinctions that also influence women's role in the public sphere. Indeed, Swain (1993) argues that underdevelopment theory only provides a partial understanding of an indigenous culture's involvement with the global economy. She contends it fails to take into account the interaction between the internal and external economic and cultural systems.

Other feminist theories that attempt to explain the gendered nature of tourism-related work incorporate class-based divisions, but they differ in the degree to which patriarchy or capitalism are identified as the pivotal catalysts of gender inequity (Sinclair 1997b). Marxist feminism focuses on class differences and relationships to the means of production. Radical feminists focus on patriarchy and heterosexuality as determining the inequalities between men and women in society. A dual-systems analysis regards patriarchy and capitalism as two separate systems that work together to oppress women's positions in society. Under patriarchal capitalism, jobs are created that conform to gender roles. Many of the jobs in tourism that reflect women's domestic roles, such as chambermaids, would be an example of this. McKay (1993) found that Caribbean men view women's role in the tourism industry as an extension of their mothering role. Norris and Wall (1994) suggest that in some instances tourism as an external force may actually change the gendered division of labor in a society. For example, to meet the needs of the tourists, the number of men available to fill certain positions may surpass the supply and, therefore, women may be brought in to fill these positions, although to what extent this is a permanent change is not addressed. According to Kinnaird and Hall (1996) "gender is essentially structural and relational and [it] needs to be positioned within analyses which address systematic change over time" (p. 95). Norris and Wall also point to the scale of tourism development in a country as influencing women's role in the tourism industry. With mass-tourism development, the jobs open to women are low-paid, service-sector positions, whereas with small-scale-tourism development there may be opportunities for women to have more autonomy in the tourism industry through running their own guest accommodations or cottage-industry craft production. Even so, they may still lack political control, and many of the jobs conform to gender roles. Agrotourism, which has become an increasingly popular form of rural-tourism development, is one area where women have played an integral role.

Garcia-Ramon, Canoves, and Valdovinos (1995) studied the role of women in the development of agrotourism as a response to the decline of agriculture in Spain. In interviews with women who participate in agrotourism in Galicia and Catalonia, the authors found that women were largely responsible for cleaning, laundering, and cooking for their guests. They spent an average of eight and half hours a day in tourism-related tasks, although the women had trouble distinguishing their tourism-related tasks from their domestic responsibilities. "In effect, they perceive the work related to agro-tourism to be an amplification or extension of domestic duties" (p. 274). While the number of overall hours worked had increased for these women, like the women in Barbados, their work was felt to be less physically demanding than agricultural work. Also, the women reported that their contribution to the family economically had raised the visibility of their work and, hence, their value. By interacting with people from outside the family and community, the women felt more connected to the outside world. The increase in family income had also raised their standard of living. The authors concluded by suggesting that the introduction of rural tourism may have reinforced traditional gender work roles. However, if you read the women's responses in the interviews, and if Foucault's (1984) notion of agency and resistance is invoked in the analysis, the macro structure may not have changed significantly, but the everyday nature of these women's world seems to have benefitted somewhat. In a similar study, Iakovidou and Turner (1995) investigated the role of women's cooperatives in the development of agrotourism in Greece. Like the women in Spain, agrotourism has provided rural women with some financial independence and raised their social position and their confidence. The cooperatives have professionalized women's domestic skills. By working together the women have successfully initiated home-based tourism lodging facilities and have contributed to the revitalization of rural areas.

While these two case studies have investigated women's tourism-related roles in developed countries, the findings can be generalized to tourism in the developing world. Also, the critique of relying solely on macrostructural theories to understand women's roles in the tourism-production process is equally applicable. Fairbairn-Dunlop (1994), in a study of tourism development in Western Samoa, illustrates these points well. She argues that the macroeconomic-development models, which have been used to analyze women's role in tourism, frequently conclude that women have been negatively affected by modernization and development (e.g., Monk and Alexander 1986). However, in Samoa, where local small-scale tourism initiatives have been encouraged, women have had the opportunity to become entrepreneurs. While some of the women's favorable experiences may be attributed to Western Samoa's stage of tourism development (Plog 1974), the explanation is a little more complex. Fairbairn-Dunlop found that by retaining autonomous control over the development of tourism, the Samoans have maintained their traditional way of life. Women constitute about 80 percent of the formal tourism workforce, largely in the hospitality sector. Taxi driving is the only male-dominated sector of the tourism industry. Thus, there is still gender segregation in jobs, as women have traditionally been responsible for hospitality in the villages and, so, their roles in tourism could be construed as conforming to gender roles. However, as Fairbairn-Dunlop points out, it is crucial when examining women's experiences that the prevailing gender ideologies that underlie the sexual division of labor in a society be analyzed. Likewise, Swain (1993) argues, "It is not enough to view international tourism as a patriarchal structure, part of a global capitalistic system, to explain who benefits from tourism within the commoditizing group and at the state level. Each indigenous group reflects specific environmental, historical, and sociocultural factors including its own gender system" (p. 35). Furthermore, Miller and Branson (1989,) studying the role of women and tourism in Bali, argue that to attain a comprehensive analysis of women's experiences in the tourism industry, attention must be given to the religious and political ideologies that prevail in the country. In addition to accommodations, women are frequently involved in the production of ethnic arts for the tourism industry. Kinnaird and Hall (1994) suggest that the ways in which individual societies deal with the commercialization of their culture may be profoundly gendered, and women and men play different roles in the selling of their traditions.

In a study of indigenous Kuna tourism, Swain (1989) investigated the gendered nature of tourism involvement by Kuna men and women. Like the Samoans, the Kuna maintain tight control over their tourism. In Kuna society, women are responsible for producing *mola* artwork, which was the catalyst for tourism development. As the popularity of *mola* artwork increased, the *mola* trade developed from a subsistence activity to a marketable commodity for tourists. Swain found that although the Kuna maintain a "complimentarity of female and male status in Kuna society " (p. 92), men and women have different roles in the tourism industry that have differing amounts of power associated with them. Female *mola* production frequently takes place in the home and it is the males who market the *mola* and are active in the political sphere. Nonetheless, under indigenous-tourism development, Swain found that there are opportunities for women to assume a more active role in the public domain. For example, through the formation of a female cooperative to manufacture and market their *molas*, Kuna women have gained a forum for discussion and have attained leadership skills. In fact, Swain found that some women had become junior officials in their village *congressos*. Similarly, Cone (1995) found that participation in tourism-related crafts was also viewed as empowering for two Highland Mayan women. She found that through their contact with tourists they had changed their relationships with their crafts and their self-identities. Women in Mayan society stay mainly in the domestic realm, but through craft production for the tourism industry Cone found that Mayan women were able to play a role in public life. However, because of their entrepreneurship, these women frequently found themselves on the fringes of their own society, while at the same time being seen as the "exotic other" by many of the tourists. Thus, on the one hand participation as artisans in the tourism industry seems to accord Kuna and Mayan women some measure of financial and political independence, but in their interactions with Western tourists they are still perceived as somehow different and socially inferior. Postcolonial theory may be one way of analyzing the complexities of women tourism producers in the developing world.

Feminist theories have long been criticized for being Eurocentric, white, and middle-class (e.g., Collins 1990; Hooks 1984). With regard to tourism producers in the developing world, we are faced with groups of women who have a different "lived experience" from the Western tourist and the Western academic. Subaltern studies use Gramsci's (1978) concept of the subaltern or powerless groups that are outside of mainstream economic production to analyze the legacy of colonial relations in the developing world. Wearing (1998) explains that critical subaltern studies seek to construct alternative views of history rather than the history written from the colonialists' point of view. Critical subaltern studies or postcolonial theory draws upon Foucault's (1984) concepts of power and resistance and Derrida's (1976) ideas on difference or "otherness" and the binary oppositions that are inherent in Western thinking. Postcolonial theory may be the best way to understand the experiences of the female tourism producers in the context of their own cultures. In this light, the tourism-related, women-centered cooperatives may be construed as the beginnings of communal action and empowerment. As Collins wrote about black American women, "While individual empowerment is the key, only collective action can effectively generate lasting social transformation of political and economic institutions" (p. 23).

Another area of study of the effects of tourism on gender roles is the change in values and norms within a community as a result of interaction with people from another culture. Picard (1993) points out that it is frequently assumed that the sociocultural impacts of tourism on the host destination is "uni-directional," when, in fact, change is the result of interactions between local people and tourists and the influence on the acceptability of different types of behavior in a community. Tourism may invoke change in a number of facets of community life, including family structure and child-rearing patterns, employment patterns, income, marriage and dating patterns, and behavioral expectations. Kousis (1989) found that tourism development in Crete led to changes in the family in landownership, family size, women's paid work outside the home, and patterns of family life. Wilkinson and Pratiwi (1995), in a study of Pangandaran, Indonesia, found that as long as women's roles in the tourism industry resembled their domestic roles (accommodation and food-related jobs), women took an active role in tourism while at the same time maintaining responsibility for child rearing. However, Wilkinson and Pratiwi found that the villagers did not regard the job as a tourist guide as appropriate for a woman. In fact, five women who were tourist guides were regarded as prostitutes, as their interaction with the tourists was not appropriate behavior for a local woman.

The difference in gender-appropriate behavior and interaction with tourists can be seen in a number of studies. Moore (1995) examined changes in alcohol consumption among young residents of Arachova, a Greek tourist town. The establishment of new bars and discos for the tourists provided young Arachovian women with places in which to drink and behave in ways not sanctioned by their own society. Likewise, Scott (1995) used the concepts of "insider groups" and "outsider groups" to examine the relationship between foreign women who come to work in tourism-related positions in Northern Cyprus. Scott explained that the behavior of the outsider group is evaluated against the behavioral expectations of the insider group. However, because of the foreign women working in jobs and dressing and behaving in ways that push the boundaries of local convention, they are gradually changing the local value system and opening up opportunities for local women that may not have been sanctioned in the past. Another line of investigation examines the relationships that form between local men and foreign female tourists. When the investigation turns to young female locals and foreign men we talk of sex tourism. The question might be asked: How can you distinguish between the two?

Cohen (1971) investigated the relationships between Arab young men and young foreign tourist women in Israel. Cohen found that the female tourists provided the young Arab men with contact with the outside world and also opportunities for romantic and/or sexual relationships that were not available to them in their own society because of religious mores. A relationship with a foreign woman also gave the man status among his peers, and for some it may have provided him with access to a foreign country. Wagner (1977), using Turner's (1974) concept of liminoid, found similar relationship patterns among Scandinavian women and Gambian men. More recently, a number of studies have investigated the encounters between young local males and foreign female tourists. Karsch and Dann (1996) examined the phenomenon of the beach boy in Barbados, using a symbolic interactionism framework. They found that "the white [female] tourist stands as a symbol [of escape] from the drudgery of the Third World and access to a better life" (p. 179). Karsch and Dann suggest that the relationships between the beach boys and the female tourists should be examined from within the framework of the dependency of the Third World on the First World for economic survival and the power and racial relations between the two systems.

Pruitt and LaFont (1995) studied the relations between female tourists and local males in Jamaica. They suggest that for the First World women such relationships afford them opportunities to engage in behavior not approved of in their own societies. Thus, vacations may provide First World women with a heterotopia in which they can experiment with new identities. The authors label these liaisons "romance tourism" and explain how they differ from sex tourism. Neither the local men nor the tourist women regard these relationships as prostitution, the emphasis being on courtship rather than paying for sex. When viewed from the angle of empowerment and resistance, these liaisons provide women with a chance to rewrite gendered scripts, a fact that Pruitt and LaFont say is the crucial distinction between romance tourism and sex tourism. Sex tourism reinforces gender and power relations, whereas romance tourism provides an arena for change. Perhaps the foreign women are still being exploited in these relationships with local men, but the romantic script is masking the true nature of the relationships. Indeed, Wearing (1994) suggests that women may lose themselves in romantic novels and soap operas to fulfill some of their needs for love and understanding that may be lacking in their everyday lives. On vacation, the romantic scripts not available in everyday life may come to fruition for these women. The possible exploitative nature of these relationships is found in Meisch's (1995) study of young American women who engage in relationships with Otavalenos men in Ecuador. Again, the women operate under a romantic script that exults in the "noble savage" mystique of the Otavalenos male. Meisch found that in some cases the relationships are purely equitable, without misconceptions on either side. However, in other cases the Otavalenos men may be married but they do not tell their "gringa" girlfriends. This deception may even continue when some of the Otavalenos men visit their foreign girlfriends in the United States, behavior Meisch categorized as exploitative. Thus, as Meisch points out, the Otavalenos is an example of the complexities and contradictory nature of modern tourism in the developing world.

Another extremely complex issue is the analysis of sex tourism. As I asked previously, What is the difference between romance tourism and sex tourism? Should the women who work in sex tourism be categorized as tourism producers, or have they been commoditized by male pimps? Oppermann (1999), in a review of the sex-tourism literature, suggests a more comprehensive conceptualization of sex tourism should include purpose of travel, length of time, relationship, sexual encounter, and a profile of the sex tourist, in addition to the monetary exchange. He argues that the traditional way of viewing sex tourism as a subset of prostitution is inadequate. He advocates including romance tourism and casual-sexual encounters as part of the sex-tourism classification. Oppermann asks, "Who exploits whom in a tourist-prostitute relationship? . . . Obviously prostitutes are usually placed in the position of the exploited as their body is bought for the pleasure of the customer. However, some authors have questioned if men, for example, get what they wanted" (p. 254). The problem with adopting a motivation and behavioral approach to analyzing sex tourism is that it fails to address the issues of power and subordination that are an integral part of sex tourism, particularly in the developing world. Also, proposing a definition of sex tourism as including encounters with others who are not just sex workers clouds rather than clarifies the study of sex tourism. Casual-sexual encounters and holiday romances may have some of the same motivational forces, but in sociological terms they do not have the same consequences for the actors involved.

Sex tourism is generally associated with male tourists from the developed world visiting the Third World to engage in commercial sex (Hall 1994). Hall (1992) explains that sex tourism generally occurs in two forms: (1) the casual or independent type, in which tourists make their own contacts with sex workers (Hanson [1997] documents this type of sex tourism in New Zealand); and (2) the packaged variety, predominantly from Japan to Southeast Asia (Muroi and Sasaki 1997).

Sex tourism is particularly well developed in the Third World, somewhat due to the international division of labor, but also because of the attraction of the exotic "othered" women. Countries such as Thailand, Korea, the Philippines, and Taiwan are renowned for their sex tourism, although some of the "red-light districts" in the Western world, such as in Amsterdam in The Netherlands, are part of this trade. Jeffreys (1998) argues that sex tourism along with Internet pornography and the trade in mail-order brides is part of the international trafficking and exploitation of women as products in the global economy. Urry (1990) suggests that sex tourism cannot be analyzed fully without addressing issues of gender and racial subordination. Hall (1994) advocates using a gender framework to analyze sex tourism, as such an approach will examine the sexual politics and power relations at work. Taking a lead from Rosen (1982), he points out that "any oversimplified utilitarian justification for prostitution may obscure the gender and class interests associated with tourism prostitution" (p. 147).

Moreover, Hall (1994) explains that any analysis should also take into consideration the international division of labor and the rampant consumerism in the Third World. Many of the women who work in sex tourism came to the cities seeking employment in manufacturing and were forced into prostitution by the lack of jobs. At the same time, the governments of Southeast Asia recognized the potential that sex tourism had for economic development. Arising out of Japanese colonialism and American militarism, a formalized international sex trade was established in Southeast Asia (Hall 1992, 1994; Leheny 1995; Muroi and Sasaki 1997). Over the last twenty years various women's groups have protested against sex tourism, with mixed success. The concern over health-related issues such as AIDS has invoked some reform in the sex-tourism industry, but Hall points out that real change will not occur without the transformation of gender relations in the host countries, the retreat of the American military, and an alternative economic-development plan that attracts foreign exchange through other means. Interestingly, as changes in Japanese society have occurred and more Japanese women are traveling, many Southeast Asian countries have changed their marketing strategies to attract this new group of tourists (Leheny 1995; Muroi and Sasaki 1997).

GENDERED CONSTRUCTION OF TOURISM

Gendered and sexualized representations in tourism marketing are one way the tourism industry uses gendered and often racial and ethnic forms to construct images of a destination or vacation package. Urry (1990) points out that in the United Kingdom the advertising materials produced by travel companies use three dominant images:

the family holiday, the heterosexual couple, and the fun holiday with young same-sex groups looking for heterosexual adventures. Single individuals, single-parent families, homosexual and lesbian couples, the disabled, and ethnic minorities are not represented in the images used to sell vacations. Kinnaird and Hall (1994) suggest that the marketing of tourism is infused with representations of women. On the one hand women from developing countries are shown as submissive and available to male tourists, and on the other hand Western women tourists are portrayed as "potent yet independent." Likewise, Enloe (1989) points out that the signs, symbols, fantasies, and myths used to market tourism are male oriented. Women and sexual imagery are used to convey the exoticness of the destination.

Cohen (1995) examined the marketing materials for the British Virgin Islands. She found that the BVI relies heavily upon sexual imagery in marketing. The images used represent the BVI as a gendered (female), natural, pristine environment that is made available for possession by the tourist. Oppermann and McKinley (1997) concentrated on the images of tourists and locals used in travel brochures for the Pacific Rim countries: "Bikini clad tourists, exotic locals and heterosexual couples" (p. 117) and smiling female flight attendants promising submissive service predominate. In their analysis, they found three general types of promotion used: body shots, suggestive postures, and sexual innuendo in language. Body shots of indigenous people or female tourists were prevalent. The indigenous people were usually young and beautiful, clothed in traditional dress, and presented in such a way that they appeared exotic and objectified for the gaze of the tourists. Female tourists were pictured scantily clad and their fair skin was used to contrast them with the locals. When male tourists are pictured it is usually in conjunction with female tourists, pictured in such a way that romance and heterosexual couplehood is the dominant image. Oppermann and McKinley found that the Pacific Island nations were more likely to use sex in their tourism promotion materials and the developed countries were least likely.

As Kinnaird, Kothari, and Hall (1994) suggest, the contrast between the First and Third World in tourism is indicative of the inequitable power relationships in international tourism. Perhaps this is also reflected in the way they promote themselves for tourist consumption, although the First World is not exempt from using gendered images in their tourism promotion. Marshment (1997) found that images used in holiday brochures in the United Kingdom serve to reinforce patriarchal relations. Women, either alone, in a couple, or in a family group, are usually pictured wearing swimsuits. Marshment suggests that this image of "woman in swimsuit" conjures up images of idleness, luxury, and pleasure. All of the images of the women conform to socially acceptable notions of sexual attractiveness, and the situations women are pictured in do not challenge the pervasive gender-role ideology. For beach holidays, the local people are rarely shown, and if they are, it is in a service-oriented capacity. In brochures for "long-haul" destinations, the locals are shown as the exotic other. Thus, in the images used for marketing the promotion of the other either as female or as exotic or foreign lends itself to postcolonial theorizing. The images are imbued with power differences along gender lines and in terms of First World versus Third World.

The way tourism destinations are constructed is another area for gender analysis. This avenue of research is not that well developed, but studies of heritage tourism, particularly Stirling in Scotland (Aitchison 1996; Edensor and Kothari 1994), lead the way for future investigations of the gendering of tourism attractions in developing nations. Again, concepts of space and place from cultural geography could provide the theoretical framework for such studies. Both Aitchison and Edensor and Kothari show how, in the case of Stirling, women's contribution to history is invisible. The construction of Stirling's history is based around militarism and masculinity. Aitchison goes on to suggest any critique of heritage tourism sites should encompass six elements: (1) construction of "the other," (2) the male "tourist gaze," (3) the iconography of gendered tourism, (4) nationalism and gendered heritage, (5) militarism and gendered heritage, and (6) masculinist myth making. Aitchison suggests that this framework may not only be applied to the analysis of existing attractions, but could also be used during the planning of new ones. She maintains that the construction of masculine forms instead of feminine ones is another way male supremacy is reinforced in societies. As such, it is another from of gender inequality in tourism. In terms of the First World tourist gaze on the Third World tourist attraction, attention to the forces of neocolonialism should also be part of the analysis.

CONCLUSION

The study of gendered tourists, gendered producers, and the gendered construction of tourism has come a long way in the last ten years. At the start of the new millennium, the available scholarship in this area has grown and the sophistication of the theoretical approaches taken has increased. However, there is still a lot of work to be done, especially in relation to the gendered nature of tourism in the developing world. As this work moves forward, we might well remember that "gender theories may help us analyze a situation but there is no single theory that can fit all occasions" (Henderson 1994, 133). Also, as Antrobus (1990) points out, tourism is frequently seen as a way of incorporating developing countries into a largely exploitative global economy. Thus, not only should future studies adopt a gender-aware framework, such work should also be contextualized with the culture of the host society (Swain 1993), and within the structure of the global marketplace.

REFERENCES

Aitchison, C. (1996). Gendered tourist spaces and places: The masculinization and militarization of Scotland's heritage. Paper presented at the LSA/ VVS 1996 Conference, Accelerating Leisure? Leisure, Time and Space in a Transitory Society, 14 September, Wageningen, Netherlands.

Aitchison, C., and F. Jordan. (1998). Gendered power in leisure and tourism: Theories of resistance. Paper presented at the Fifth Congress of the World Leisure and Recreation Association, 26–30 October, Sao Paulo, Brazil.

Anderson, L., and M. Littrell. (1995). Souvenir-purchase behavior of women tourists. *Annals of Tourism Research* 22: 328–348.

Anderson, L., and M. Littrell. (1996). Group profiles of women as tourists and purchasers of souvenirs. *Family and Consumer Sciences Research Journal* 25: 28–56.

Antrobus, P. (1990). Gender issues in tourism. Paper presented at the CTRC Conference on Tourism and Socio-Cultural Change in the Caribbean, 25–28 June, Port of Spain, Trinidad.

Bartos, R. (1982). Women and travel. *Journal of Travel Research* 20: 3–9.

Birkett, D. (1989). *Spinsters Abroad: Victorian Lady Explorers*. New York: Basil Blackwell.

Britton, S. (1996). Tourism, dependency and development: A mode of analysis. In *The Sociology of Tourism; Theoretical and Empirical Investigations*, edited by Y. Apostolopoulos, S. Leivadi, and A. Yiannakis. London: Routledge.

Butler, K. (1995). Independence for Western women through tourism. *Annals of Tourism Research* 22: 487–489.

Cohen, C. B. (1995). Marketing paradise, making nation. *Annals of Tourism Research* 22: 404–421.

Cohen, E. (1971). Arab boys and tourist girls in a mixed Jewish–Arab community. *International Journal of Comparative Sociology* 12: 217–233.

Cohen, E. (1974). Who is a tourist? A conceptual clarification. *Sociological Review* 22: 527–555.

Collins, P. H. (1990). *Black Feminist Thought: Knowledge, Consciousness, and the Politics of Empowerment*. New York: Unwin.

Cone, C. (1995). Crafting selves: The lives of two Mayan women. *Annals of Tourism Research* 22: 314–327.

Creighton, M. (1995). Japanese craft tourism: Liberating the crane wife. *Annals of Tourism Research* 22: 463–478.

Crick, M. (1989). Representations of international tourism in the social sciences: Sun, sex, sights, savings, and servility. *Annual Reviews in Anthropology* 18: 307–344.

Davidson, P. (1996). The holiday and work experiences of women with young children. *Leisure Studies* 15: 89–103.

Deem, R. (1996a). No time for a rest? An exploration of women's work, engendered leisure and holidays. *Time and Society* 5: 5–25.

Deem, R. (1996b). Women in the city and holidays. *Leisure Studies* 15: 105–119.

Derrida, J. (1976). *Of Grammatology*, translated by Gayatri Chakravorty Spivak. Chicago: University of Chicago Press.

Edensor, T., and U. Kothari. (1994). The masculinization of Stirling's heritage. In *Tourism: A Gender Analysis*, edited by V. Kinnaird and D. Hall. Chichester: Wiley.

Enloe, C. (1989). On the beach: Sexism and tourism. In *Bananas, Beaches and Bases: Making Feminist Sense of International Politics*, edited by C. Enloe. London: Pandora.

Fairbairn-Dunlap, P. (1994). Gender, culture and tourism development in Western Samoa. In *Tourism: A Gender Analysis*, edited by V. Kinnaird and D. Hall. Chichester: Wiley.

Foucault, M. (1984). Space, knowledge and power. In *The Foucault Reader*, edited by P. Rainbow. New York: Pantheon.

Garcia-Ramon, M., G. Canoves, and N. Valdovinos. (1995). Farm tourism, gender and the environment in Spain. *Annals of Tourism Research* 22: 267–282.

Gibson, H. (1989). Tourist roles: Stability and change over the life cycle. Master's thesis, University of Connecticut, Storrs.

Gibson, H. (1994). Some predictors of tourist role preference for men and women over the adult life course. Ph.D. diss., University of Connecticut, Storrs.

Gibson, H. (1996). Thrill seeking vacations: A lifespan perspective. *Loisir et Société/Society and Leisure* 19: 439–458.

Gibson, H., and F. Jordan. (1998a). Shirley Valentine lives! The experiences of solo women travelers. Paper presented at the Fifth Congress of the World Leisure and Recreation Association, 26–30 October, Sao Paulo, Brazil.

Gibson, H., and F. Jordan. (1998b). Travelling solo: A cross-cultural study of British and American women aged 30–50. Paper presented at the Fourth International Conference of the Leisure Studies Association, 16–20 July, Leeds, U.K.

Gibson, H., and A. Yiannakis. (1993). Patterns of tourist role preference across the life course. Paper presented at the Leisure Studies Association Third International Conference, 14–18 July, Lougborough University, U.K.

Graburn, N. (1989). Tourism: The sacred journey. In *Hosts and Guests: The Anthropology of Tourism*, edited by V. Smith. Philadelphia: University of Pennsylvania Press.

Gramsci, A. (1978). *Selections from Political Writing: 1921–1926*. New York: International Publishers.

Grosz, E. (1995). Women, chora, dwelling. In *Postmodern Cities and Spaces*, edited by S. Watson and K. Gibson. Oxford: Basil Blackwell.

Hall, C. M. (1992). Sex tourism in Southeast Asia. In *Tourism and the Less Developed Countries*, edited by D. Harrison. London: Bellhaven.

Hall, C. M. (1994). Gender and economic interests in tourism prostitution: The nature, development and implications of sex tourism in South-East Asia. In *Tourism: A Gender Analysis*, edited by V. Kinnaird and D. Hall. Chichester: Wiley.

Hall, D., and V. Kinnaird. (1994). A note on women travelers. In *Tourism: A Gender Analysis*, edited by V. Kinnaird and D. Hall. Chichester: Wiley.

Hanson, J. (1997). Sex tourism as work in New Zealand: A discussion with Kiwi prostitutes. In *Pacific Rim Tourism*, edited by M. Oppermann. Wallingford: CAB International.

Hawes, D. (1988). Travel-related lifestyle profiles of older women. *Journal of Travel Research* 27 (2): 22–32.

Henderson, K. (1994). Perspectives on analyzing gender, women and leisure. *Journal of Leisure Research* 26: 119–137.

Hooks, B. (1984). *Feminist Theory: From Margin to Center*. Boston: South End Press.

Iakovidou, O., and C. Turner. (1995). The female gender in Greek agro-tourism. *Annals of Tourism Research* 22: 481–484.

Jeffreys, S. (1998). Globalizing sexual exploitation: Sex tourism and the traffic in women. Paper presented at the Leisure Studies Association 1998, The Big Getto: Gender Sexuality and Leisure, 16–20 July, Leeds Metropolitan University, U.K.

Karsch, C., and G. Dann. (1996). Close encounters of the Third World. In *The Sociology of Tourism: Theoretical and Empirical Investigations*, edited by Y. Apostolopoulos, S. Leivadi, and A. Yiannakis. London: Routledge.

Kinnaird, V., and D. Hall. (1994). Conclusion: The way forward. In *Tourism: A Gender Analysis*, edited by V. Kinnaird and D. Hall. Chichester: Wiley.

Kinnaird, V., and D. Hall. (1996). Understanding tourism processes: A gender-aware framework. *Tourism Management* 17 (2): 95–102.

Kinnaird, V., U. Kothari, and D. Hall. (1994). Tourism: Gender perspectives. In *Tourism: A Gender Analysis*, edited by V. Kinnaird and D. Hall. Chichester: Wiley.

Kousis, M. (1989). Tourism and the family in a rural Cretan community. *Annals of Tourism Research* 16: 318–332.

Leheny, D. (1995). A political economy of Asian sex tourism. *Annals of Tourism Research* 22: 367–384.

Lett, J. (1983). Ludic and liminoid: Aspects of charter yacht tourism in the Caribbean. *Annals of Tourism Research* 10: 35–56.

Levinson, D. (1996). *The Seasons of a Woman's Life*. New York: Knopf.

Levinson, D., C. Darrow, E. Klein, N. Levinson, and B. McKee. (1978). *The Seasons of a Man's Life*. New York: Knopf.

Levy, D., and P. Lerch. (1991). Tourism as a factor in development: Implications for gender and work in Barbados. *Gender and Society* 5 (1): 67–85.

Marshment, M. (1997). Gender takes a holiday: Representation in holiday brochures. In *Gender, Work and Tourism*, edited by M. T. Sinclair. London: Routledge.

Massey, D. (1994). *Space, Place and Gender*. Minneapolis: University of Minnesota Press.

McGehee, N., L. Loker-Murphy, and M. Uysal. (1996). The Australian international pleasure market: Motivations from a gendered perspective. *Journal of Tourism Studies* 7 (1): 45–57.

McKay, L. (1993). Gender and tourism in Negril, Jamaica. In *Women and Change in the Caribbean: A Pan-Caribbean Perspective*, edited by J. Momsen. Bloomington: Indiana University Press.

Meisch, L. (1995). Gringas and Otavalenos: Changing tourist relations. *Annals of Tourism Research* 22: 441–462.

Miller, D., and J. Branson. (1989). Pollution in paradise: Hinduism and the subordination of women in Bali. In *Creating Indonesian Cultures*, edited by P. Alexander. Sydney: Oceania.

Monk, J., and C. Alexander. (1986). Free port fallout: Gender, employment, and migration on Margarita Island. *Annals of Tourism Research* 13: 393–413.

Moore, R. (1995). Gender and alcohol use in a Greek tourist town. *Annals of Tourism Research* 22: 300–313.

Mowl, G., and J. Towner. (1995). Women, gender, leisure and place: Towards a more "humanistic" geography of women's leisure. *Leisure Studies* 14 (2): 102–116.

Muroi, H., and N. Sasaki. (1997). Tourism and prostitution in Japan. In *Gender, Work, and Tourism*, edited by M. T. Sinclair. London: Routledge.

Norris, J., and G. Wall. (1994). Gender and tourism. In *Progress in Tourism, Recreation and Hospitality Management*, edited by C. Cooper and A. Lockwood. Chichester: Wiley.

Oppermann, M. (1999). Sex tourism. *Annals of Tourism Research* 26: 251–266.

Oppermann, M., and S. McKinley. (1997). Sexual imagery in the marketing of Pacific tourism destinations. In *Pacific Rim Tourism*, edited by M. Oppermann. Wallingford, U.K.: CAB International.

Picard, M. (1993). Cultural tourism in Bali: National integration and regional differentiation. In *Tourism in South-East Asia*, edited by M. Hitchcock, V. King, and M. Parnwell. London: Routledge.

Plog, S. (1974). Why destination areas rise and fall in popularity. *Cornell Hotel and Restaurant Administration Quarterly* 14: 55–58.

Pruitt, D., and S. LaFont. (1995). For love and money: Romance tourism in Jamaica. *Annals of Tourism Research* 22: 422–440.

Richter, L. (1994). Exploring the political role of gender in tourism research. In *Global Tourism: The Next Decade*, edited by W. Theobold. London: Butterworth Heinemann.

Robinson, J. (1990). *Wayward Women: A Guide to Women Travellers*. Oxford: Oxford University Press.

Rosaldo, M. (1980). The use and abuse of anthropology: Reflections on feminism and cross cultural understanding. *Signs* 5: 389–417.

Rosen, R. (1982). *The Lost Sisterhood*. Baltimore: Johns Hopkins University Press.

Scott, J. (1995). Sexual and national boundaries in tourism. *Annals of Tourism Research* 22: 385–403.

Sinclair, M. (1997a). Gendered work in tourism: Comparative perspectives. In *Gender, Work and Tourism*, edited by M. T. Sinclair. London: Routledge.

Sinclair, M. (1997b). Issues and theories of gender and work in tourism. In *Gender, Work and Tourism*, edited by M. T. Sinclair. London: Routledge.

Smith, V., ed. (1989). *Hosts and Guests: The Anthropology of Tourism*. 2d ed. Philadelphia: University of Pennsylvania Press.

Squire, S. (1994). Gender and tourist experiences: Assessing women's shared meanings for Beatrix Potter. *Leisure Studies* 13 (3): 195–209.

Swain, M. (1989). Gender roles in indigenous tourism: Kuna Mola, Kuna Yala, and cultural survival. In *Hosts and Guests: The Anthropology of Tourism*, 2d ed., edited by V. Smith. Philadelphia: University of Pennsylvania Press.

Swain, M. B. (1993). Women producers of ethnic arts. *Annals of Tourism Research* 20: 32–51.

Swain, M. B. (1995). Gender in tourism. *Annals of Tourism Research* 22: 247–266.

Turner, V. (1974). Liminal to liminoid in play, flow, and ritual: An essay in comparative symbology. *Rice University Studies* 60: 53–92.

Urry, J. (1990). *The Tourist Gaze*. London: Sage.

Valentine, G. (1989). The geography of women's fear. *Area* 21: 385–390.

Wagner, U. (1977). Out of time and place: Mass tourism and charter trips. *Ethnos* 42: 38–52.

Wearing, B. (1994). The pain and pleasure of gendered leisure. *World Leisure and Recreation*, Fall, 4–10.

Wearing, B. (1998). *Leisure and Feminist Theory*. London: Sage.

Wearing, B., and S. Wearing. (1988). "All in a day's leisure": Gender and the concept of leisure. *Leisure Studies* 7 (2): 111–123.

Wearing, B., and S. Wearing. (1996). Refocusing the tourist experience: The flâneur and the choraster. *Leisure Studies* 15 (4): 229–243.

Wilkinson, P., and W. Pratiwi. (1995). Gender and tourism in an Indonesian village. *Annals of Tourism Research* 22: 283–299.

Wolff, J. (1985). The invisible flâneuse: Women and the literature of modernity. *Theory, Culture and Society* 2: 37–45.

World Tourism Organization. (1997). *Yearbook of Tourism Statistics*. Madrid: Author.

Yiannakis, A., and H. Gibson. (1988). Tourist role preference and need satisfaction: Some continuities and discontinuities over the life course. Paper presented at the Leisure Studies Association Conference, 29 June–3 July, Brighton, U.K.

Yiannakis, A., and H. Gibson. (1992). Roles tourists play. *Annals of Tourism Research* 19: 287–303.

PART **II**

WOMEN IN THE MATURE
TOURIST DESTINATIONS

3

Island Is a Woman: Women as Producers and Products in British Virgin Islands Tourism

Colleen Ballerino Cohen

In a TV commercial aired early in 1999 by on-line brokerage firm Discovery Brokerage, a businessman with car trouble is picked up by a t-shirted tow truck driver, Bob. As Bob drives along in his somewhat junky tow truck, he tells his incredulous passenger that he really only drives his truck to keep busy, that through his on-line trading he has actually made enough money to buy his own tropical island. Bob shows his passenger a photograph of his pristine island paradise, and muses aloud about what to name it—perhaps he'll name it Bob, after himself. The commercial concludes with Bob returning the photo to its place in the sun visor, and ending the conversation with the punch line, "Technically, it's a country." On the surface, this commercial seems to be telling a story about democracy and hard work in the new age of e-commerce: With a little savvy and entrepreneurial drive, *anyone* can make enough money day trading to buy a tropical island. But when one considers the joke of the "technicality" of the island's sovereignty, the allure in Bob's being able to name the island after himself, and the fact that the conversation about the island takes place between two white men of different social classes, what emerges is a reassuring story in the cyber age about the stability of white male privilege and the endurance of colonial imperative. Of course, no matter how one reads it, what makes the commercial work is that it employs a familiar trope to concretize a fantasy about wealth, power, and possession. Centering a tropical island as the object of consumer desire, the commercial deploys a Western semiotic that conflates tropical locales with women's bodies as key signifiers of difference, and as naturally enticing objects to be explored, known, and possessed.

Depictions of tropical islands as enticing objects to be explored, known, and possessed are the mainstay of advertisements and brochures marketing tourism in the Caribbean (Pattullo 1996, 142–144). This chapter explores this semiotic, looking in particular at the way that it is deployed in tourism campaigns marketing the British Virgin Islands, a British Dependent Territory in the Eastern Caribbean.[1] As is the case for the majority of Caribbean countries, the British Virgin Islands economy depends heavily on the tourism industry, and tourism has had a considerable impact on British Virgin Islands society and culture. The chapter begins with an overview of tourism in the Caribbean and of tourism development in the British Virgin Islands in particular, with special reference to the link between tourism development and British Virgin Islands nationalism, and to the role that women play in both as producers of cultural products, events, and ideals. This overview is followed by an examination of the ideology of sexual difference underlying representations of the British Virgin Islands, and an analysis of the links between descriptions of the British Virgin Islands as a place of special allure and erotic attraction and male Western subjectivity. The chapter concludes with an assessment of the ways in which the discourse of naturalized heterosexual desire that eroticizes British Virgin Islands geography as a commodity for Western consumption also animates an ideology of the British Virgin Islands nation— and citizenship in it—as natural facts.

TOURISM DEVELOPMENT IN THE
BRITISH VIRGIN ISLANDS

The British Virgin Islands consists of over fifty islands, rocks, and cays located sixty miles east of Puerto Rico in the Lesser Antilles chain in the Eastern Caribbean. Settled by the British in 1672, the British Virgin Islands was one of the poorest, most scantily populated, and least economically profitable of all of Britain's Caribbean colonies (Dookhan 1975; Harrigan and Varlack 1988). In the years immediately following World War II the British Virgin Islands economy experienced dramatic and rapid growth due to the development in the 1960s of a successful tourist economy and in the 1980s of a strong financial-services sector. During this same period, the British Virgin Islands achieved enhanced political autonomy—marked by the 1967 formation of a fully representative ministerial system of government—and experienced rapid population growth and demographic change. Of the present-day British Virgin Islands population of 20,000, half are non–British Virgin Islanders (mostly from other Caribbean countries), drawn to work in its burgeoning tourist and financial-services economies. While the specific impacts of tourism and financial-services development have varied by race, gender, and nationality, throughout this period of rapid growth the British Virgin Islands has maintained a high degree of political and social stability and its per capita income of over $18,000 is exceeded only by the per capita incomes of the Bahamas, Bermuda, and the Cayman Islands.[2] The economic development that fostered radical demographic and social change has gone hand in hand with a growing sense of the British Virgin Islands as a distinct national community, made up of people of "own kind" (Williams 1993, 153). Increasingly one hears talk of the need to prepare for independent political status.[3]

The post–World War II tourism boom in the British Virgin Islands mirrors in many important respects developments throughout the region. Tourism in the Caribbean traces to the late nineteenth century, when wealthy Europeans first established winter residences there and wealthy Americans began to make it a regular stop on their winter yacht sojourns (Pattullo 1996). Cuba and the Bahamas became favored destinations of elite Western tourists between the wars, but it wasn't until after World War II that tourism became the major foreign-exchange earner regionwide, with mass tourism—cruise ship, chain-hotel based, and tour-operated tourism—accounting for most of the growth (Pattullo 1996, 11). In 1959, 1.5 million tourists visited the region; between 1970 and 1991 the number of visitors to the region increased from 4.24 million to 11.65 million (Momsen 1994, 107–108); by 1994, the number of tourists to the Caribbean had increased to 16 million annually (Pattullo 1996). Today tourism revenues constitute an important segment of the GDP of every country in the Caribbean, with tourism accounting for more than 50 percent of the national income of Antigua, the Bahamas, Barbados, the British Virgin Islands, Grenada, St. Kitts-Nevis, and the Dominican Republic (Pattullo 1996, 12).

This growth in Caribbean tourism is a direct result of factors and forces originating from outside the region: the introduction of nonstop international jet service, the investment of foreign capital in large-scale resorts and chain hotels like Hilton and Sheraton, and the development of cruise ship tourism. Thus, although tourism has resulted in selected infrastructural development in the form of new roads, airports, docks, and so on, external interests control vast sectors of the industry. Similarly, while Caribbean national incomes have risen as a result of tourism development, and while many countries report over 25 percent of their working population employed in tourism (Momsen 1994; Pattullo 1996), local participation in the profits of the tourism industry is limited. Moreover, according to Momsen's (1994) study of tourism and gender in the Caribbean, "Most of these workers in tourism are young, semi-skilled and increasingly likely to be female" (p. 111).

Women's participation in tourism in the Caribbean has been shaped in large measure by their roles in Caribbean society at large. Thus, where women have traditionally been involved in market activity or in craft work, they tend to become engaged in the tourist economy as vendors or producers of tourist craft goods. Throughout the region the stereotypical association of women with the domestic sphere has also resulted in women entering the tourism service sector as landladies running guest houses, or as owner–operators of small restaurants (McKay 1993; Momsen 1994). Although advertisements for Caribbean tourism frequently feature pictures of women whose dress and demeanor suggest that they are sexually available and ready to serve, female prostitution directed toward tourists is in fact less frequent in the Caribbean than "beach boy" sex tourism directed toward women tourists. I address this aspect of tourism in some detail later in this chapter. Rather, as Momsen (1994) has demonstrated, "The main form of employment for women in the tourist industry is as maids in hotels" (p. 112). Moreover, although more women are employed in tourism regionwide than men, men experience higher levels of training, advancement, and job security than women (p. 113).

The development of the British Virgin Islands tourism industry was also made possible by massive foreign investment, but the British Virgin Islands government had an early hand in shaping the nature and extent of British Virgin Islands tourism. In this and in the factors shaping women's participation in tourism, the British Virgin Islands experience is somewhat different from the experience of most other Caribbean countries. Tourism development in the British Virgin Islands traces to the 1953 Hotels Aid Ordinance that provided tax incentives to potential investors in tourist-oriented enterprises, and to a 1966 government-commissioned report targeting tourism as the most viable development option for the British Virgin Islands. The opening in 1964 of the Rockefeller-owned Little Dix Bay resort on the British Virgin Islands island of Virgin Gorda marked the beginning of the development of the modern British Virgin Islands tourism industry (O'Neal 1983, Bowen 1976), and initiated a boom in the construction of similarly upscale resorts on Virgin Gorda. The 76.7-percent increase in the local population of this one island from 1970 to 1991 (Development Planning Unit 1991) is a direct result of the development of these largely foreign-owned enterprises. The major focus of British Virgin Islands tourism development is "elite tourism" (Smith 1989), concentrated on charter yacht tourism, small luxury beach resort tourism, and short- and long-term private villa rentals.[4] In 1981 the British Virgin Islands had the highest tourist per capita ratio of all island countries world- wide; in 1989, annual tourist arrivals (177,074) exceeded by ten times the total British Virgin Islands population (Encontre 1989, 98).

Most of the British Virgin Islands' largest tourist-based enterprises are foreign owned, and much of the labor in the service sector of all components of the British Virgin Islands tourist economy is performed by nationals from other islands (British Virgin Islands Department of Labor 1990). Nevertheless, a development policy of controlled growth backed by legislation impeding land speculation and prohibiting the sort of large-scale development associated with mass tourism have resulted in some locally owned tourism-related businesses in the form of restaurants, guest houses, taxi services, and long-term housing for off-island labor.[5] One of the most important consequences of this leg- islation has been the retention by British Virgin Islanders of their land: Today close to 70 percent of British Virgin Islands land is held by Brit- ish Virgin Islanders of all classes. Similarly, although the most profit- able British Virgin Islands yacht chartering companies are foreign owned, national legislation—and a recently opened community col- lege—have provide a structure for local residents to secure increased involvement at the managerial level of these and other foreign-owned companies (Coopers and Lybrand Consultants 1996, 2–6). Finally, yacht chartering has drawn some locals into its economy as skippers, yacht managers, and small marina owners. In this respect, yacht chartering, like the small-scale guest-house development in Dominica documented by Weaver (1991), can represent a viable form of alternative tourism development.

WOMEN AND TOURISM IN THE BRITISH VIRGIN ISLANDS

Notwithstanding the British Virgin Islands being singled out by one scholar as one of the few Caribbean micro states that has had some success in exerting local control over tourism development (Wilkinson 1989), a 1996 report commissioned by the British Virgin Islands gov- ernment as part of a national tourism development strategy found that "the emergence of BVI's tourism economy was largely funded by offshore investment . . . [and] at the present time, the critical mass of the most visible land-based and sea-based tourism assets are foreign owned" (Coopers and Lybrand Consultants 1996, 7-7). As one might expect, the growth of tourism in the British Virgin Islands has created internal divisions in the labor market and a related intensification of class stratification. Government legislation gives British Virgin Islanders first preference in hiring, and most public-sector occupations are held by British Virgin Islanders. Meanwhile, British Virgin Islanders are underrepresented in the tourism workforce. While the entry to middle-level positions in the private sector are shared by British Virgin Islanders and non–British Virgin Islanders from other Caribbean countries, senior positions in the private sector are held principally by non–British Virgin Islanders, who are for the most part white British and Canadian expatriates. Although available census data do not provide a further breakdown by gender, anecdotal evidence and my own observations suggest that women's participation in tourism follows a similar pattern, with British Virgin Islands women contributing to tourism through their positions in the public sector (e.g., as managers of tourist board departments, as managers and middle managers in ministries of government, and as educators) or in the private sector as managers of small hotels or villas or as supervisors in service businesses such as car rental agencies, tourist-oriented shops, restaurants, hotels, and bars. The lower-paid, less secure, and largely unregulated positions of maids, cooks, waitresses, and street vendors are filled predominately by non–British Virgin Islands Afro-Caribbean women.

During the past two decades, jobs in tourism have exceeded the local labor supply (Coopers and Lybrand Consultants 1996), and so many of the Caribbean women who come to the British Virgin Islands seeking work in its tourism industry stay, setting up households and sometimes marrying or having children with British Virgin Islands men. If a non–British Virgin Islands woman marries a British Virgin Islands man, she receives the full rights of citizenship accorded him, and although she will always be identified by her nation of birth (e.g., as "from Anguilla" or "from Nevis"), her children will be reckoned as "Belongers," a legal term for British Virgin Islands citizenship that also conveys the cultural ascription of being of British Virgin Islands descent.[6] However, within five years of divorce or her husband's death, the woman's rights to British Virgin Islands citizenship may be revoked. A child born to non–British Virgin Islands parents or outside of a legal marriage union to a non–British Virgin Islands woman and a British Virgin Islands man is not a citizen of the British Virgin Islands (see also Maurer 1997), but is deemed a citizen of the mother's country of origin. For such a child to be formally accorded this citizenship, however, requires that the birth be registered in the mother's country of origin, and that proper citizenship papers be acquired. This is a lengthy and costly procedure, frequently requiring several trips off-island, and there are countless children residing in the British Virgin Islands today who are "without papers"; that is, without legal citizenship anywhere. The magnitude of this problem is reflected in the fact that the coveted British Virgin Islands Calypso King crown was won in 1991 by a St. Kitts national, Benji V., with a song, "Where We Born Is Where We From," that detailed the dilemma of these children. As its title suggests, this song presents an argument against British Virgin Islands citizenship law, claiming instead that "where a baby first see sun, that country must be their own, they must have the rights like anybody born in the same region."

As this brief overview of British Virgin Islands tourism is meant to suggest, the factors contributing to the internal divisions in the contemporary British Virgin Islands economy and society are varied and complex, with race and nationality figuring as crucially as gender in determining opportunities for economic and social success. Moreover, while it is non–British Virgin Islands women who are most likely to work cleaning the rooms at British Virgin Islands upscale resorts where British Virgin Islands women work as desk managers and white expatriate women keep the books, "to this day a significant mass of the Islands' high visibility tourism enterprises are in the private sector and owned by expatriates, many of whom live offshore" (Coopers and Lybrand Consultants 1996, 7-2). Thus, for example, I know of one British Virgin Islands woman who Monday through Friday works in a relatively high-status job as an associate in a real estate company that manages vacation rentals, and weekends works in a lower-status job as a clerk for a yacht-chartering company. Both of the companies for whom the woman works are owned by white expatriates residing in the British Virgin Islands. However, as a British Virgin Islander, this woman is assured that her child will be educated through high school, and, should he qualify, that he will receive government scholarship support for college. A non–British Virgin Islands woman from another Caribbean country who might have a similar occupational profile has no such assurances. Indeed, in response to the overcrowded conditions in all British Virgin Islands primary schools and its two public high schools, the British Virgin Islands government regularly warns individuals seeking entry to the British Virgin Islands for work in its prosperous tourism economy that they cannot be assured that there will be a space for their school-age children in BVI schools.

The ability of women to assert control over the tourist economy and its impacts is structured similarly, with British Virgin Islands women in a far better position than most non–British Virgin Islands women to take advantage of legislative policies that limit alien landownership and regulate the allocation of trade licenses to, for example, open small tourist-oriented shops, restaurants, or guest houses. On the whole, however, policies giving preference to British Virgin Islanders in all hirings, land purchases, and the awarding of trade licenses have not significantly altered the profile of British Virgin Islander participation in the tourist economy. The reasons for this are multiple and varied, but seem to trace to several interconnected factors: an entrenched pattern of and reliance on offshore investment in the British Virgin Islands tourist industry, the long-term practice of importing workers to fill high- and low-end jobs in tourism, a reluctance on the part of British Virgin Islanders to enter the tourism workforce at the lower levels, and a lack of capital or credit necessary for investment in tourism, either through existing banking institutions or the British Virgin Islands Development Bank, established for that purpose.[7] One particular site within which local negotiations for control can and do take place is the cultural arena. And in this arena, British Virgin Islands women are a visible and influential presence.

With economic prosperity at home, fewer British Virgin Islanders today emigrate abroad for work, and those who have been away—for work or for education—are returning to take up permanent residence. In conjunction with increasing British Virgin Islands political autonomy, local economic stability, and a declining economic dependence on Great Britain, the demographic changes resulting from economic prosperity have abetted the growth of national pride and nationalist sentiment. The conception of the British Virgin Islands as a national homeland to a people with a shared heritage is foregrounded in electoral debates about British Virgin Islands independence, in government reports warning that "the BV Islander is precariously close to being a minority in his own country" (Coopers and Lybrand Consultants 1996, 2-1), and in cultural events, such as National Education Week and British Virgin Islands Festival that showcase British Virgin Islands culture and provide opportunities for expressions of British Virgin Islands national identity. Meanwhile, even as British Virgin Islands tourist-industry prosperity depends upon wide-scale importation of labor from other Caribbean nations, its continued success as a tourist destination depends upon its being able to distinguish itself from the other islands from which these workers originate, in a market in which potential tourists have a demonstrated inability to differentiate between one Caribbean island and the next (Pattullo 1996, 147). Hence, the same venues that provide opportunities for expressions of British Virgin Islands national identity also serve to exhibit to tourists what is unique and special about the British Virgin Islands.

The labor of British Virgin Islands women, as government officials, as educators, and as public-spirited citizens, has been central to the development of the British Virgin Islands cultural "product" in both respects. British Virgin Islands women fill most of the top positions on the tourist board, both in the British Virgin Islands and in its tourist board offices in the United States and Europe, and a British Virgin Islands woman currently holds the post of director of the tourist board. The post of Minister of Education and Culture is held by the British

Virgin Islands woman who held the first official position directing British Virgin Islands tourism development, as head of the Tourism Advisory Board, established in 1961. In 1979 this same woman also founded the BVI Heritage Dancers, a dance company that performs at most national cultural events and represents the British Virgin Islands at regional cultural festivals as well as at international tourism trade shows. Finally, a British Virgin Islands woman innovated and implemented "BVI Nice," a tourist board program that trains taxi drivers to provide information and behave toward their customers in ways that accord with tourism representations of the British Virgin Islands and its people as yet untouched by the forces of development.

The image promulgated by the BVI Nice campaign is consonant with the description with which the 1993 edition of *Fodor's Caribbean* opens its section on the British Virgin Islands: "Serene, seductive, and spectacularly beautiful even by Caribbean standards, the British Virgin Islands are happily free of the runaway development that has detracted from the charm of so many West Indian islands" (Simon 1993, 159). *Fodor's* portrayal of the BVI as unique among other Caribbean destinations is mirrored in the British Virgin Islands tourist board motto around which early tourism advertising campaigns were centered: "Yes We Are Different." It is also consistent with a marketing strategy that stresses the "freshness" of the British Virgin Islands product (PKF Consulting 1992, II-19), and government policies that seek, in the words of a government-commissioned report, "to strike a balance between the need to develop . . . tourist attractions for the benefit of the economy, without at the same time destroying what make[s] them attractive in the first place" (Shankland Cox 1972, 43, quoted in O'Neal 1983, 114).[8] Of course, in contrasting the "runaway development" characterizing other Caribbean destinations with the serene environment of the British Virgin Islands, this portrayal also corresponds with a nationalist discourse that can and does differentiate between British Virgin Islanders and non–British Virgin Islanders. Hence, the "nice" British Virgin Islands taxi driver (who may or may not be a native of the British Virgin Islands), enacts at once a behavior expected by the tourists and at the same time a nationalist sensibility that casts British Virgin Islanders as different from individuals from other Caribbean countries (see also Cohen and Mascia-Lees 1993).

A principal arena for simultaneously expressing national pride and identity and demonstrating what is special about the British Virgin Islands is the annual festival commemorating the August 1, 1834, emancipation from slavery. Marked by a three-day national holiday, Festival is an occasion for family reunions, for honoring local personages notable for their civic contributions, and for putting on public demonstrations of British Virgin Islands cuisine, music, and dance. Festival also serves as a bellwether of national sentiment and pride. A "good" Festival is one at which all elements—from number of parade troupes, to variety and elaborateness of costumes, to number of contestants participating in Festival's calypso and queen shows, to whether or not the Festival parade starts on time—are considered to have provided a worthy representation of British Virgin Islands culture and society.[9] In this respect, concerns to put on a good Festival overlap with concerns to put on a Festival that will appeal to tourists who visit the British Virgin Islands during the summer off-season. The 1998 consolidation of all Festival planning and events under the Ministry of Education and Culture was effected in large measure so that the government might have more direct control of the cultural product, which is both marketed to tourists and constitutive of the British Virgin Islands sense of itself as a nation (Cohen 1998).

British Virgin Islands women occupy most of the key positions of the Festival and Fairs Planning Committee, the government body responsible for organizing and carrying out Festival events. In this capacity they determine the annual Festival theme, create publicity for the Festival, and head up the committees responsible for securing Festival entertainment, putting on Festival parades, and organizing Festival competitions. Among the most anticipated of Festival events is the Miss British Virgin Islands Queen Show, a contest that selects the national beauty queen, who represents the British Virgin Islands at the Miss Universe contest and other regional and international competitions. Because it highlights a local aesthetic and local standards of comportment, and because it can elevate the social standing of its participants and their families, the Miss British Virgin Islands contest is a key site for exhibiting ideal standards of British Virgin Islands womanhood (Cohen 1996). For the same reasons, the women sitting on the Queen Show Committee and who screen candidates, solicit prizes, put together the panel of judges, and so on, can and frequently do wield a good amount of influence in the local political cultural arena (Cohen 1998, 1996).

Because it selects a candidate to represent the British Virgin Islands at the Miss Universe contest, the Miss British Virgin Islands contest also plays out on a more global stage, where the reigning Miss British Virgin Islands serves as ambassador of her country. Primary among her duties in this capacity is promoting her country as a tourist destination. In an interview for a British Virgin Islands newspaper, Miss British Virgin Islands 1990 was quite explicit about the connection between her participation in the Miss Universe Contest as her nation's representative and the British Virgin Islands competing for Caribbean tourist dollars: "I am happy to have sold tourism for the British Virgin Islands. My sash indicated my place of origin and allowed me to explain the Territory's geographical location and the natural beauty it possesses" ("Miss British Virgin Islands" 1991).[10] Yet even as Miss British Virgin Islands 1990 was preparing to depart for the Miss Universe contest, another article appeared in the local British Virgin Islands paper reporting the use of a photograph taken of Miss Bermuda lounging on a Bermudan beach for a Barbados tourist brochure inviting Western tourists to "Play the Bajan Way." This case of mistaken identity points, finally, to the difficulty of Miss British Virgin Islands' task. For even as she strives to distinguish the attractions of her homeland from the attractions of other Caribbean tourist destinations, she works within an ideological economy that lumps all Caribbean countries together and casts them all as exotic objects of erotic allure.

TROPICAL ISLANDS AND SEXUAL DESIRE

The advertisement about Bob and the tropical island that his online trading enabled him to buy aired at about the same time the 1999 *Sports Illustrated* swimsuit issue came out. As in swimsuit issues before it, the 1999 *Sports Illustrated* swimsuit issue was devoted to the display of women's bodies in a format associated more with *Playboy* than with *Sports Illustrated*. Shot on location in the British Virgin Islands, the 1999 swimsuit issue announced its content with a cover subcaption replete with sexual innuendo: "The Not So Virgin Islands." Apart from this cover reference and a frontispiece description that conflates the British Virgin Islands with the Fantasy Island of television fame, the only other references to the British Virgin Islands appear in articles that construct it as outside of time, with no local social or political history. Indeed, like the women displayed lounging on its beaches, the British Virgin Islands appearing on the pages of the 1999 swimsuit issue is portrayed as existing solely for pleasure or consumption.[11]

One of the articles on the British Virgin Islands, entitled "Dissipation Row," features Bomba, a local British Virgin Islander, and his "Shack," a beach bar on the British Virgin Islands island of Tortola that is famous for its full-moon parties and psychedelic mushroom tea. Claiming that "there are few more seductive places to do nothing in style than Bomba's" (Lidz 1999, 134), the article describes Bomba in terms that evoke images of the classic "primitive" (Torgovnick 1990); that is, as simultaneously "wild and . . . filled with an old old knowledge" (Lidz 1999, 130). Similarly, although the article refers to Bomba's place of birth and residence on Tortola, the largest and most densely populated of the British Virgin Islands, it characterizes Bomba himself as "blissfully forgetful" of the particulars of his personal history— "time and me's one big ball"—who lives only to oversee the "Dionysian rapture" of the Shack (Lidz 1999, 130, 132). As for Tortola—the center of one of the region's most successful tourism and financial-services economies—the article attributes its allure to "its Sartrean sense of nothingness" (Lidz 1999, 134).

The only other article in the swimsuit issue that makes reference to the British Virgin Islands is a short piece that appears as part of a longer article on Richard Branson, CEO of Virgin Atlantic Airlines. This piece, entitled "An Island of One's Own" (Nack 1999), describes Branson's purchase of Necker Island, a small island in the British Virgin Islands, and details the negotiations and financial terms of the sales transaction. Like the commercial about Bob and his island, this article makes island buying look easy. As the article submits, "As fast as Branson could make out a check, Necker Island was his" (196). To make buying a piece of the British Virgin Islands plausible, the article purges Necker Island of any meaning apart from its existence as a commodity. "Never heard of them," Branson is reported to have said when first told about the British Virgin Islands (p. 196). This dismissal opens the article and, like the textual strategies of nineteenth-century travelers into the "unmapped" and "unnamed" interiors of South America (Pratt 1992), it also opens the British Virgin Islands for whatever meaning we wish to inscribe on it. In this case, what is depicted as "a mostly barren shank of rock" occupied by "a herd of belligerent wild goats" is transformed "into what [Branson] now calls 'my private island paradise.' And it has cost him only $20 million" (p. 196).

The construction in the *Sports Illustrated* swimsuit issue of a British Virgin Islands that exists solely for the pleasure of Western consumers—who party in its hot spots or buy its islands—goes hand in hand with the construction of the women for whose bodies the British Virgin Islands provide a picturesque backdrop. In one photo essay entitled "Island of Plenty" a naked model is sprawled on what looks like a food platter surrounded by tropical fruits; a subtitle suggests that this main dish is "the most delectable fruit" ("Island of Plenty" 1999, 158). This same model is elsewhere in the magazine referred to as an "exemplary specimen" who is "on our cover but 'off the market,'" as she recently married sitcom star John Stamos (Murphy 1999). A two-page advertisement that appears in the middle of the article on Branson also makes explicit the way in which deserted tropical islands are made to stand in for women in order to pique consumer desire. The first page of this advertisement shows a deserted tropical beach, turquoise waves breaking gently on white sand. The caption running across the top of this picture reads, "Of all the curvaceous, sexy frames in this magazine." Upon turning the page, one sees the same tropical beach, but now there is a mountain bike on its sands. The caption on this page completes the caption from the previous page: "Here's one you can actually get your hands on."

The marketing strategy that sells a mountain bike by piquing sexual desire works because it draws upon a convention that associates lush tropical islands with erotic pleasure. "Islands As Aphrodisiacs" is the title of a 1994 Conde Nast Traveler article that begins, "Islands are sexy. By nature they are" (p. 106). A 1993 article in Outside magazine describes more explicitly the imagined connection between the tropics and sex that animates the mountain bike ad. Referring to the tropics as "those latitudes synonymous with passion," the article asserts

It's a barometric conspiracy of the soul down there, below the belt of northern proprieties, where everything is ripe, tumescent, sticky, and all sensory information seems deliberately lascivious: the phallic fruits and the labial blossoms; the skunky, primal ooze of the mangrove swamps; the steamy jungle. . . . This is the climate of decadence so organic, so outrageously seductive, that desire takes no prisoners. It's an all-or-nothing affair. (Shacochis 1993, 74)

Of course, the mountain bike advertisement also works because, in addition to piquing desire, it holds forth the possibility of possession: "Here's one you can actually get your hands on." Erotic pleasure and the will to possess are linked in the Western imagination (Hulme 1992; McClintock 1995; Pratt 1992), and as key signifiers of "difference" to the Western subject, tropics and tropical islands emerge as potent sites for the expression of male sexual desire. In this capacity, as well, tropical islands are easily conflated with woman as erotic object of desire. As Chambers (2000) has recently pointed out in a discussion of tourism as a gendered activity,

The traveler's "eye" is an extension of a masculine will to conquer and control. . . . One needs only to scan a handful of tourist brochures from almost any part of the world, but especially from "hot and sexy" places like the tropics, to discover that there are merits to this interpretation. Consider how typically women are depicted in the roles of hosts or entertainers and how readily their images meld into those of a region's landscape, becoming a part of that which is different and picturesque about a place. (p. 60)[12]

NATURE'S LITTLE SECRETS

The association between tropical islands and sexual desire that was used in the *Sports Illustrated* swimsuit issue to sell a mountain bike is replicated in British Virgin Islands tourism advertisements, which play extensively upon the term "virgin." In most British Virgin Islands tourism advertisements, the seductiveness of the "serene" and "spectacularly beautiful" British Virgin Islands is posited as a factor of its being "unsullied" by forces that have defiled other Caribbean countries, as in the *Fodor's Caribbean* description of the British Virgin Islands, or as in a 1995 tourist board advertisement that proclaims more explicitly, "Our Virgin Islands Are Still Virgin." In 1990 the British Virgin Islands tourist board launched a $770,000 advertising campaign around the slogan, "Discover Nature's Little Secrets" ("$770,000 Ad Campaign" 1991). Combined with references to the untouched beauty of the British Virgin Islands, this invitation to discovery offers up the British Virgin Islands for the taking. A memo from the advertising agency that developed the Discover Nature's Little Secrets campaign confirms this intention, highlighting the BVI as "virgin holiday territory . . . one of the few remaining outposts of the old British Empire" (FCB/Inter-Marketing 1989).

The opening narrative of a promotional video produced to kick off the Nature's Little Secrets campaign suggests the same in more cultivated prose, as follows: "Surviving intact through centuries of man's excess, the islands look now much as they did when the first visitors arrived. Today's visitors say this pristine beauty calls them back again and again. Will the British Virgin Islands cast their spell on you?" ("Discover Nature's Little Secrets" 1991). In the Discovery Brokerage commercial, the appeal of owning a tropical island disguised the fact that what was really being sold was the power that comes with wealth. In similar fashion, the promotional video's invitation to tourists to discover "for yourself" an "intact" landscape and a "pristine" beauty sells the British Virgin Islands as a tourist destination by appealing to male sexual desire and the will to possess.

Sexual desire is, as Cynthia Enloe (1990) has noted, a central component of tourism ideology, and the desire to know another place is conflated in the touristic imagination with women "as the quintessence of the exotic . . . something to be experienced" (p. 28). Likewise, as a manifestation of sexual desire for an exotic other, tourism is not just about escape, it is also about power (p. 40). Not only is tourism embedded in the economic inequalities between the countries from which tourists originate and the countries of their destination, but the sexual ideology underlying tourism's representations of destinations such as the British Virgin Islands draws its effectiveness from notions of the naturalness of sexual difference and inequality. Pattullo (1996) makes a similar point when she attributes tourist fantasies about the Caribbean as an edenic paradise "of daytime indolence beneath the palms and a nighttime of pleasure through music, dance and sex" to racist stereotypes that draw their effectiveness from assumptions of the naturalness of racial difference and inequality (p. 142). In either case, raced and sexed bodies emerge as key sites for assertions of the "naturalness" of difference, and hence for normalizing Western subjectivity (cast as normatively male) and power (see also Cohen and Mascia-Lees 1993; Hulme 1992; McClintock 1995; Pratt 1992).

While allusions to the sexiness of tropical locales like the British Virgin Islands characteristically center male libidinal desire—positioning women as objects of that desire—it bears noting that Western women tourists are not immune to the messages so prevalent in Caribbean tourism advertisements. Studies of sexual encounters between Western women tourists and Caribbean men, while scant and frequently anecdotal, suggest that such encounters comprise an important aspect of some Western women's tourist experiences. Such sexual encounters are, of course, not limited to Caribbean tourism. Studies of sexual encounters between Western women tourists and local men elsewhere in the world suggest that they result in part from the women's sense of freedom from moral constraints that they might feel at home and in part from a local perception that Western women are more "available" and interested in short-term sexual relations than local women (Bowman 1989; Tucker 1997, 113–114). In particular respect to the Caribbean, the association of the region with a colonized and raced other and the marketing of the region as a place whose residents are experts at catering to Western desire conspire to eroticize the power differential between white Western tourists and the locals with whom they mingle. As Polly Pattullo (1996) points out in her comprehensive study of Caribbean tourism, the possibility that Caribbean men and women might be available to Western tourists as sexual partners "is made more seductive by received images, laced with racism: the 'exotic,' easy 'native' woman with a hibiscus behind her ear; or the beach boy whose sexual prowess has been defined by white culture" (p. 87).

The particular nature of British Virgin Islands tourism, with its dual emphasis on yacht chartering and long-term stays at elite resorts or rented villas, draws more families and couples to the British Virgin Islands than the single white women who are most likely to be looking for sexual encounters with local men. Thus, the sort of sex tourism that has come to be associated with Jamaica (see especially Pattullo 1996, 88; Pruitt and LaFont 1995) is neither as prevalent nor as visible in the British Virgin Islands. Surely, the possibility of a sexual encounter with a local man is one of the attractions of Bomba's Full-Moon Party, and the regularity of such encounters is sufficient to draw occasional letters of protest or outrage to the local newspapers. Such an encounter even inspired a poem by a local writer.[13] Most British Virgin Islanders with whom I have spoken disdain these encounters, finding them not just morally repugnant but also mystifying, as the men that women tourists usually become involved with are poorer and less well educated than their tourist partners. Those British Virgin Islanders who take a more benign view of such encounters tend to speak of them as just one of the many edifying experiences that a British Virgin Islands vacation offers. In this they mirror the rhetoric of tourist ads that cast the British Virgin Islands as a special place with special experiences in store.

British Virgin Islands advertisements have changed very little since I first started fieldwork there in 1990. Taking as their starting point the slogan "Discover Nature's Little Secrets," most advertisements play on the West's desire for a "natural" beauty—whether woman or island—by emphasizing the British Virgin Islands' "unmatched natural splendour . . . [its] unspoilt beaches, coves and bays . . . a water-sports paradise relatively untouched by civilization" (*Bon Appétit* 1991). Brochures depicting the British Virgin Islands as a natural paradise also tend to depict the people occupying the British Virgin Islands as "naturally" friendly and accommodating, as in an advertisement from a 1995 British Virgin Islands tourist board brochure that claims, "Learning water sports takes on a new dimension, and not just for unmatched scenery. . . . Instructors make the big difference. Typical BVI citizens, they care a lot. Teaching you to enjoy the water is not just what they do, it's what they *are*" (italics original); or in a press release that conflates the "natural" beauty of the BVI geography with the "natural" friendliness of the BVI people and offers them both as natural secrets "yet to be discovered": "Although peopled by some of the friendliest faces in the Caribbean, the little known British Virgin Islands and its many little secrets of nature have yet to be discovered by the traveling masses" ("Discover Nature's Little Secrets" 1991). By positing the British Virgin Islands and its residents as "naturally" what they are—pristine Caribbean landscapes occupied by people who exist to give pleasure to tourists—such descriptions assume the same function as the articles on the British Virgin Islands in the *Sports Illustrated* swimsuit issue. They construct a British Virgin Islands that is outside of time, devoid of any specific historical past or political volition.

These textual strategies that naturalize the British Virgin Islands and its residents are consistent with an ideology that postulates as natural the opposition between a primitive dark-skinned "other" and a civilized white-skinned "self." Thus, promoting the British Virgin Islands as a "secret" appeals to the elite tourists targeted by the advertisements because it invokes the notion of dominant white culture as normative and in possession of truth. Insofar as the historic "discovery" of the islands of the Caribbean "mark[s] the moment when 'the West' became a conceptual entity" (Mintz 1989, xxi) and establishes the conceptual basis for Western hegemonic authority through the ensuing centuries of imperial expansion (Hulme 1992), what is being held out for discovery is as much a sense of a powerful knowing self as an untouched exotic other. To be among the first to "know" the British Virgin Islands in this sense is to recapture the moment when local histories were obliterated and rewritten to stabilize the West as the center of power and knowledge.

It is in this sense that the pristine British Virgin Islands constituted in tourist industry representations also works to "cast its spell." Naturalized within relations of sexual difference as female and eroticized through references to the allure of virginity, the British Virgin Islands is rendered a site where to "discover nature's little secrets" is to achieve the transcendence of the knowing male subject (Beauvoir 1953). This aspect of British Virgin Islands allure is reinforced in the words with which the promotional video closes: "Xeno, a famous Greek philosopher who lived more than 2000 years ago, once said that the goal of life is living in agreement with nature. It may well take us another 2000 years to achieve that goal. But isn't it worthwhile starting to work on it right now? Come to the British Virgin Islands and discover nature's little secrets for yourself" ("Nature's Little Secrets" 1991).

CONCLUSION

The contemporary British Virgin Islands experience is conditioned by its being a place whose territory and residents are marketed worldwide as representative of an idealized tropical paradise; where, on any given day during tourist season, foreign "visitors" may outnumber local residents ten to one; and where its primacy in the global offshore banking community involves it minute by minute in an international electronic flow of information and money. Simultaneously, the contemporary British Virgin Islands experience is conditioned by its implication in the very local project of nation-building. This is a project that finds its people deeply engaged in the cultural practices and discursive productions that give meaning to their understanding of themselves as part of a British Virgin Islands nation and, most crucially, that establish exclusionary categories for membership in that nation.

The question of how local and global economies and interests intersect and diverge is central in contemporary tourism studies, which have moved from an initial concern with defining the field to a concern with understanding "the various meanings that are shaped and produced by the dynamic interchange that constitutes tourism encounters" (Abram and Waldren 1997, 6; see also Chambers 2000). In the British Virgin Islands, tourism development has resulted in a strong economy and has also abetted the development of strong nationalist sentiments. Materially, efforts to develop the British Virgin Islands tourism product have gone hand in hand with efforts to nurture and support British Virgin Islands culture, and the labor of British Virgin Islands women has been central to both developments. As crucially,

British Virgin Islands tourism and nationalism are both deeply gendered activities that draw extensively on a discourse of naturalized heterosexual desire. Thus, for example, even as Western tourists visiting the British Virgin Islands are enticed by the sexual innuendoes in the invitation to "discover nature's little secrets," British Virgin Islanders assert their "natural" citizenship in the British Virgin Islands nation through claims to having "a piece of Virgin."

The transformation of what were historically diverse and widespread communities and islands into the British Virgin Islands nation is a consequence of political changes in the 1950s and 1960s that resulted in the British Virgin Islands assuming greater control over its internal affairs, and of the development in the 1970s and 1980s of a successful tourism industry. The economic prosperity resulting from tourism increased the British Virgin Islands' material wealth, even as the influx of laborers from other Caribbean islands raised concerns over who should properly have access to this wealth. During this period, initiatives promoting a national culture were also launched, muting long-standing distinctions between different communities of British Virgin Islanders. The establishment in 1954 of a national beauty contest, in 1957 of St. Ursula's Day as a national holiday, in 1979 of a national folk dance troupe, and in 1982 of a Culture Officer, and the publication in 1984 of a comprehensive collection of British Virgin Islands folktales, songs, and recipes all provided bases for the people inhabiting the British Virgin Islands to think of themselves and their relations to each other in new ways.

A key component of the conceptualization of the British Virgin Islands as "nation" is the construction of a "natural" British Virgin Islands nation and—in opposition to the outsiders swelling the population—a "natural" British Virgin Islander. In this respect, some of the same initiatives developed to sell the British Virgin Islands as a tourist destination can also authenticate assertions about the "naturalness" of British Virgin Islands citizenship. We have seen how programs such as BVI Nice, which are meant to enhance the British Virgin Islands tourism product, can also abet a nationalist project. In the case of BVI Nice this is accomplished through a rhetoric that distinguishes the British Virgin Islands from other Caribbean destinations by reference to the "friendliness" of the people providing the service. Likewise, the tourist brochure that promises the tourist that BVI citizens care conflates an assertion about natural characteristics—"it's not just what they do, it's what they *are*"—with a legal status—"BVI citizens." The adjective "typical" turns this into a statement about national character: "They care a lot." Like magazine advertisement or tourist brochure narratives that mask differences in power by evoking the naturalness of desire for an exotic "other," constructions of the British Virgin Islands as a "natural" community of citizens establish a strong cultural basis for the social and economic divisions that have ensued with the growth of the tourism economy.

The conceptualization of the British Virgin Islands as a "natural" grouping of "natural" British Virgin Islanders is also accomplished through conceptualizing the British Virgin Islands as a pristine and timeless space. Such a conceptualization is not unlike the British Virgin Islands to which tourists are invited to travel for full-moon parties and mushroom tea or that are rendered rhetorically ready for purchase and transformation into personal tropical paradises. However, where the pristine British Virgin Islands of tourism's constructions invites discovery and possession by stimulating desire for an eroticized and sexualized "other," the British Virgin Islands that emerges in nationalist discourse is constituted as a motherland whose respectability—framed in terms of cultural integrity—must be safeguarded against outside influence. This conceptualization of the British Virgin Islands is most evident in official documents and newspaper accounts that point with alarm to the prospect that "the influx of persons from abroad if not adequately monitored could lead to the indigenous population being outnumbered to the detriment of the preservation of the local heritage and culture" (Secretary of State for Foreign and Commonwealth Affairs 1994, 21). But it also emerges in popular discourse that bemoans the increase in children of "mixed" (i.e., BVI and non-BVI) parentage (see also Maurer 1997), or that asks rhetorically, "How can you be a British Virgin Islander without having a piece of the virgin?" In this respect, representations of the British Virgin Islands as woman that ground assertions of British Virgin Islands identity reflect a general tendency to depict the nation as a female body whose violation must be defended against. And, as Parker, Russo, Sommer, and Yaeger (1992) point out, this tendency "depends for its representational efficacy on a particular image of woman as chaste, dutiful, daughterly, or maternal" (p. 6; see also Yuval-Davis and Anthias 1989).

Their superficial differences notwithstanding, each construction of the British Virgin Islands—as an exotic female other, as a nation of own kind with autochthonous origins in an ancient motherland—is embedded within a conceptual framework that works to naturalize the British Virgin Islands, and thus to normalize and homogenize differences in history, race, ethnicity, and power. In the case of tourism's construction of the British Virgin Islands as an exotic other to the Western self, naturalizing the British Virgin Islands stabilizes historic relations of exploitation and power. In the case of constructions of the British Virgin Islands as the homeland of a people of shared heritage, naturalizing the British Virgin Islands as nation blurs differences among

British Virgin Islanders and fixes an absolute difference between British Virgin Islanders and non–British Virgin Islanders, and hence establishes fixed categories of people who may or may not lay claim to its prosperity and rewards. In each case, it is by constituting the British Virgin Islands as female—as sexual object or as primordial motherland—that difference is naturalized. In each case, finally, a physical place is constituted as a particular kind of space, and each space shapes subjectivities within it according to its particular logic (Kirby 1996), be it the logic of the "national" space of the BVI as "natural" nation, the "primitive" vacation space of the BVI as "Sartrean nothingness," or the "colonial" space of the BVI as "my own private tropical island."

Meanwhile, women's participation in today's British Virgin Islands tourist economy is structured by very particular historical and material circumstances. These circumstances mean that women experience real differences in their access to jobs, social services, and wealth according to their race, nationality, marital status, and so forth. Such difference in lived experience means that women necessarily understand their relationship to the "space" of the British Virgin Islands differently, and will have greater or lesser agency in altering or shaping that space. Similarly, the appeal of sexual conquest or possession may be expected to register differently with tourists who are nonwhite and/or who are women.[14] The analysis here of the images of the British Virgin Islands disseminated in magazine articles, tourism advertisements, and nationalist discourses points to the centrality of an ideology of natural sexual and racial difference in establishing and fixing as "natural" historically contingent differences in power and wealth. In light of the concrete differences in material circumstances described here, the analysis also underscores the importance of understanding tourism as one among many linked forces in the context of which people negotiate their individual realities and collective identities.

NOTES

1. The ethnographic fieldwork on which this chapter draws was initiated in the summer of 1990 and continues to the present, funded by the Vassar College Ford Scholars Program and Vassar Faculty Research Grants. I am indebted to my many British Virgin Islands friends and colleagues who so generously help me in my work.

2. From 1962 (when the British Virgin Islands government targeted tourism as a primary economic development strategy) to 1965 British Virgin Islands tourism was responsible for a 40-percent increase in the British Virgin Islands GDP, from $2,251,000 to $3,157,000. By 1970 visitor expenditures and construction associated with tourism development had pushed the GDP of the British Virgin Islands to $15,947,000 (O'Neal 1983, 113), by 1992 the gov-

ernment was reporting a GDP of $105.7 million (Development Planning Unit 1991), and by 1994 the government was reporting a GDP of $320 million (*Offshore Finance Annual* 1996). Beginning in the late 1970s the British Virgin Islands began to develop the financial-services sector of its economy; by 1994 revenues from offshore banking constituted 35 percent of British Virgin Islands GDP, and direct and indirect revenues from tourism constituted 50 percent of British Virgin Islands GDP (Coopers and Lybrand Consultants 1996, 2-9–2-12).

3. Indeed, the status of the British Virgin Islands as a country surfaced as the major issue in the national elections held in May 1999. A new political party that highlighted the youth and worldliness of its candidates set the tone of the debates during campaigning, which tended to ask not whether independence, but rather when and under whose leadership.

4. Yacht chartering is a specialized tourist industry in which crewed and uncrewed sailing yachts are rented out to tourists on a per-week basis; yacht charterers in the British Virgin Islands usually spend one to two weeks in the area sailing from island to island, with overnight stays at marinas or sheltered anchorages (Lett 1983; O'Neal 1983). Although the British Virgin Islands experienced an increase of cruise ship visitors beginning in the late 1980s, the most recent available data from 1992 show overnight arrivals outnumbering cruise ship arrivals almost three to one, and hotel tourists outspending charter yacht tourists (51.1 percent versus 36.5 percent), even though the number of charter yacht tourists visiting the British Virgin Islands exceeded the number of hotel tourists (50,478 versus 42,773) (Coopers and Lybrand Consultants 1996).

5. A 1968 nationwide demonstration to protest the long-term leasing of public land to outside developers resulted in a historic U.K.–funded buyback of the leases. This historic incident impelled the government to pass legislation that closely regulates land sales to non–British Virgin Islanders and operates symbolically in the present-day context to inspire continued vigilance with regard to British Virgin Islands public land.

6. British Virgin Islands labor statistics do not record country of origin, but anecdotal evidence and school enrollment records suggest that most emigration to the BVI is from the neighboring Eastern Caribbean countries of Nevis, St. Kitts, Anguilla, Antigua, and Santo Domingo; other Caribbean countries with a notable representation in the BVI population are Guyana, Trinidad, St. Lucia, and Jamaica. By law, only British Virgin Islands citizens have the unrestricted right to buy and hold land, and British Virgin Islands citizens are usually given preference in hiring and in the awarding of trade licenses, college scholarships, and low-interest development-bank loans. Following provisions of the 1981 British Nationality Act and of the British Virgin Islands Constitution, British Virgin Islands citizenship is acquired in one of two ways: one may be made a citizen or born a citizen. One is made a citizen by being granted Belonger status. This is usually a long and complicated process preceded by long-term residence (and prior legal Residence status), and requiring demonstration of moral integrity and productivity. More commonly, one is born a citizen through birth to parents in a legal marriage union, when one of the

parents is a British Virgin Islander, or through birth, legitimate or otherwise, to a British Virgin Islands woman. A child born outside of a legal marriage union to a non–British Virgin Islands woman and a British Virgin Islands man is not automatically a citizen (see also Maurer 1997). In terms of daily practice and local knowledge, however, a Belonger may also be marked literally by who one "belongs to": by what family and part of the British Virgin Islands one comes from, and even by one's physical—and frequently behavioral—characteristics. While it is conventional to carry the surname of one's father (except in instances where the father refuses to acknowledge paternity), one is assumed to "belong" to the lines of both father and mother. In this sense, "belonging" means being of the British Virgin Islands, nation of birth or nationality of mother notwithstanding.

7. These trends were culled from a lengthy report, commissioned by the government and completed by Coopers and Lybrand Consultants (1996), entitled, "National Tourism Development Strategy 1996–2005." The report is a remarkable combination of alarmism—stressing the dire consequences for British Virgin Islanders if they continue to import "foreign" labor to work in tourism—and condescension—placing the blame for the low numbers of British Virgin Islands owners and managers on the shoulders of British Virgin Islanders who, the report claims, "have made choices, and often their choice largely was not to invest their money in the tourism industry. This is probably due to the lack of training and knowledge of the industry" (p. 7-7) and "have not chosen to undertake the education and training regimens that qualify them for many of the positions in the Industry. . . . We have been unable to identify many BVIslanders who have enrolled in [the numerous post-secondary hotel management programs and hospitality programs available]. We understand that one of the reasons for this is the lack of knowledge on the part of possible candidates that these opportunities exist" (p. 7-11). In light of the overall tone of the report, it warrants quoting in full its assessment of the investment opportunities to British Virgin Islanders: "The data seem to indicate that during the last three decades BVIslanders have not had the pools of capital, nor sources of credit, at their disposal to develop intermediate to large scale tourism products. The creation of the Development Bank has not had an overall positive impact on this situation" (p. 7-7).

8. Claims about the pristine and serene British Virgin Islands landscape can also be read as so much hype targeted at the tourist consumer who, in the words of one British Virgin Islands Chief Minister, has "the inherent need to get away from the pressures of city and business life to escape to paradise, even if for only a short while" (FCB/InterMarketing 1989). On the other hand, tourist responses to a tourism consulting-firm questionnaire that rank the British Virgin Islands highest on the statements, "is a good place to relax at the beach," "is a visually attractive island," and "is a safe place to visit" (PKF Consulting 1992, V-33) suggest a certain correspondence between this characterization and tourist experience.

9. Particularly in comparison to other Festivals around the region. Indeed, a good deal of the debate over the quality of any BVI Festival event is based on comparisons that are made by nationals from other Caribbean countries

residing in the British Virgin Islands between their "home" Festivals and the British Virgin Islands Festival. A major concern of organizers of the British Virgin Islands Festival is to put on an event that is both distinctive and high quality; a major dilemma is how to do so in a way that will invite the participation of non–British Virgin Islanders while at the same time be a distinctive national British Virgin Islands product.

10. Barnes's (1997) study of Jamaican beauty contests demonstrates a similar and long-standing connection between beauty contests and the interests of the Jamaican tourist board.

11. Maurer (1997) makes a similar point in his book on British Virgin Islands law and citizenship. Referring to a cruise ship advertisement that begins, "There is no law that says you can't," and then lists the activities one can do while anchored in the BVI, Maurer asserts, "To the tourist, the BVI is a territory apart from the law, a virgin land of sun, sand, the sea, and servants" (pp. 8–9).

12. Judith Williamson's (1986) analysis of print advertisements marketing tropical products and tropical vacations underscores the significance of sexual difference in stimulating desire, with special attention to the role that racial difference also plays in normalizing the Western male prerogative to possess women or territory. According to Williamson, advertisements use images of women with light (as opposed to very dark) brown skin to stand for "exotic" products because they can stimulate desire while masking any actual difference in power between the "other" (who is not too much "other") and the Western subject. This erotically charged "natural" difference also asserts the continuity of Western hegemony while it simultaneously functions ideologically to conceal and control social difference (such as the social inequalities of class) and historical difference (such as the inequalities of power between colonizer and colonized). Hulme (1992) makes a similar point in his discussion of the role of nineteenth-century fictionalized accounts of reciprocal love between slave women and European slave owners in masking the horrors of slavery.

13. This poem, by Patricia Turnbull (1992), is a conversation between the mother of a white tourist girl and the mother of a local youth with whom the girl has taken up. In the poem, the mother of the girl exclaims, "Your island is indeed a paradise/what girl from a mill town in New/Hampshire would not fall/prey to playing mermaid/earth child and sun goddess/all at once?" The boy's mother responds, "Now, tell me, what these people take we for?/They t'ink we savage just because we poor!/I'll have that woman, that . . . that Jezebel/ understand I too raised a decent child."

14. One of the most intense debates to have surfaced recently is over whether to repeal a law that prohibits entry into the British Virgin Islands of any individual with dreadlocks. Passed in the mid-1980s when the British Virgin Islands tourism economy was undergoing its most rapid period of growth and advertising campaigns were stressing British Virgin Islands difference from other Caribbean islands, the law was seen as a means to safeguard the British Virgin Islands (and tourists to the British Virgin Islands) from the presumably harmful influences of Rastafarianism. Today, after several embarrassing situations in which wealthy and famous Afro-Americans were kept from entering the British Virgin Islands, there is a growing movement to wipe the law off the books.

REFERENCES

Abram, S., and J. Waldren. (1997). Introduction: Tourists and tourism—identifying with people and places. In *Tourists and Tourism: Identifying with People and Places*, edited by S. Abram, J. Waldren, and D.V.L. Macleod. Oxford and New York: Berg.

Barnes, N. B. (1997). Face of the nation: Race, nationalisms, and identities in Jamaican beauty contests. In *Daughters of Caliban: Caribbean Women in the Twentieth Century*, edited by C. Lopez-Springfield. Bloomington: Indiana University Press.

Beauvoir, S. de. (1953). *The Second Sex*. New York: Doubleday.

Bon Appétit. (1991). Advertisement. March, 21.

Bowen, W. E. (1976). Development, immigration and politics in a pre-industrial society: A study of social change in the British Virgin Islands in the 1960s. *Caribbean Studies* 16 (1): 67–85.

Bowman, G. (1989). Fucking tourists: Sexual relations and tourism in Jerusalem's old city. *Critique of Anthropology* 9 (2): 77–93.

British Virgin Islands Department of Labor. (1990). *Labour Department Statistics for the Year of 1990*. Road Town: Government of the British Virgin Islands, Department of Labor.

Chambers, E. (2000). *Native Tours: The Anthropology of Travel and Tourism*. Prospect Heights, Ill.: Waveland Press.

Cohen, C. B. (1996). Contestants in a contested domain: Staging identities in the British Virgin Islands. In *Beauty Queens on the Global Stage: Gender, Contests, and Power*, edited by C. B. Cohen, R. Wilk, and B. Stoltje. New York and London: Routledge.

Cohen, C. B. (1998). "This is de test": Festival and the cultural politics of nation building in the British Virgin Islands. *American Ethnologist* 25 (2): 189–214.

Cohen, C. B., and F. E. Mascia-Lees. (1993). The British Virgin Islands as nation and desti-nation: Representing and siting identity in a post-colonial Caribbean. *Social Analysis* 33 (September): 130–151.

Coopers and Lybrand (Caribbean) Consultants, Inc. (1996). *National Tourism Development Strategy 1996–2005, Final Report*. Road Town: Government of the British Virgin Islands Chief Minister's Office.

Development Planning Unit. (1991). *1990 Population and Housing Census, Preliminary Count*. Road Town: Government of the British Virgin Islands.

Discover nature's little secrets. (1991). Brochure. Road Town: British Virgin Islands Tourist Board.

Dookhan, I. (1975). *A History of the British Virgin Islands 1672–1970*. Epping, Essex, England: Caribbean Universities Press.

Encontre, P. (1989). *Why Does the Tourist Dollar Matter? An Introduction to the Economics of Tourism in the British Virgin Islands*. Road Town: British Virgin Islands Tourist Board.

Enloe, C. (1990). *Bananas, Beaches, and Bases: Making Feminist Sense of International Politics*. Berkeley and Los Angeles: University of California Press.

FCB/InterMarketing. (1989). Discover nature's little secrets. Press releases. New York.

Harrigan, N., and P. Varlack. (1988). *The Virgin Islands Story*. Epping, Essex, England: Caribbean Universities Press.

Hulme, P. (1992). *Colonial Encounters: Europe and the Native Caribbean, 1492–1797*. New York and London: Routledge.

Island of plenty. (1999). *Sports Illustrated*, Swimsuit ed. (Winter): 158–184.

Islands as aphrodisiacs. (1994). In *Conde Nast Traveler*. New York: Conde Nast.

Kirby, K. (1996). Defining the space of the subject. In *Indifferent Boundaries: Spatial Concepts of Human Subjectivity*, edited by K. Kirby. New York: Guilford Press.

Lett, J. (1983). Ludic and liminoid aspects of charter yacht tourism in the Caribbean. *Annals of Tourism Research* 10: 35–56.

Lidz, F. (1999). Dissipation row. *Sports Illustrated*, Swimsuit ed. (Winter): 130–139.

Maurer, B. (1997). *Recharting the Caribbean: Land, Law, and Citizenship in the British Virgin Islands*. Ann Arbor: University of Michigan Press.

McClintock, A. (1995). *Imperial Leather: Race, Gender, and Sexuality in the Colonial Context*. New York and London: Routledge.

McKay, L. (1993). Women's contribution to tourism in Negril, Jamaica. In *Women and Change in the Caribbean*, edited by J. H. Momsen. Bloomington: Indiana University Press.

Mintz, S. (1989). *Caribbean Transformations*. New York: Columbia University Press.

Miss British Virgin Islands returns from Las Vegas. (1991). *The Island Sun* 1617 (1 June): 1, 12.

Momsen, J. H. (1994). Tourism, gender, and development in the Caribbean. In *Tourism: A Gender Analysis*, edited by V. Kinnaird and D. Hall. Chichester: Wiley.

Murphy, A. (1999). The not so Virgin Islands. *Sports Illustrated*, Swimsuit ed. (Winter): 8–16.

Nack, W. (1999). An island of one's own. *Sports Illustrated*, Swimsuit ed. (Winter): 196.

Nature's little secrets. (1991). Video. Road Town: British Virgin Islands Tourist Board.

Offshore Finance Annual. (1996). Road Town: British Virgin Islands Tourist Board.

O'Neal, M. (1983). British Virgin Islands transformations: Anthropological perspectives. Ph.D. diss., Union Graduate School, Cincinnati, Ohio.

Parker, A., M. Russo, D. Sommer, and P. Yaeger. (1992). Introduction. In *Nationalisms and Sexualities*, edited by A. Parker, M. Russo, D. Sommer, and P. Yaeger. New York and London: Routledge.

Pattullo, P. (1996). *Last Resorts: The Cost of Tourism in the Caribbean*. London: Cassell.

PKF Consulting. (1992). *The British Virgin Islands Tourism and Cruiseship Study*. Prepared for the Office of the Chief Minister, British Virgin Islands. Miami: PKF Consulting.

Pratt, M. L. (1992). *Imperial Eyes: Travel Writing and Transculturation*. New York and London: Routledge.

Pruitt, D., and S. LaFont. (1995). For love and money: Romance tourism in Jamaica. *Annals of Tourism Research* 22: 422–440.

Secretary of State for Foreign and Commonwealth Affairs. (1994). *British Virgin Islands: Report of the Constitutional Commissioners 1993*. London: HMSO.

770,000 ad campaign unveiled: Putting the BVI's "best foot forward." (1991). *BVI Beacon* 7 (35): 1, 8.

Shacochis, B. (1993). The tropics. *Outside* 17 (3): 74–75.

Shankland Cox and Associates. (1972). *Tortola, British Virgin Islands: A Development Plan for Wickhams Cay*. London: Shankland Cox and Associates.

Simon, J. (1993). The British Virgin Islands. In *Fodor's Caribbean*. New York: Fodor Publishing.

Smith, V. (1989). Introduction. In *Hosts and Guests: The Anthropology of Tourism*. 2d ed., edited by V. Smith. Philadelphia: University of Pennsylvania Press.

Torgovnick, M. (1990). *Gone Primitive: Savage Intellects, Modern Lives*. Chicago: University of Chicago Press.

Tucker, H. (1997). The ideal village: Interactions through tourism in Central Anatolia. In *Tourists and Tourism: Identifying with People and Places*, edited by S. Abrams, J. Waldren, and D.V.L. Macleod. Oxford and New York: Berg.

Turnbull, P. (1992). Two mothers. In *Rugged Vessels: Poems by Patricia Turnbull*. British Virgin Islands: Archipelago Press.

Weaver, D. E. (1991). Alternative to mass tourism in Dominica. *Annals of Tourism Research* 18: 414–432.

Wilkinson, P. F. (1989). Strategies for tourism in island microstates. *Annals of Tourism Research* 16: 153–177.

Williams, B. (1993). The impact of the precepts of nationalism on the concept of culture: Making grasshoppers of naked apes. *Cultural Critique* 24 (Spring): 143–191.

Williamson, J. (1986). Woman is an island: Femininity and colonization. In *Studies in Entertainment: Critical Approaches to Mass Culture*, edited by T. Modleski. Bloomington: Indiana University Press.

Yuval-Davis, N., and F. Anthias, eds. (1989). *Woman–Nation–State*. New York: St. Martin's Press.

4

Destabilizing "Maturity": Women as Producers of Tourism in Southeast Asia

Sara Kindon

Postcolonial Southeast Asia is a diverse and complex region characterized by uneven capitalist development.[1] It also exhibits depeasantization, labor migration, a newly affluent middle class and growing consumer culture, and the persistence of relatively strong state governments (Ong and Peletz 1995). In 1996 Southeast Asia experienced 31 million tourist arrivals worth $29,664 million in receipts (World Tourism Organization 1998), and seven of the ten countries in the region were recently in the top twenty earners of international tourism receipts in the East Asia and Pacific region (Fletcher and Latham 1997, 203). Tourism has fueled government elites' obsession with economic growth and modernization and is an increasingly important source of foreign exchange earnings (Hall 1994b, 68). It has been seen as a "soft" development option with which to attract foreign direct investment (Brohman 1996), spread economic benefits to peripheral areas (Hitchcock, King, and Parnwell 1993), extend political authority (Lowenhaupt-Tsing 1993), and manage low-intensity conflicts within national borders (Ong and Peletz 1995).

Increasingly, Southeast Asia is described as a mature touristic destination within developing regions of the world because it is considered to be well-integrated into the world economy and able to cater to diverse market segments, and it offers a wide range of integrated tourist products. Certainly, when compared with other developing regions Southeast Asia has a longer history of tourism development and is more integrated into world tourism circuits. However, there is no comprehensive view of the social, economic, cultural, environmental, and political issues, processes, and problems associated with tourism development in Southeast Asia (Hitchcock, King, and Parnwell 1993, 4; Wall 1998), and when trying to systematically investigate women's experiences, the picture is even more partial. This is despite increasing calls to recognize the gendered nature of tourism globally (Kinnaird and Hall 1994; Richter 1994, 1995; Swain 1995; Wall 1996; Sinclair 1997).

Within Southeast Asia the relatively high status of women is often considered an important feature underlying the region's cultural diversity and, at the local level, there is commonly a degree of gender equality and fluidity (Atkinson and Errington 1990; Blanc Szanton cited in Gardiner Barber 1996). However, at the national level there are emerging struggles to create more uniform gender imageries (Suryakusuma 1991; Ledgerwood 1996). These national gender imageries tend to reflect middle-class and neoconservative ideologies and draw on the symbolic structuring of gender relations according to binary oppositions such as prestige and stigma, the spiritually potent and the spiritually weak, and the disciplined and the disruptive (Atkinson and Errington 1990). Such imagery and symbolism are aligned with efforts to develop economically and are reinforced in state guidelines and development plans (Sen and Stivens 1998). In these, femininity is associated with the domestic sphere, chastity, modesty, duty, and hard work, and masculinity is associated with the public sphere, leadership, sexual prowess, and violence (Chant 1997; Kindon 1995; Ledgerwood 1996).

However, Errington (1990) has argued that "gender is not the difference that makes a difference" in Southeast Asia because prestige systems are not explicitly framed in gendered terms, but are linked to the activities people engage in or the spiritual power they exhibit or fail to exhibit. Thus, women encounter ambiguous and contradictory messages as they seek employment in new spaces opened up by tourism. This ambiguity presents opportunities and constraints for women to rework cultural meanings associated with femininity and masculinity. Not surprisingly, issues of family, gender, home, and work have become central sites for the expression of concerns about the cultural costs of modernity associated with tourism and other forms of capitalist development (Stivens 1998).

Consequently, when considering women in tourism in Southeast Asia it is important to acknowledge their positions within complex webs of power relations at different scales, for as Enloe (1989) has argued, "Paying serious attention to women can expose how much power it takes to maintain . . . [a] political system in its present form" (p. 3). In this chapter I focus on women as a way of questioning the concept of maturity as it is currently applied to the region as a touristic destination.[2] I argue that this concept and its application reinforces hegemonic development discourse. This discourse reflects measures of masculine involvement in tourism, thus positioning women's economic participation as absent, marginal, or deviant. I draw on published research about women as tourism producers in Southeast Asia to demonstrate how their participation destabilizes maturity and reveals the gendered-power relations inherent in tourism development and its classification at different scales.[3] Finally, I propose that utilizing "liminality" may recalibrate the concept of maturity when considering Southeast Asia as a touristic destination.

SOUTHEAST ASIA: A MATURE DESTINATION?

Tourism has a long history in Southeast Asia, dating back to the travel associated with European colonial expansion, and to the "R & R requirements" of U.S. and Japanese military staff based throughout the region in the twentieth century (Richter 1989). Since the 1980s the Association of Southeast Asian Nations (ASEAN) has been promoting the region worldwide and, in 1992, led a marketing campaign with the slogan, "ASEAN: The world's only 6-in-1 tropical paradise" (Walton 1993). The campaign was particularly aimed at attracting male business and convention travelers (Richter 1993).

The concept of maturity as it is applied to Southeast Asia reflects tourism's role as a major contributor to the region's economy, with its high numbers of tourist arrivals and receipts, its increasingly modern and sophisticated infrastructure development, and its diverse and integrated market segments and products (see Table 4.1). Moreover, the historical legacy of tourism in the region means that it has demonstrated the ability to weather individual market or seasonal fluctuations, stagnating or declining tourist arrivals, and the recent economic crisis to maintain a stable market share of tourism receipts within the Asia Pacific region (Wall 1998; World Tourism Organization 1998). Well-integrated promotions and the careful consolidation or rejuvenation of specific tourist products (Butler 1980) have been essential to maintaining the region's profile and arrivals (Urry 1990; Hall 1994b; Goad and Crispin 1999).

From this overview, it would appear that the basic framework for tourism development in Southeast Asia is "mature" or "set" (Hitchcock, King, and Parnwell 1993, 190). However, the notion of maturity needs to be questioned. It relies upon formal economic measures of growth

Table 4.1
Economic Indicators of Southeast Asia's Tourism (1996)

Country	Tourist Arrivals (thousands)	Tourism Receipts ($ millions)	Tourism Receipts Average Annual Growth Rate 1980–1996 (percent)	Share of Receipts within Asia Pacific Region (percent)
Thailand	7,192	8,664	15.47	10.65
Malaysia	7,138	3,926	18.35	4.83
Singapore	6,608	7,961	11.31	9.79
Indonesia	5,034	6,087	22.21	7.48
Philippines	2,049	2,700	14.26	3.32
Vietnam	1,607	87	N/A	0.11
Brunei Dar	837	38	N/A	0.05
Cambodia	260	118	N/A	0.15
Myanmar	172	33	N/A	0.04
Lao PDR	93	50	N/A	0.06
Southeast Asia Region	30,990	29,664	15.05	36.48
Asia Pacific Region	89,186	81,352	14.98	100.00
World	594,827	433,863	9.25	—

Source: World Tourism Organization, Yearbook of Tourism Statistics (Madrid: Author, 1998).

and modernization in a few "core" destinations and countries for its definition and purchase, masking inequalities at smaller scales. The term "mature" misleadingly signifies a uniform or homogenous indication of tourism development, when, as Teo and Chang (1998) observe, "Classifying the region as a single destination area belies the fact that its member countries are at differing stages of the tourism development cycle" (p. 120). "Maturity" also conveys a stage of development to which states and communities should aspire, and can be equated with linear notions of "progress" and "modernity" favored in modernist development discourse (Crush 1995). Such discourse values the elimination of "underdevelopment" and peripherality of people and places through their increased integration into the capitalist world economy (Harrison 1992). A recent example of this discourse can be seen in Var, Toh, and Khan's (1997) brief report on tourism and ASEAN economic development, in which they note, "Singapore [has] the *best and most modern* infrastructure with Vietnam *lagging far behind*" (p. 195, italics added).

However, many places in Southeast Asia do not reflect characteristics of maturity (Twining-Ward and Baum 1998; Dahles and Bras 1999). In Laos, Cambodia, and Vietnam, for example, war and conflict have stifled the development of their tourist infrastructure, human resources, and organizational structures and planning until recently (Wagner cited in Lam 1998; Lieper 1998; Biles, Lloyd, and Logan 1999). They more closely exhibit the involvement, exploration, and development stages of Butler's (1980) tourist-area life-cycle model and the associated characteristics of underdevelopment or "peripherality" discussed by Wanhill and Buhalis (1999). In addition, even in the more "developed" or "core" destinations like Indonesia, the Philippines, and Thailand there are areas with unconsolidated tourism services, products, and markets (Hall 1994b; Kindon and Hume-Cook 1997; Goad and Crispin 1999) because certain localities have been promoted at the expense of others (Chon and Oppermann 1996).

In addition to the spatial variations obscured by the discourse of maturity, it is imperative to question the activities maturity represents. The description of an area or destination as mature currently relies upon the measurement of labor, products, and markets associated with formal economic and infrastructural development, and their integration into national and world economies. While it is an oversimplification to dichotomize the economy into two distinct sectors—formal and informal—it is a useful heuristic device (Timothy and Wall 1997).[4] Moreover, it is important to work with this dichotomy, as governments only recognize the formal sector in their provision of financial and other assistance and in their calculations of revenue, taxes, and employment. The informal sector is generally absent from their planning or is viewed as marginal or deviant and is preferably destined to disappear with increasing modernization (Timothy and Wall 1997, 324).

At present, more men participate in the formal sector than women, even with the rapid feminization of manufacturing in recent years (Ong 1990). Women predominate in informal-sector activities throughout the region and often work as unpaid labor within family enterprises (see Table 4.2).

Economic measures of tourism development upon which the notion of maturity is constructed do not, therefore, account for women's participation in and experiences of tourism, or the often contradictory ways in which it positions them (Jones cited in Murray 1991). In fact, it is extremely difficult to ascertain national and regional statistics on women's participation in tourism as either producers or consumers. Thus, it is men's labor and products that are recognized within development discourses and assessments about the maturity or otherwise of a touristic destination (Selwyn 1993). Consequently, the label of

Table 4.2
Percentage Distribution of Workers by Class and by Sex
in Southeast Asia

Country	Employer	Employee	Own Account/ Self-Employed	Unpaid Worker
Brunei 1991				
Male	85	—	75	56
Female	15	—	25	44
Indonesia 1993				
Male	83	18	73	37
Female	17	82	27	63
Malaysia 1990				
Male	92	64	73	36
Female	8	36	27	64
Philippines 1994				
Male	52	47	53	54
Female	48	53	47	46
Singapore 1990				
Male	81	48	80	50
Female	19	42	20	50
Thailand (no date)				
Male	81	60	70	34
Female	19	40	30	66

Source: Adapted from Association of Southeast Asian Nations Secretariat, *The Advancement of Women in ASEAN: A Regional Report* (Jakarta: Author, 1996), 12.

Note: National figures come from different years of observation. No date specified for Thai figures.

maturity as it has been applied to the region reflects and privileges masculine activities within tourism development as normal and desirable. The absence of attention to gender in regional tourism analyses of Southeast Asia as a mature destination also constructs a degree of homogeneity and uniformity that negates the diverse sociospatial realities of women at smaller scales. These realities are described in more detail in the next section.

WOMEN AND TOURISM IN SOUTHEAST ASIA

The advertising imagery and marketing strategies associated with tourism in Southeast Asia promote opportunities for leisure, relaxation, and exotic and erotic exploration (Kontogeorgopoulos 1998). Such images clearly reinforce stereotypical and colonial images of Southeast Asia as a source of cheap labor and as "other" to the civilized West (Said 1978; Selwyn 1993; Oppermann and McKinley 1996; Carter 1998, 355).[5] In addition, tourists' exotic activities and potentially erotic behavior rely on the commodification of women's labor and sexuality (Enloe 1989; Truong 1990; Hall 1994a).

Within national-development discourses in the region, women are ambiguously positioned as commodified workers and their cultures' moral guardians (Association of Southeast Asian Nations Secretariat 1996).[6] They are desirable as workers because of stereotypical assumptions about their personal and economic attributes (Sadli 1992; Ong 1990). Yet they are reminded not to forsake their primary duties as wives and mothers and they may face the reassertion of patriarchal control if they are thought to have transgressed these norms of femininity (Suryukusuma 1991; Kindon 1993, 1995; Yeoh and Huang 1995; Chant and McIlwaine 1995; Ledgerwood 1996; Stivens 1998). They also continue to receive fewer resources for health, education, and training than men, which further constrains their employment opportunities (Ranck 1992; Truong 1996).

Given that tourism works within these wider development discourses, women are frequently positioned as secondary income earners for their families and associated with activities that reinforce their subordination within localized prestige systems (Errington 1990). The formal sector is therefore segmented in terms of gender-related wage differentials, in which women are often paid less than men for the same work or confined to lower echelons and lower pay (Richter 1994). This segmentation turns "the existing comparative advantage [of Southeast Asia's cheap labor] into the comparative advantage of women's disadvantage" (Department for Policy Coordination and Sustainable Development 1995, 15). It often forces women into the informal sector, where they work as casual, short-term, and seasonal wage laborers, street traders, or homeworkers (Chant and McIlwaine 1995; Ong and Peletz 1995; Gardiner Barber 1996; Wong 1996; Sittirak 1998). In particular, many women work as unpaid labor in family businesses connected with small-scale production or move into prostitution and personal services. They remain invisible within formal calculations of revenue, taxes, and employment (Department for Policy Coordination and Sustainable Development 1995).

Women's Experiences in Formal-Sector Tourism: The Philippines and Indonesia

In the Philippines, Chant and McIlwaine (1995) argue that tourism's formal-sector employment is less "feminized" than other sectors and there is more equal employment and remuneration between women and men. However, there are important gender differences. In a survey of four major hotels in Cebu, they found that only 39 percent of employees were women; a low figure compared with export-manufacturing

(75-percent female) and the entertainment industry (90-percent female). Within these hotels, women were concentrated in administration and accounts, and in front-desk duties as receptionists, cashiers, and telephone operators. In a related study of six hotels in Boracay, they found that 37 percent of workers in the top two hotels were women and 49 percent were women in the four smaller hotels. Generally, women formed the majority of workers in housekeeping, laundry, accounting, and front-desk duties. Women were underrepresented in gardening, maintenance, security, food, and beverages, and as drivers (Chant 1997).

In these hotels, women were favored for jobs that reinforced normative constructions of femininity. There was a strong emphasis on servile and/or frontline work where they would provide a "pleasing sight to customers" (Chant and McIlwaine 1995, 210). In addition, in Boracay, single and childless women were favored by employers because motherhood was considered incompatible with full-time employment (Chant and McIlwaine 1995). In other areas of the formal sector, such as restaurants and tourist shops, women were employed as the majority of waitstaff and assistants because they were thought to attract more custom through their social and physical attributes (Chant 1997). Overall, women earned less than men, as they were largely concentrated in lower echelons and types of work where they had less opportunities to earn gratuities (Chant and McIlwaine 1995, 186).

In Bali, substantially more men than women are formally employed in tourism (Cukier 1996). For example, there were ten times more male than female tour guides registered in 1997 (Directorate General Tourism Bali 1998), reflecting men's greater access to education and training and the greater social acceptability for them to travel unaccompanied away from home (Cukier, Norris, and Wall 1996). With respect to hotel employment, a United Nations Development Programme study found that the proportion of men to women employed in Balinese hotels was three to one (Ranck 1992). However, in a study of tourism employment in Kedewatan village, Norris (1994) observed that only 25 percent of employees in the more exclusive hotels were women, although in other hotels women constituted 31 percent of employees. The gendered division of labor was similar to that described for the Philippines (Chant and McIlwaine 1995), and women generally earned less than men (Cukier 1996).

Women's Experiences in Informal-Sector Tourism: The Philippines and Indonesia

In the Philippines women are frequently positioned within narrowly bound tourism labor markets as prostitutes, entertainment workers, menial service workers, and commercial traders (Chant and McIlwaine

1995). In Boracay Chant and McIlwaine found that women dominated as ambulant vendors, but were concentrated in the sale of clothes, food, and personal services where there was a less ready market for their goods than for those sold by men (fish, ice cream, and newspapers). In addition, women were generally older than those employed in the formal sector and more likely to be married and involved in home-based enterprises, where they could simultaneously take care of their families. When profits were good, female ambulant vendors and home-based entrepreneurs earned more than the wages (and tips) of male and female employees in hotels, shops, or restaurants. However, across all sectors, men earned more than women and were positioned in more stable and less arduous work (Chant and McIlwaine 1995).

A similar situation was documented in Pangandaran, Java (Wilkinson and Pratiwi 1995) and Bali, where women constituted a large portion of the informal tourism sector, working in small-scale handicrafts, jewelry, and garment production (Ariani, Arjani, Wiasti, Parwata, and Sukranatha 1993), as independent vendors of clothing, food, and other objects (Norris 1994), and in hawker cooperatives selling massages, hair braiding, and manicures (Cukier-Snow and Wall 1993; Cukier 1996). These occupations were especially convenient for married women, who combined work with family and religious obligations (Wilkinson and Pratiwi 1995; Cukier, Norris, and Wall 1996, 264). In addition, women worked as entrepreneurs and managers of their families' small-scale enterprises (Ariani et al. 1993) and accommodation businesses (Long and Wall 1995; Wall and Long 1996; Long and Kindon 1997). In these roles, they tapped directly into the wealth of their consumers (Cukier 1996, 57), but still had to negotiate its allocation with their husbands.

As in Boracay, in Kuta and Sanur in Bali there were gender divisions evident within the informal sector related to what goods were sold, how much was earned, and where people worked. Cukier (1996) recorded that the majority of individual vendors selling goods to tourists on the streets were young men from Java, whereas more Balinese women participated as beach hawkers and kiosk workers (Cukier and Wall 1995). Male vendors earned higher incomes than female hawkers, but women kiosk workers earned more than men (Cukier and Wall 1995). In Yogyakarta in Java Timothy and Wall (1997) also noted that 70 percent of street vendors were men, with female street vendors being confined to the sale of foodstuffs. They commented on the increasing role of government in the regulation of commercial and spatial activities of vendors.

Similar intervention in Bali has regulated some informal-sector activities through the spatial concentration of hawkers into designated areas or markets. In Bras and Dahles's (1998) study of Sanur's beachwalk installation, they observed that some women (usually older and married) were authorized by hotels to have access to their beachwalk space and provide guests with services. Their work was increasingly "professional-ized" and secure. Others, who were younger mobile vendors, were ex-cluded from the same space and forced into a more marginal and less secure enterprise of attracting tourists walking along the beach.

Women's Experiences in the Hospitality Sector: Thailand, the Philippines, and Indonesia

Domestic prostitution has a long history throughout most of South-east Asia, with women working as courtesans, concubines ("little wives"), and prostitutes in many countries (Swain 1995, cited in Lieper 1998). However, there has been a rapid growth in international de-mand for prostitution services since the stationing of U.S. military troops in the region during World War II and the Vietnam War (Lee 1991). Today, the hospitality industry, and international sex tourism in particular, is in an ambiguous position. Prostitution, while illegal, continues to be promoted as a major generator of national revenue (Bell 1992). Yet there is a growing resistance to its promotion and aware-ness that it could present a major problem for the region's future tour-ism development (Dunn 1994; Esichaikul and Baum 1998; Skrobanek, Boonpakdi, and Chutman 1997; Teo and Chang 1998).[7] Estimates of how many women are involved as commercial sex workers are prob-lematic because of the nature of the industry. In addition, it is impor-tant to remember that tourist-oriented prostitution is only undertaken by a minority of women, who can be considered to be elite in terms of their flexible lifestyles and larger incomes (Richter 1989).[8] Table 4.3 provides recent estimated total numbers of commercial sex workers in six countries in the region.

The women involved in commercial sex work with tourists are most commonly constructed as a "problem" within national-development discourses, especially with the increase in cases of HIV–AIDS. Women are also frequently positioned as victims of exploitative social and eco-nomic relations that force them into the industry because of poverty or lack of occupational skills, or because they are tricked or trafficked into entering (Bell 1992; Boonchalaski and Guest 1994). However, such stereotypical images can reflect the masculinist character of tourist, academic, and state gazes (Urry 1990; Rose 1993) and fix crude and artificial binaries of rich/Western/powerful/male/oppressor versus poor/Asian/disempowered/female/victim (Law 1997, 119). They also foreclose a more nuanced analysis of the gendered power relations at play at different scales.

From more recent empirical studies, it would seem that male sex tourists encounter women who are usually far from the colonial im-age of "passive, exotic, oriental Third World woman" (Mohanty 1988),

Table 4.3
Estimated Numbers of Female Commercial Sex
Workers in Southeast Asia (1997)

Country	Total Women and Children (thousands)	Children (thousands)
Thailand	2,000–3,000	40-60
Vietnam	600	72
Indonesia	500	100
Philippines	300	75
Malaysia	142	28.2
Cambodia	20–30	7–10

Source: T. Mehrain, Sex trade and trafficking of women and girls in Thailand, Gender Studies (Hong Kong: Chinese University of Hong Kong, 1997).

Note: The definition of "child" was not supplied by Mehrain and is likely to vary from country to country.

and who represent many different occupational groups depending on their class and the spaces in which they work (Murray 1991; Cohen 1993; Boonchalaski and Guest 1994; Hall 1994a; McIlwaine 1996; Chant 1997; Law 1997; Askew 1998). Many of these women choose to engage in sex work because they can gain considerably higher incomes than from other jobs available to them (Murray 1991; Cohen 1993; Rigg 1997; Sittirak 1998). Moreover, their choice to work is often strategic. In Jakarta, Indonesia, sex work may be a temporary way for young women to meet immediate material and consumeristic desires (Murray 1991). In Thailand and the Philippines it can enable women to gain important social merit by sending remittances to their distant families (Truong 1990; Dunn 1994; Cook 1998). Sex work, according to one ethnographic account, may also enable some women to recover self-value and attain "cultural capital relating to economic status, sexuality and modernity" (Askew 1998, 133). For example, some women in Cebu in the Philippines have positioned themselves as prospective wives, cultural ambassadors, and city guides in their relations with their customers (Law 1997, 121); in Bangkok, Thailand, some have appeared to enjoy the risk and skill involved in attracting men, the control and manipulation involved in extracting money from them, and the possibility of leaving "the game" altogether with an affluent male partner (Cohen 1993, 172).

However, while it is possible for these women to earn higher incomes than other women in formal and informal sectors, and possibly gain important cultural capital, many find their opportunities to be short lived and emotionally demanding. In addition, as they age, marry, or have children, they are less likely to attract foreign men and may face discrimination if they try to enter formal tourism employment. They generally remain confined to informal-sector activities that are poorly paid, seasonal, and insecure (Chant and McIlwaine 1995).

Women's frequent positioning within low-status occupations in both formal and informal sectors reflects capitalism's grip on their laboring bodies (Ong and Peletz 1995) and draws heavily on Western masculinist stereotypes about Southeast Asian women (Chant 1997). It also reflects the intersections of patriarchal and nationalistic gender imagery with localized symbolic systems of prestige and stigma, whereby women's recruitment into tourism activities further crystallizes and intensifies their subordinate positions within the industry and their societies more generally (Chant 1997).

RECALIBRATING MATURITY
UTILIZING LIMINALITY

In this chapter I have argued that at the regional level the discourse of maturity obscures tourism's spatially and socially uneven development in Southeast Asia. First, it homogenizes spatial and social differences at the national and local levels behind such "objective" measures as regional economic growth and figures of tourist arrivals, which remain undifferentiated by sex or subregion. Second, it fails to acknowledge the embodied geographies of power represented in pronounced spatial concentrations of investment, authority, and wealth (Richter 1994). Effectively, the discourse of maturity represents a rational, Western, masculinist, and disembodied approach to the categorization of the Earth's surface that privileges "objective," "scientific," and quantifiable measures of economic "progress" above locally embedded meanings, values, and experiences (Rose 1993).

The examples of women's activities as tourism producers in the region, and their associated meanings within national and local prestige systems, reveal their frequent positioning within tourism and its wider development discourse as absent, marginal, and deviant. Women's absence from conceptions of the region as mature can be related to their concentration in informal-sector activities that remain unintegrated into national and regional assessments of tourism development. Their concentration within these activities also means that they are often marginalized within Southeast Asia's maturity, as prestige systems inform gendered practices of tourism employment and consumption. Women in the informal sector are also the most likely to encounter further marginalization as their "deviant" work in tourism is increasingly professionalized, spatially segregated, or regulated by state authorities in their efforts to modernize (Bras and Dahles 1998). Yet women's persistent presence as marginal and "deviant" tourism producers also serves to destabilize regional classifications of Southeast Asia as a mature destination.

Maturity thus needs recalibrating in light of the ambiguous ways in which tourism development involves the (re)negotiation of women's activities and identities at the edges of acceptable society on different scales (the body, family, civil society, nation, and transnational) (Ong and Peletz 1995; McIlwaine 1996). To understand the importance of these edges requires attention to the concept of liminality and the recognition that there are always liminal spaces and people within any classification of a region as mature. Liminality allows for the preservation of ambiguity in classification and enables a consideration of development that is not necessarily linear and unidirectional. As Turner (cited in Ryan and Kinder 1996) has noted, "The attributes of liminality or of liminal *personae* ("threshold people") are necessarily ambiguous, since the condition of these persons elude or slip through the network of classification that normally locate states and positions in cultural [and economic] space" (p. 508, italics in original).

As this chapter has shown, the activities of most female tourism producers in the informal sector in Southeast Asia currently "slip through" the hegemonic networks of classification that locate the region as mature. Their liminality is reflected in their contradictory and ambiguous positioning as absent, marginal, or "deviant" workers who are simultaneously central to the character and forms of tourism in the region on different scales. Thus, I would conclude by arguing that the integration of liminality as a concept within tourism analyses is imperative if the gendered patterns of wealth, power, and prestige on different scales in Southeast Asia (Ong and Peletz 1995, 2) are to be more fully understood, and if Southeast Asia's classification as a mature touristic destination is not to perpetuate hegemonic development discourse any longer.

NOTES

I would like to acknowledge the constructive comments of Geoffrey Hume-Cook on an earlier draft of this chapter and the ongoing support of Putu Hermawati. Responsibility for any errors remains my own.

1. Given the colonial heritage of much regional geography, the contested nature of the term "region," and the presence of regions at the subnational scale, any definition of Southeast Asia is somewhat arbitrary. For the purposes of this chapter, I adopt Teo and Chang's (1998) classification, which includes Brunei, Cambodia, Indonesia, Lao Democratic Republic, Malaysia, Myanmar, the Philippines, Singapore, Thailand, and Vietnam.

2. By focusing on women, I am not assuming that they form an homogenous category for analysis. Nor am I suggesting that gender is an analytically discrete domain of inequality or difference (Peletz 1995, 77), for it clearly intersects with other axes of difference, such as ethnicity, class, age, sexuality, and relationship status.

3. Research for this chapter draws on published material from a range of disciplines. Their methods and scales of analysis are not comparable in many cases. In addition, while the chapter focuses on Southeast Asia, most published material has focused on Thailand, Indonesia, and the Philippines and these are the main examples drawn upon. Gaps remain on other countries and peripheral areas of core destinations. In addition, research on gender and tourism in the region to date has focused on the gendered division of labor and women in international sex tourism. There is a dearth of information on women as tourism consumers (with the exception of Lette 1996; Dahles and Bras 1999), so they are not discussed here. Unfortunately, at a conference, "Southeast Asian Tourism in the 21st Century," held in Singapore, September 6–7, 1999, there were no papers that addressed women or gender and tourism in the region, and it remains an important oversight in many analyses of the region.

4. The informal sector has been categorized by small-scale activities, individual or family ownership and operations, high labor intensity and flexibility, and reliance on indigenous resources and skills acquired outside of the formal sector (Timothy and Wall 1997, 336).

5. For Hall (1992, 74) this commodification of the region's labor and its incorporation into the capitalist world economy primarily through sex tourism has effectively coded it as "feminine" within oppressive and exploitative economic relationships with the "masculine and developed West."

6. Moser (1989) has observed that where gender and development intersect, women are often positioned in contradictory ways as invisible, problematic victims, wives and mothers, effective implementers of state development programs, "untapped" economic resources, and/or political actors who need surveillance.

7. In Vietnam and Cambodia, too, there are growing concerns about the flourishing sex industry (Lam 1998), and the possible "tarnishing" of these countries' international images (Truong 1996; Lieper 1998). Cambodia is of special concern because it is now the leading destination for pederasts from Australia, Europe, and the United States (Sherry et al. cited in Lam 1998), who go there because of the lower cost of sex compared with neighboring countries in the region.

8. Meyer (cited in Harrison 1992) estimated that less than 10 percent of Southeast Asian sex workers depend on international clients for their livelihood.

REFERENCES

Ariani, G., N. Arjani, N. Wiasti, O. Parwata, and A. Sukranatha. (1993). The impacts of tourism upon the status and role of women in gold and silver handicraft production in Desa Celuk, Kabupaten Gianyar. In *Report of the Bali Sustainable Development Project Gender and Development Training Workshop*. Research Paper Series #48, edited by S. L. Kindon. Toronto: University Consortium on the Environment.

Askew, M. (1998). City of women, city of foreign men: Working spaces and reworking identities among female sex workers in Bangkok's tourist zone. *Singapore Journal of Tropical Geography* 19 (2): 130–150.

Association of Southeast Asian Nations Secretariat. (1996). *The Advancement of Women in ASEAN: A Regional Report*. Jakarta: Author.

Atkinson, J., and S. Errington, eds. (1990). *Power and Difference in Island Southeast Asia*. Stanford, Calif.: Stanford University Press.

Bell, P. (1992). Gender and economic development in Thailand. In *Gender and Economic Development in Southeast Asia*, edited by P. Van Esterick and J. Van Esterick. Montreal: Canadian Council for Southeast Asian Studies.

Biles, A., K. Lloyd, and W. Logan. (1999). "Tiger on a bicycle": The growth, character, and dilemmas of international tourism in Vietnam. *Pacific Tourism Review* 3: 11–23.

Boonchalaski, W., and P. Guest. (1994). *Prostitution in Thailand*. Salaya, Thailand: Institute of Population and Social Research, Mahidol University.

Bras, K., and H. Dahles. (1998). Women entrepreneurs and beach tourism in Sanur, Bali: Gender, employment opportunities and government policy. *Pacific Tourism Review* 1: 243–256.

Brohman, J. (1996). New directions in tourism for Third World development. *Annals of Tourism Research* 23: 48–70.

Butler, R. (1980). The concept of a tourist area cycle of evolution: Implications for management of resources. *Canadian Geographer* 24 (1): 5–12.

Carter, S. (1998). Tourists' and travellers' social construction of Africa and Asia as risky locations. *Tourism Management* 19 (4): 349–358.

Chant, S. (1997). Tourism employment in Mexico and the Philippines. In *Gender, Work and Tourism*, edited by M. T. Sinclair. London: Routledge.

Chant S., and C. McIlwaine. (1995). *Women of a Lesser Cost: Female Labor, Foreign Exchange and Philippine Development*. London: Pluto Press.

Chon, K., and M. Oppermann. (1996). Tourism development and planning in the Philippines. *Tourism Recreation Research* 21 (1): 35–44.

Cohen, E. (1993). Open-ended prostitution as a skillful game of luck: Opportunity, risk and security among tourist-oriented prostitution in a Bangkok soi. In *Tourism in Southeast Asia*, edited by M. Hitchcock, V. King, and M. Parnwell. London: Routledge.

Cook, N. (1998). "Dutiful daughters," estranged sisters: Women in Thailand. In *Gender and Power in Affluent Asia*, edited by K. Sen and M. Stivens. London: Routledge.

Crush, J., ed. (1995). *Power of Development*. London: Routledge.

Cukier, J. (1996). Tourism employment in Bali: Trends and implications. In *Tourism and Indigenous Peoples*, edited by R. Butler and T. Hinch. London: International Thomson Business Press.

Cukier, J., J. Norris, and G. Wall. (1996). The involvement of women in the tourism industry of Bali, Indonesia. *Journal of Development Studies* 33: 248–270.

Cukier, J., and G. Wall. (1995). Tourism employment in Bali: A gender analysis. *Tourism Economics* 1: 389–401.

Cukier-Snow, J., and G. Wall. (1993). Tourism employment: Perspectives from Bali. *Tourism Management* 14 (4): 195–217.

Dahles, H., and K. Bras. (1999). Entrepreneurs in romance: Tourism in Indonesia. *Annals of Tourism Research* 26: 267–293.

Department for Policy Coordination and Sustainable Development. (1995). *Women in a Changing Global Economy: 1994 World Survey on the Role of Women in Development*. New York: United Nations.

Directorate General Tourism Bali. (1998). *Tourism Statistics*. Denpasar: Ministry of Justice, Bali.

Dunn, C. (1994). *The Politics of Prostitution in Thailand and the Philippines*. Melbourne: Monash University Press.

Enloe, C. (1989). *Bananas, Beaches and Bases: Making Feminist Sense of International Politics*. London: Pandora.

Errington, S. (1990). Recasting sex, gender and power: A theoretical and regional overview. In *Power and Difference: Gender in Island Southeast Asia*, edited by J. Atkinson and S. Errington. Stanford: Stanford University Press.

Esichaikul, R., and T. Baum. (1998). The case for government involvement in human resource development: A study of the Thai hotel industry. *Tourism Management* 19 (4): 359–370.

Fletcher, J., and J. Latham. (1997). East Asia and the Pacific databank. *Tourism Economics* 3 (2): 201–205.

Gardiner Barber, P. (1996). Modes of resistance: Gendered responses to global impositions in coastal Philippines. *Asia Pacific Viewpoint* 37 (2): 181–194.

Goad, G., and S. Crispin. (1999). Wish you were here. *Far Eastern Economic Review*, 30 September, 60–62.

Hall, C. M. (1992). Sex tourism in Southeast Asia. In *Tourism and the Less Developed Countries*, edited by D. Harrison. Chichester: Wiley.

Hall, C. M. (1994a). Gender and economic interests in tourism prostitution: The nature and development implications of sex tourism within Southeast Asia. In *Tourism: A Gender Analysis*, edited by V. Kinnaird and D. Hall. Chichester: Wiley.

Hall, C. M. (1994b). *Tourism in the Pacific Rim: Developments, Impacts and Markets*. Melbourne: Longman.

Harrison, D., ed. (1992). *Tourism and the Less Developed Countries*. Chichester: Wiley.

Hitchcock, M., V. King, and M. Parnwell, eds. (1993). *Tourism in Southeast Asia*. London: Routledge.

Kindon, S. L. (1993). *From Tea Makers to Decision Makers: Applying Participatory Rural Appraisal to Gender and Development in Rural Bali, Indonesia*. Paper #16. Toronto: University Consortium on the Environment.

Kindon, S. L. (1995). Balinese gender relations and the state: National transformation of a local system? In *Managing Change in Southeast Asia: Local Identities, Global Connections*, edited by J. DeBernardi, G. Forth, and S. Niessen. Edmonton: University of Alberta Press.

Kindon, S. L., and G. Hume-Cook. (1997). Unpublished field notes. January, Lovina, Bali.

Kinnaird, V., and D. Hall, eds. (1994). *Tourism: A Gender Analysis*. Chichester: Wiley.

Kontogeorgopoulos, N. (1998). Tourism in Thailand: Patterns, trends, and limitations. *Pacific Tourism Review* 2: 225–238.

Lam, T. (1998). Tourism in Cambodia: An overview of Cambodian international tourism and its development potential. *Pacific Tourism Review* 1: 235–241.

Law, L. (1997). Dancing on the bar: Sex, money and the uneasy politics of third space. In *Geographies of Resistance*, edited by M. Keith and S. Pile. London: Routledge.

Ledgerwood, J. (1996). Politics and gender: Negotiating conceptions of the ideal woman in present day Cambodia. *Asia Pacific Viewpoint* 37 (2): 139–152.

Lee, W. (1991). Prostitution and tourism in Southeast Asia. In *Working Women: International Perspectives on Labor and Gender Ideology*, edited by N. Redclift and T. Sinclair. London: Routledge.

Lette, H. (1996). "Changing my thinking with a Western woman": Javanese youths' constructions of masculinity. *Asia Pacific Viewpoint* 37 (2): 195–207.

Lieper, N. (1998). Cambodian tourism: Potential, problems, and illusions. *Pacific Tourism Review* 1: 285–297.

Long, V., and S. Kindon. (1997). Gender and tourism development in Balinese villages. In *Gender, Work and Tourism*, edited by M. T. Sinclair. London: Routledge.

Long, V., and G. Wall. (1995). Small scale tourism development in Bali. In *Island Tourism: Management, Principles and Practice*, edited by M. Conlin and T. Baum. Chichester: Wiley.

Lowenhaupt-Tsing, A. (1993). *In the Realm of the Diamond Queen: Marginality in an Out-of-the-Way Place*. Princeton: Princeton University Press.

McIlwaine, C. (1996). The negotiation of space among sex workers in Cebu City, the Philippines. *Singapore Journal of Tropical Geography* 17 (2): 150–164.

Mohanty, C. (1988). Under Western eyes: Feminist scholarship and colonial discourses. *Feminist Review* 30: 61–88.

Moser, C. (1989). Gender planning in the Third World: Meeting practical and strategic gender needs. *World Development* 17: 1799–1825.

Murray, A. (1991). *No Money, No Honey: A Study of Street Traders and Prostitutes in Jakarta*. Singapore: Oxford University Press.

Norris, J. (1994). Gender and tourism in rural Bali: Case study of Kedewatan Village. Master's thesis, University of Guelph, Guelph, Ontario, Canada.

Ong, A. (1990). Japanese factories, Malay workers class and sexual metaphors in West Malaysia. In *Power and Difference in Island Southeast Asia*, edited by J. Atkinson and S. Errington. Stanford: Stanford University Press.

Ong, A., and M. Peletz, eds. (1995). *Bewitching Women, Pious Men: Gender and Body Politics in Southeast Asia*. Berkeley and Los Angeles: University of California Press.

Oppermann, M., and S. McKinley. (1996). Sex and image: Marketing of tourism destinations. In *Pacific Rim Tourism 2000: Issues, Interrelations, Inhibitors*, edited by M. Oppermann. Rotorua: Waiariki Polytechnic.

Peletz, M. (1995). Neither reasonable nor responsible: Contrasting representations of masculinity in Malay society. In *Bewitching Women, Pious Men: Gender and Body Politics in Southeast Asia*, edited by A. Ong and M. Peletz. Berkeley and Los Angeles: University of California Press.

Ranck, D. (1992). Women and tourism. In *Comprehensive Tourism Development Plan for Bali: Annex 16*. Denpasar: United Nations Development Programme.

Richter, L. (1989). *The Politics of Tourism in Asia*. Honolulu: University of Hawaii Press.

Richter, L. (1993). Tourism policy making in Southeast Asia. In *Tourism in Southeast Asia*, edited by M. Hitchcock, V. King, and M. Parnwell. London: Routledge.

Richter, L. (1994). Exploring the political role of gender in tourism research. In *Global Tourism: The next Decade*, edited by W. Theobold. Oxford: Butterworth Heinemann.

Richter, L. (1995). Gender and race: Neglected variables in tourism research. In *Change in Tourism: People, Places and Processes*, edited by R. Butler and D. Pearce. London: Routledge.

Rigg, J. (1997). *Southeast Asia*. London: Routledge.

Rose, G. (1993). *Feminism and Geography: The Limits of Geographical Knowledge*. Minneapolis: University of Minnesota Press.

Ryan, C., and R. Kinder. (1996). Sex, tourism and sex tourism: Fulfilling similar needs? *Tourism Management* 17 (7): 507–518.

Sadli, S. (1992). Professionalization of women in cultural tourism. In *Universal Tourism Enriching or Degrading Culture*, edited by J. Ave, J. Hillig, and K. Hardjasoemantri. Yogyakarta: Universitas Gadjah Madah.

Said, E. (1978). *Orientalism*. New York: Pergamon Press.

Selwyn, T. (1993). Peter Pan in South-East Asia: View from the brochures. In *Tourism in Southeast Asia*, edited by M. Hitchcock, V. King, and M. Parnwell. London: Routledge.

Sen, K., and M. Stivens, eds. (1998). *Gender and Power in Affluent Asia*. London: Routledge.

Sinclair, M. T., ed. (1997). *Gender, Work and Tourism*. London: Routledge.

Sittirak, S. (1998). *Daughters of Development: Women in a Changing Environment*. London: Zed Books.

Skrobanek, S., N. Boonpakdi, and J. Chutman. (1997). *The Traffic in Women: Human Realities of the International Sex Trade*. London: Zed Books.

Stivens, M. (1998). Sex, gender and the making of the new Malay middle classes. In *Gender and Power in Affluent Asia*, edited by K. Sen and M. Stivens. London: Routledge.

Suryakusuma, J. (1991). State Ibuism: The social construction of womanhood in the Indonesian new order. *Asian Visions* 4 (2): 46–71.

Swain, M. B. (1995). Gender in tourism. *Annals of Tourism Research* 22: 247–266.

Teo, P., and T. Chang. (1998). Critical issues in a critical era: Tourism in Southeast Asia. *Singapore Journal of Tropical Geography* 19 (2): 119–129.

Timothy, D., and G. Wall. (1997). Selling to tourists: Indonesian street vendors. *Annals of Tourism Research* 24: 322–340.

Truong, T. (1990). *Sex, Money and Morality: Prostitution and Tourism in Southeast Asia*. London: Zed Books.

Truong, T. (1996). *Uncertain Horizon: The Women's Question in Viet-nam Revisited*. The Hague: Institute of Social Studies.

Twining-Ward, L., and T. Baum. (1998). Dilemmas facing mature island destinations: Cases from the Baltic. *Progress in Tourism and Hospitality Research* 4: 131–140.

Urry, J. (1990). *The Tourist Gaze*. London: Sage.

Var, T., R. Toh, and H. Khan. (1997). Tourism and ASEAN economic development. *Annals of Tourism Research* 24: 195–196.

Wall, G. (1996). Gender and tourism development. *Annals of Tourism Research* 23: 721–722.

Wall, G. (1998). Reflections upon the state of Asian tourism. *Singapore Journal of Tropical Geography* 19 (2): 232–237.

Wall, G., and V. Long. (1996). Balinese homestays: An indigenous response to tourism opportunities. In *Tourism and Indigenous Peoples*, edited by R. Butler and T. Hinch. London: International Thomson Business Press.

Walton, J. (1993). Tourism and economic development in ASEAN. In *Tourism in Southeast Asia*, edited by M. Hitchcock, V. King, and M. Parnwell. London: Routledge.

Wanhill, S., and D. Buhalis. (1999). Introduction: Challenges for tourism in peripheral areas. *International Journal of Tourism Research* 1: 295–297.

Wilkinson, P., and W. Pratiwi. (1995). Gender and tourism in an Indonesian village. *Annals of Tourism Research* 22: 283–299.

Wong, D. (1996). Foreign domestic workers in Singapore. *Asian and Pacific Migration Journal* 5: 117–138.

World Tourism Organization. (1998). *Yearbook of Tourism Statistics*. Madrid: Author.

Yeoh, B., and S. Huang. (1995). Childcare in Singapore: Negotiating choices and constraints in a multicultural society. *Women's Studies International Forum* 18: 445–461.

5

Power, Women, and Tourism Development in the South Pacific

Tracy Berno and Trudy Jones

The importance of women to tourism in the South Pacific is seldom critically acknowledged. This chapter explores key issues pertaining to the topic of women as producers and consumers of tourism in the South Pacific, the primary emphasis being upon women in their role as producers. Stereotypical representations of women in the Pacific are contrasted with the roles they actually play in tourism. In the context of planning and management of tourism, the politics of gender in South Pacific tourism will be examined. Questions such as who gets what, linked to who already has what, and when and how that is distributed, will be addressed in relation to women's involvement in tourism development in the South Pacific.

TOURISM IN THE SOUTH PACIFIC

The South Pacific is often referred to as though it was an amorphous, homogenous entity sprawled across the expanse of the southern region of the Pacific Ocean. In reality, the South Pacific is comprised of thousands of individual islands organized as island states and nations. They reach from Hawaii along the Tropic of Cancer—technically in the North Pacific but included as part of Polynesia—to New Zealand

and the Chatham Islands, well below a longitude of 40 degrees south. There are a dozen separate nations and states in the South Pacific divided into two geographical regions: Melanesia (southwest) and Polynesia (east). Contrary to the ubiquitous images of the South Pacific as a uniform and homogenous "tropical paradise," the regions of the South Pacific differ significantly in land mass and type, resources, flora and fauna, sociocultural organization and custom, history and colonization, and tourism profiles. Of marked contrast are the differences between Melanesia and Polynesia, the two geographical regions of the South Pacific on which this chapter focuses (Berno and Douglas 1998).

In global terms, the South Pacific as a whole accounts for only 0.15 percent of the world's international tourist arrivals, but this small number is enough for tourism to be the mainstay of the region's economy. Tourist numbers for Melanesia are higher than those for Polynesia, with Melanesia having received 361,137 holiday visitors in 1995 and Polynesia 226,021 (see Table 5.1). Observed in isolation, this statistic presents a picture contrary to expectations, for it is the reputation and imagery of Polynesia that are most commonly promoted and with which both the traveling public and the travel operators are most familiar (Douglas and Douglas 1996; Pacific Asia Travel Association 1982, n.d.). It is the inclusion of Fiji in Melanesia that causes the distortion. If, as has been proposed by a number of scholars, Fiji is not really part of Melanesia, then the statistical picture changes entirely. Tourist arrivals to Melanesia proper would now total 176,895 in 1995; Fiji's figures could either stand alone or be incorporated into Polynesia. Perhaps the tourist slogan "Fantastic Fiji" could be abbreviated to "Fantesia," thus designating a new South Pacific region for tourism statistical purposes. Indeed, this is consistent with the homogenous way the South Pacific is often portrayed in the tourism advertising media. For example, a recent advertisement for a family holiday in Rarotonga, Cook Islands (Polynesia) offered *leis* (an Hawaiian word, the Cook Island Maori word is *ei*) and a free *sulu* (a Fijian word, the Cook Island Maori word is *pareu*) for each child who traveled (cited in Berno and Douglas 1998).

The majority (59 percent) of the tourists traveling to the Pacific region come from other Pacific countries. A large number of the tourists to the South Pacific come from Australia (19 percent), New Zealand (15 percent), and other Pacific Islands (9 percent), from which the Pacific Islands are "short-haul" destinations. Traditionally, these were the main tourism-generating countries in the South Pacific, but with the introduction of flights from North America and Europe the profile of tourist arrivals has shifted, with increased numbers of tourists from outside the Pacific. It is interesting to note, however, that despite this shift the main tourist-generating countries are those that have had

Table 5.1
Tourism in Polynesia and Melanesia

	POLYNESIA						MELANESIA				
	Cook Islands	French Polynesia	Niue	Tonga	Tuvalu	Western Samoa	PNG	Solomon Islands	Vanuatu	New Caledonia	Fiji
Arrivals	**48,500**	**172,179**	**2,161**	**29,520**	**922**	**67,954**	**37,734**	**11,918**	**42,140**	**85,103**	**318,874**
Purpose of visit:											
Holiday	40,255	146,310	1,021	15,722	184	22,529	9,888	3,892	31,217	60,167	255,973
Business	3,152	9,295	503	5,194	523	7,612	15,963	4,364	6,379	7,601	23,849
VFR	2,565	9,662	524	8,553	92	27,513	6,190	648	3,179	10,704	21,348
Receipts*	28.3	177.2	1.6	10.4	0.4	30.7	49.2	6.7	30.8	74.6	283.6
Hotels	56	201	8	43	9	28	130	20	44	76	221
Rooms	652	3,829	48	544	45	565	2,700	405	780	1,888	5,003

Source: Tourism Council of the South Pacific, 1995 visitor statistics for TCSP member countries. *South Pacific On-Line*, March 1997. Available <http://www.infocentre.com/spt> or <http://www.tcsp.com/spt>.

Note: These Polynesian and Melanesian countries comprise member countries of the Tourism Council of the South Pacific (TCSP). Accurate tourism statistics for other countries are not available.

*Receipts in $ millions.

colonial ties with countries in the South Pacific, and the Asian markets are very poorly represented (Tourism Council of the South Pacific 1997).

IMAGE MAKING AND MARKETING
IN SOUTH PACIFIC TOURISM

Representation of Women and Impacts on
Tourism Consumers and Providers

Many authors have identified and explored the representations of women in tourism and how these impact upon the perceptions and expectations of tourism consumers (see, for example, Cohen 1995; Goss 1993; Momsen 1994; Wilson 1994). In regard to the portrayal of South Pacific island people in tourism, it has been observed that "Pacific island people suffer from an image problem" (O'Grady 1990, 24), which is sometimes promoted by their own governments, but more often by overseas marketers and tourism operators. Brochures often feature photos of scantily clad, passive Polynesian women. This gives support to the popular misconception that South Pacific island women are "willing and available" (O'Grady 1990, 24), as well as serving to "Polynesianize" the women of the culturally diverse South Pacific region (Berno and Douglas 1998). Marketing images such as these have long served as promotional devices for South Pacific destinations because they have proved to be a successful marketing strategy, enticing potential tourists to "consume" the "products" portrayed in these images. Women of the South Pacific have been employed as "geographical markers" in the task of creating and maintaining tourist motivations to visit South Pacific islands (Schellhorn 1998).

The portrayal of South Pacific women as the "exotic other" is not just a contemporary phenomenon, however. The recent history of much of the South Pacific region includes a prolonged period of exploration and colonization by Europeans. Since the earliest contact between the different cultures, understandings, assumptions, and representations have been made by both sides. Last century, the romanticization by sailors, and the domestication of women associated with missionary practices in the region, together paved the way for persistent appropriation and stereotyping surrounding the supposedly simple, carefree existence in these paradisical tropical islands (Selwyn 1996). These deep-rooted Eurocentric myths serve the tourist industry well by ignoring the social realities and challenges facing Pacific Island communities and the complexity of women's multiple roles within those societies.

These myths, promoted in contemporary tourism marketing, also act to perpetuate the patronizing conceptualizations regarding the roles of Pacific women. The constructed images focus upon male fantasy projections predominantly directed at the Western heterosexual male market or honeymooning couples and, less often, family groups. Representations of Pacific women as languid, seductive service providers inevitably influence the expectations of visitors to the region. The use of women as geographical markers in tourist brochures helps to perpetuate the cognitive association by tourism consumers between a particular region and a romanticized female archetype. The stereotypical "Pacific–Polynesian fantasy women," narrowly defined and passively presented in this marketing discourse, becomes part of the aesthetic appeal and geographic otherness of the Pacific Islands (Schellhorn 1998). As Suaalii (1997) elaborates, "Tourism . . . effectively assists in commodifying and perpetuating the orientalised female beauty of the Pacific Islands as the sensual/sexual exotic other of the West, by subversively preserving, homogenising, mystifying—and managing—selective parts of the Pacific cultures and cultural practices" (p. 81).

Through the images portrayed in tourist marketing, the tourism consumer is encouraged to perceive South Pacific women as decorative and at leisure and, by implication, ready and willing to wait upon the visiting tourist. Such portrayals limit understandings of Pacific women, presenting them in a unidimensional role as service providers with the implicit suggestion that service can be interpreted in the widest sense to include the fulfilment of sexual fantasies (Schellhorn 1998). The effects of these representations upon consumer demands and expectations have not yet been widely documented in the academic research literature.

Women of the South Pacific are often portrayed in tourist brochures and ethnographic postcards in passive roles, decorating turquoise lagoons and isolated sandy beaches. In contrast, men are often pictured in active roles, working rather than at leisure (Schellhorn 1998; Edwards 1996). This false dichotomy is revealed as remarkably inaccurate when the realities of life in the Pacific nations are observed. In fact, women are active producers of much more than tourist-industry-focused fantasy fulfilment. They are key figures in most areas of the formal and informal economy, from textile production to agriculture, as well as playing crucial roles in community and resource management (Jones 1999). Also in direct contrast with the projection of eroticized images, for much of the South Pacific religious and moral beliefs censure public displays of sexuality, and modesty in dress is often strictly adhered to. These more accurate and realistic images, however, contradict the commonly held tourist images of a "South Pacific paradise," and directly challenge the motivations and expectations of tourism consumers in the region. As long as they are perceived to promote tourism successfully, it is unlikely that these representations of Pacific Island women will change to any great extent (O'Grady 1990).

On the other side of the equation, representations of Western women that are seen in the Pacific Islands are also limited and distorted by the nature of the cross-cultural contact engendered by tourism. Impressions of Western women as sexually available are reinforced through the type of videos available in the islands as well as the beach fashion and sexual behavior displayed by some tourists. These impressions also inform understandings of gender roles cross-culturally and can contribute to misunderstandings and the increased likelihood of incidents of sexual harassment for solo female travelers (Berno 1995; Jones and Pinheiro 1997; Stanley 1993). Hence, there are misunderstandings and misrepresentations that affect women as producers and consumers of tourism in the South Pacific.

THE ACTIVE ROLE OF WOMEN IN
TOURISM IN THE SOUTH PACIFIC

Labor Roles

There are contradictory reports regarding the role of tourism-related work as a tool for increasing women's status (Cukier and Wall 1995; Lim 1993). The underpinning issue behind this variability lies in the concept of control and whether work opportunities give women as producers of tourism greater or less control over their lives.

The popular image of South Pacific women as being languid, seductive service providers is important in understanding the impacts of tourism on women in the region, and contributes in a range of ways to women's roles in the industry. For example, on Bora Bora in French Polynesia, local women went to work in a new hotel wearing their "Sunday best" clothes: long dresses of calico with long sleeves and a high neckline. The hotel advised the women that this form of dress was unacceptable. To be consistent with the popular tourist perception of Polynesian women, the hotel management instructed the women to wear a *pareu* (a piece of fabric wrapped around as a strapless dress) to work. For these women, the *pareu* was a garment worn exclusively around the home, a type of robe or housedress worn when doing the cleaning or laundry. Afraid of losing their jobs at the hotel, the women did not complain to management; rather, they went to the men in their community. The men took the issue to the Council of Deacons on behalf of the women, who then in turn met with the hotel management. It was made clear by members of the community that the dress style required by management was totally unacceptable to local values. As a result of this meeting, a compromise was reached (Biddlecomb 1981, as quoted in O'Grady 1990, 25). While dress codes may appear superficial to the tourists or tourism operators, they can in fact signify profound meaning to the indigenous wearer.

In addition to clothing that is culturally significant, women's traditional tattooing is enjoying a renaissance in parts of the Pacific; for example, Samoa and Tahiti. This revival in body tattoos has arisen from a renewed sense of pride in traditional practices in the postindependence era. However, it also has implications for tourism, in that dancers in hotel resorts are reported to be earning more if they can display genuine markings (Lee 1997). Thus, this resurgence of tattooing as a traditional practice serves to reinforce women's cultural identity and self-esteem, as well as expanding their opportunities in tourism.

The choreography and costuming of women's dancing in the South Pacific is often adjusted to appeal to tourist expectations. This has often been thought to be a negative impact of tourism on Pacific Island women. These changes in response to tourists' expectations, however, have been heralded as "helping save [traditional] sensual Cook Islands dancing" (Buchanan 1998, 4). A top Cook Islands female dancer reported that "while the Cook Islands dance culture is changing with the times, traditions don't change. Traditional themes and the techniques are intact, unchanged by tourism" (Georgina Keenan Williams, quoted in Buchanan 1998, 4). There has also been an emphasis on using natural fibers and shells for costumes, rather than plastic or fake flowers (Buchanan 1998). This renaissance of traditional dancing in response to tourism is not isolated in the Cook Islands. There is a great deal of cultural exchange and borrowing between the Cook Islands, Tahiti, and more recently Hawaii, suggesting that these islands also may be benefitting from tourists' expectations and interests in traditional South Pacific dancing.

Despite these positive advances for women in tourism in the South Pacific, the service industry is notorious for providing part-time, low-paid employment, and women make up a significant percentage of this workforce (Kinnaird and Hall 1994; Meleisea and Meleisea 1980). In every country the jobs undertaken predominantly by women are the least well paid and have the lowest status (Tinker 1990). Women generally have the majority of the jobs at the base of the tourism employment hierarchy, while men have most of the jobs at the middle and top (Richter 1994). In the Pacific, as elsewhere, women tend to fulfil nurturing as well as productive and community-management roles (Momsen 1994). However, in relation to tourism employment, the focus tends to be quite narrow, as a result of assumed natural capabilities. "Caring for the comfort and welfare of others and preparing and serving food are quintessentially sex-typed 'women's work' calling for the exercise of tacit skills widely assumed to reflect 'inherent aptitudes' possessed by the majority of women" (Purcell 1997, 41). In a general sense, this is a worldwide phenomenon. Often the forms of paid employment that are available to them are extensions of this assumed "natural role," and do not perform the function of empowering women or their communities to create positive change in the quality of their lives.

Conceptualizations regarding appropriate male and female roles within a society can be challenged by the introduction of tourism as a source of livelihood. In particular, misleading representations of women in host communities can have a profound impact upon gender relations within the local population. There are many instances in which tourism employment has created a dramatic shift in traditional gender roles, with concomitant impacts upon gender relations. There are documented cases that illustrate the potentially negative outcomes resulting from women involved in increased levels of waged labor outside of the home (see, for example, Jones 1999; Petit-Skinner 1977; Swain 1995).

While women may aspire to tourism-related employment beyond the domestic sphere in order to improve the quality of life for themselves and their families, in reality the work opportunities available may be quite different. Traditionally, labor roles in the South Pacific have been clearly defined along lines of gender. Social status, age, and geographical location (for example, coastal versus inland areas) have also had significant influence upon the specific jobs allocated to men and women involved in subsistence-based lifestyles of the South Pacific (Schoeffel and Kikau 1980). In general, development projects, including tourism, have been criticized for failing to acknowledge the burden of women's triple roles of reproduction, production, and community management. In terms of the economic-development options available to women in the Pacific, there has been a tendency for business-development initiatives to focus on low-profit, culturally legitimate "women's enterprises." Such initiatives often fail to increase standards of living and in association serve to erode the traditional value associated with women's domestic work. In this context, the meaning that a society gives to handicraft production can be significantly altered as a result of the move from production for social exchange purposes to retail purposes. In some instances tourist interest in locally produced handicrafts can prompt a renewed level of interest in traditional skills and designs, which has the potential to boost the status of those involved in producing the handicraft items (Pearce 1982).

Division of Labor

Traditionally, work roles in much of the Pacific have been clearly delineated along gender lines. In subsistence-based economies this division of labor is crucial to ensure fulfilment of basic needs, and cooperation between the sexes is crucial for survival. In this context, flexibility of roles may be limited to maximize efficiency for the benefit of the collective. To varying degrees this ethos remains, especially in rural areas of the Pacific (Schoeffel and Kikau 1980). While the practice of many traditional arts and crafts has been declining dramatically in the face of increasing availability of consumer goods, gendered roles remain for many, aspects of modern life.

In contrast to the tourism advertising and marketing portrayals of women as primarily passive and decorative adornments, much of the labor in Pacific tourist destinations is undertaken by local women from the host community. However, ideologies of social sexuality can create constraints upon the range and levels of occupation available to women (Sinclair 1997). Within the Pacific, there are varying degrees of economic benefit available as a result of increased finance entering communities through women employed in the tourism industry. However, there are also associated social risks to be managed, given the predominantly semiskilled, low-paid nature of the work available to most Pacific women. In this scenario, the prospect of overburdening women and reducing rather than improving the quality of life for them and their families is a very real risk (Auger-Andrews 1995).

To meet tourists' expectations of the South Pacific as presented in promotional materials, women are often placed on the "front line" of hotel resort services. This can leave men in the host community who are not directly involved in the industry themselves, struggling to adapt to changes in the traditional labor roles. Adjustments have to be made, partly in terms of altering work patterns as a result of changes in the gendered work-role dynamics. Families have to adapt to the prospect of women spending a significant amount of time away from the home base. External influences, cultural or material, that may otherwise not be introduced to the household or community suddenly become sources of conflict (Auger-Andrews 1995; Petit-Skinner 1977).

Given the cross-cultural contact experienced by women in the tourism service industry, there is the possibility that existing cultural values may be challenged by the beliefs, opinions, and behavior of visiting tourists with whom women in the industry have regular contact. Reciprocal social obligations are the foundation for many collectivist subsistence-based communities, and survival dictates that the collective be paramount over individual wants. The increased emphasis upon commercial concerns in tourism can impact negatively on the collective ethos upon which most Pacific cultures are based (Berno 1999).

The changing responsibilities and supporting roles that men need to play in areas such as child care and subsistence production are vital as the gendered division of labor patterns change with the growth of tourism development. In order to modify any negative impacts arising from women becoming paid providers of tourism-related services and products, men from the host communities face the prospect of adapting their roles accordingly. In some ways this aspect of social change brought about by tourism development is a secondary impact, and therefore often neglected at the policy level of tourism development. This process of change in gender relations can leave individual households and local communities struggling to balance the contemporary demands of work and family life in what continues to be a period of rapid and profound economic change for the Pacific region.

WOMEN'S ROLES IN PLANNING
AND MANAGING TOURISM

Traditional decision-making structures in the South Pacific have tended to be male dominated, and in rural areas extended families are often under the authority of the family chief and elders. Where traditional hierarchical chiefly systems have been retained, women are rarely appointed as chiefs, but in some instances this is possible, depending upon lineage patterns. In nations such as Samoa the chief's role as a family patriarch is to promote family unity and prestige, administer family lands, settle disputes among kin, encourage religious participation, and act as political spokesperson on the village council and beyond (Holmes 1984). As the previous list of responsibilities suggests, the chiefly areas of concern are multiple and there are no clear demarcation lines between religious, political, and social duties. The success of systems of chiefly rule lie partially in the assumption that each person knows their place in the scheme of things and will act accordingly (Fairbairn-Dunlop 1994).

In many South Pacific cultures prestige is increased by sharing rather than accumulating resources. A continuous exchange of goods and services lubricates social relations and is an essential aspect of ceremonies and rites of passage. Women in Samoa are key figures in the creation and presentation of mats and other exchange items. In terms of the secular–sacred division of responsibility, moral authority, ceremony, and hospitality have been a female domain and political authority, defense, and warfare have traditionally been a masculine domain (Schoeffel cited in Fairbairn-Dunlop 1994).

Given this distinction and emphasis upon women as providers of village hospitality in Samoa, it is not surprising that in a service rather than a production industry such as tourism, women tend to predominate. Also, in Samoa, as well as many other South Pacific nations, women predominantly produce handicrafts for retail to tourists. Traditional crafts have low economic potential and therefore the shift from production for ceremonial purposes to commercial production can have an associated negative impact on the status of women as producers of these crafts.

In contrast with some other South Pacific nations, the understanding that such efforts are pursued in the interest of the family as a whole has meant that Samoan women have faced limited antagonism in response to their entrepreneurial activities. For the people of Samoa, adherence to *faaSamoa* (the Samoan way) provides a strong foundation for cultural identity and pride. The principles upon which *faaSamoa* is based ensure that customary values, such as women gaining access to education and being allowed to take initiative, have facilitated women's control over tourism development in that country. Gaining the support of family has also led to women creating lucrative enterprises from small moneymaking ventures. For example, Aggie Grey's hotel, which over the years has become a thriving business initiated by a local woman, is one of Samoa's most successful hotels (Schoeffel cited in Fairbairn-Dunlop 1994).

In other nations the revival of cultural traditions has not necessarily helped to facilitate women's involvement in tourism development. In parts of Vanuatu, *kastom* has been reinforced in reaction to the introduction, through colonization, of a capitalist monetarized economy (de Burlo 1997; Jolly 1991). In moves to retain cultural integrity, women's roles have become more restricted. As a result, participation in political decision making and formal community planning has not been encouraged. In Fiji, which experienced a different form of colonialism, many British officials were committed to the preservation of traditional Fijian culture and customary land tenure was codified, enhancing the power of chiefs. The administrative body created to manage native lands was dominated by chiefly Fijians, and this in effect inverted the pattern of commoners' ownership, divesting power from them into the hands of chiefly males who have since become the rich elite entrepreneurs and ruling class in Fiji (Jolly 1991). The influence that such historical political interference has had upon the role of women in contemporary politics remains evident, with low numbers of women elected to positions in regional and national politics. Decisions regarding tourism-development policy, therefore, do not tend to incorporate women's perspectives. Some authors argue that extractive and exploitative land-use practices, which might include unsustainable hotel resort development, would be diminished if women were integrated into formal land-management strategies (Emberson-Bain 1994; Wacker 1994).

SOUTH PACIFIC WOMEN
AS CONSUMERS OF TOURISM

Little has been written about South Pacific women as consumers of tourism. Historically, people of the South Pacific have always been great travelers. Their consumption of contemporary tourism, however, is not as well known. Despite the traditional generosity of Pacific Islanders and the fact that many Islanders themselves travel, it has been suggested that tourism, as popularly understood, is not an indigenous practice in the South Pacific and is alien to indigenous ways (Biddlecomb 1981; Farrell 1982; Minerbi 1992; Patterson 1993).

Travel for many Pacific Islanders often involves traveling in groups to meet and stay with members of the extended family or friends. Often the travel has a specific purpose, such as attending a wedding, funeral, or sporting event. There are close cultural and familial relationships between many of the Pacific Islands (including New Zealand), and this is reflected in international travel patterns. For example, almost 10 percent of tourists entering the Cook Islands are returning Cook Islanders (primarily from New Zealand or Australia), and another 5 percent are nationals of other Pacific Island countries (Cook Island Tourism Corporation 1996). Similarly, 6 percent of visitors to Fiji are Pacific Islanders (Fiji Visitors Bureau 1999).

Likewise, Pacific Islanders commonly undertake a great deal of domestic travel. For example, it was found in one study in the Cook Islands that 97 percent of respondents had engaged in domestic inter-island travel. Interestingly, however, participants in this type of domestic travel did not conceptualize themselves as consumers of "tourism" (Berno 1995). Recent research in Fiji drew similar conclusions:

The question of local tourists often caused much laughter. Some people thought that it was a silly idea. People couldn't be tourists in their own country while [other interviewees] said they had never thought of local tourists but on reflexion believed that they were possible. . . . [O]ne respondent defin[ed] a tourist as someone who visited Levuka but was not a Fijian citizen. Another said that a Fijian could be a visitor but not a tourist. (Fisher 1999, 224)

Hospitality for Pacific Islanders as consumers of tourism is generally reciprocated by means such as gifts (for example, food and crafts), a financial contribution to the hosts, and/or by hosting in return. It is implicitly understood that cultural obligation dictates that at some point in the future the hosts will be reciprocated appropriately for their hospitality (Beaglehole 1957; Ross 1991; Stephenson 1979). The social and economic transactions for this type of tourism are therefore "continuous" transactions that are unbound in time and worth and do not end when the tourist–host encounter is complete. This is in contrast to the segmented and instrumental social and economic interactions implicit in most Western forms of tourism. The payment of money to purchase the tourist experience forms a discrete transaction, and tourist–host interactions, both social and economic, are entered into for specific, limited, and immediate purposes. Unlike Pacific Islanders, Western tourists rarely expect far-reaching or long-lasting consequences as a result of their transactions (Berno 1999; van den Berghe 1994).

Clearly, both South Pacific men and women are consumers of tourism as product. How they consume it, the form it takes, and the underlying meaning, motivations, and any gender differences however, are yet to be explored.

THE FUTURE OF WOMEN IN TOURISM IN THE SOUTH PACIFIC

Much hotel-resort-type tourism development in the South Pacific is owned and controlled by outside investors and provides little opportunity for women's empowerment in the tourism industry (Britton 1987). However, in many cases rural indigenous people do retain the rights to landownership, and, in some circumstances, there is the potential to develop community-based ecotourism or other small-scale tourism-related business ventures. There are many issues that must be addressed in terms of acknowledging and working with the vagaries of international market demands. These constraints must be accurately assessed to avoiding setting up local people for failure. To achieve this, outside expertise may be required in the shorter term. On the other hand, local issues, which include the need to address power relations between the genders that can limit women's opportunities as well as the strong collective social structures inherent in the South Pacific, must be acknowledged and built upon to create viable tourism ventures that ensure benefits are distributed equitably. If these fundamental issues are addressed there is the possibility of women diversifying their current economic activities in order to improve standards of living for themselves and their families without increasing their double burden.

Alongside land-management issues associated with tourism development is the connected issue of access to financial credit, often only available with land as collateral (Bolabola 1986). In the context of small-business ventures, even where credit is made available to women for tourism-related enterprises this is not necessarily an empowering mechanism when low-profit culturally legitimate "women's enterprises" that do not increase their standard of living are encouraged (Robinson 1995). In order for tourism-related credit to be empowering rather than merely adding an extra burden to the lives of Pacific women, the following measures are recommended: mechanisms to enhance women's access to credit, such as requirements for training to facilitate progression to the formal sector; networking to support women in nontraditional fields (to avoid simply increasing domestication through tourism development); and legal reforms, such as the need for a cosignatory in conjunction with changes to existing property laws (Berger 1989).

There is the need for broadening perceptions of gender activities among external agents involved in tourism development, and also the need to collectivize and politicize gender issues through "awareness raising" among local communities (United Nations Development Fund for Women 1997). These questions must be addressed before culturally appropriate and financially successful tourism ventures can be realized by women. The formation of women's credit groups through preexisting channels of women's village collectives and other community-based organizations would allow tourism development to be guided by the self-defined goals and objectives of those women who will ultimately provide most of the labor. In association, effective support mechanisms must be introduced, and carefully structured ongoing training made available to assist women to manage credit disbursements and savings and to improve general business-management skills. While entrepreneurial skills are necessary for such small-scale business ventures, the role of the individual in collectivist societies is quite different from that of most Western capitalist nations, from whom business-management strategies are usually imported and often imposed with limited success. This needs to be recognized from the outset in relation to tourism entrepreneurship in the South Pacific.

CONCLUSION

Tourism development affects men and women differently in the South Pacific as a result of their particular gender roles. This can be seen in how men and women are represented within the tourism industry and the roles they play as producers and consumers of tourism. Because tourism is by nature an export industry based upon the interaction of hosts and guests, it also affects gender relations, both inter- and intraculturally.

When discussing women and tourism in the South Pacific, generalizations cannot be made, as the South Pacific is a culturally diverse region. In order to assess the impacts of tourism development upon the women in various countries of the South Pacific, efforts must be made at policy, planning, and management levels to create valid means of verification in order to monitor the impacts of tourism development from a gender perspective.

REFERENCES

Auger-Andrews, M. L. (1995). A human dimension of tourism: The impact of hotel and resort work on the attitudes of Fijian working mothers. Master's thesis, University of the South Pacific, Suva, Fiji.

Beaglehole, E. (1957). *Social Change in the South Pacific: Rarotonga and Aitutaki.* Sydney: George Allen and Unwin.

Berger, M. (1989). Giving women credit: The strengths and limitations of credit as a tool for alleviating poverty. *World Development* 17: 1017–1032.

Berno, T. (1999). When a guest is a guest: Cook Islanders view tourism. *Annals of Tourism Research* 26: 656–675.

Berno, T. (1995). The socio-cultural and psychological effects of tourism on indigenous cultures. Ph.D. diss., University of Canterbury, Christchurch, New Zealand.

Berno, T., and N. Douglas. (1998). Tourism in Polynesia and Melanesia: A comparison. *Asia Pacific Journal of Tourism Research* 2: 65–73.

Biddlecomb, C. (1981). *Pacific Tourism: Contrasts in Values and Expectations.* Nadi, Fiji: Lotu Pacifica Productions.

Bolabola, C. (1986). Fiji: Customary constraints and legal process. In *Land Rights of Pacific Women.* Suva, Fiji: Institute of Pacific Studies, University of the South Pacific.

Britton, S. (1987). *Ambiguous Alternatives: Tourism in Small Developing Countries.* Suva, Fiji: University of South Pacific.

Buchanan, F. S. (1998). Culture—helped or held hostage by tourism? *Cook Islands Press*, 4–5 July, 5–12.

Cohen, C. B. (1995). Marketing paradise, making nation. *Annals of Tourism Research* 22: 404–421.

Cook Islands Tourism Corporation. (1996). *Visitor Arrivals.* Rarotonga: CITC.

Cukier, J., and G. Wall. (1995). Tourism employment in Bali: A gender analysis. *Tourism Economics* 1 (4): 389–401.

de Burlo, C. R. (1997). Tourism, conservation and cultural environment in rural Vanuatu. Paper presented at the VIII Pacific Science Inter-Congress, 13–19 July, University of the South Pacific, Suva, Fiji.

Douglas, N., and N. Douglas. (1996). Tourism in the Pacific: Historical factors. In *Tourism in the Pacific: Issues and Cases*, edited by C. M. Hall and S. J. Page. London: International Thomson Business Press.

Edwards, E. (1996). Postcards: Greetings from another world. In *The Tourist Image: Myths and Myth Making in Tourism*, edited by T. Selwyn. Chichester: Wiley.

Emberson-Bain, A. (1994). Mining development in the Pacific: Are we sustaining the unsustainable? In *Feminist Perspectives on Sustainable Development*, edited by W. Harcourt. London: Zed Books.

Fairbairn-Dunlop, P. (1994). Gender, culture and tourism development in Western Samoa. In *Tourism: A gender analysis*, edited by V. Kinnaird and D. Hall. Chichester: Wiley.

Farrell, B. H. (1982). The future of tourism in the South Pacific. In *The Impact of Tourism Development in the Pacific*, edited by F. Rajotte. Peterborough, ON: Environmental and Resource Studies Programme, Trent University.

Fiji Visitors Bureau. (1999). *Visitor Arrival Statistics*. Suva: FVB.

Fisher, D. (1999). Tourism as an agent of change in local economic behaviour: A case study of Levuka, Fiji. Ph.D. diss., Lincoln University, Lincoln, New Zealand.

Goss, J. (1993). Placing the market and marketing place: Tourist advertising of the Hawaiian Islands, 1972–1992. *Environment and Planning D: Society and Space* 11: 663–688.

Holmes, L. D. (1984). *Samoan Village*. New York: Holt, Rinehart and Winston.

Jolly, M. (1991). The politics of difference: Feminism, colonialism and decolonisation in Vanuatu. In *Intersexions Gender/Class/Culture/Ethnicity*, edited by G. Bottomley, M. De Lepervanche, and J. Martin. Sydney: Allen and Unwin.

Jones, R., and L. Pinheiro. (1997). *Fiji: A Lonely Planet Survival Kit*. Hawthorn, Australia: Lonely Planet Publications.

Jones, T. (1999). Talanoa and tourism, exploring the intersexions of gender and village based tourism development in Fiji: The myth of community. Master's thesis, Lincoln University, Lincoln, New Zealand.

Kinnaird, V., and D. Hall. (1994). *Tourism: A Gender Analysis*. Chichester: Wiley.

Lee, J. (1997). Women who are tattooed for their country. *She and More*, July, 22–27.

Lim, N. Z. (1993). The contribution of women to cultural tourism. In *Universal Tourism: Enriching or Degrading Culture? Proceedings on the International Conference on Cultural Tourism*, edited by W. Nuryanti. Yogyakarta: Gadjah Mada University Press.

Meleisea, M., and P. Meleisea. (1980). "The best kept secret": Tourism in Western Samoa. In *Pacific Tourism: As Islanders See It*, edited by R. Crocombe. Suva, Fiji: University of the South Pacific.

Minerbi, L. (1992). *Impact of Tourism Development in Pacific Islands*. San Francisco: Greenpeace Pacific Campaign.

Momsen, J. H. (1994). Tourism, gender and development in the Caribbean. In *Tourism: A Gender Analysis*, edited by V. Kinnaird and D. Hall. Chichester: Wiley.

O'Grady. (1990). *The Challenge of Tourism*. Bangkok: Ecumenal Coalition on Third World Tourism.

Pacific Asia Travel Association. (n.d.). *Perceptions of the South Pacific in the USA: A Survey of Tour Operators and Travel Agents on the West Coast*. San Francisco: Author.

Pacific Asia Travel Association. (1982). *Study of Potential Australian Holiday Travellers to the Pacific Area, 1981*. Sydney: Author.

Patterson, K. (1993). Aloha: Welcome to paradise. *The New Internationalist* 245: 14–15.

Pearce, P. (1982). Tourists and their hosts: Some social and psychological effects of intercultural contact. In *Cultures in Contact: Studies in Cross-Cultural Interaction*, edited by S. Bochner. Oxford: Pergamon Press.

Petit-Skinner, S. (1977). Tourism and acculturation in Tahiti. In *The Social and Economic Impact of Tourism on Pacific Communities*, edited by B. H. Farrell. Santa Cruz: Center for South Pacific Studies, University of California.

Purcell, K. (1997). Women's employment in UK tourism: Gender roles and labor markets. In *Gender, Work and Tourism*, edited by M. T. Sinclair. London: Routledge.

Richter, L. K. (1994). Exploring the political role of gender in tourism research. In *Global Tourism: The Next Decade*, edited by W. F. Theobald. London: Butterworth Heinemann.

Robinson, J. S. (1995). Finance or fatigue? Credit for rural Fijian women in microenterprise. Master's thesis, Lincoln University, New Zealand.

Ross, H. (1991). Controlling access to environment and self: Aboriginal perspectives on tourism. *Australian Psychologist* 26: 176–182.

Schellhorn, M. (1998). "There is a place where the dreams live": Portrayals of the South Seas in German language tourist brochures. Master's thesis, Lincoln University, Lincoln, New Zealand.

Schoeffel, P., and E. Kikau. (1980). Women's work in Fiji: An historical perspective. *Review: A Journal from SSED* 1: 20–28.

Selwyn, T., ed. (1996). *The Tourist Image: Myths and Myth Making in Tourism*. Chichester: Wiley.

Sinclair, M. T. (1997). Gendered work in tourism. In *Gender, Work and Tourism*, edited by M. T. Sinclair. London: Routledge.

Stanley, D. (1993). *South Pacific Handbook*. 5th ed. Chico, Calif.: Moon Publications.

Stephenson, R. A. (1979). Atiu revisited: Environmental perception in anthropology. In *Persistence and Exchange: Papers from a Symposium on Ecological Problems of the Traditional Societies of the Pacific Region*, edited by R. W. Force and B. Bishop. Honolulu: Pacific Science Association.

Suaalii, T. M. (1997). Deconstructing the "exotic" female beauty of the Pacific Islands and "white" male desire. *Women's Studies Journal* 13 (2): 75–94.

Swain, M. B. (1995). Gender in tourism. *Annals of Tourism Research* 22: 247–266.

Tinker, I. (1990). *Persistent Inequalities: Women and Development*. New York: Oxford University Press.

Tourism Council of the South Pacific. (1997). 1995 Visitor statistics for TCSP member countries. *South Pacific On-line*. Available <http://www.info centre.com/spt> or <http://www.tcsp.com/spt>.

United Nations Development Fund for Women. (1997). *UNIFEM—Pacific Annual Report*. Suva, Fiji: Author.

van den Berghe, P. L. (1994). *The Quest for the Other*. Seattle: University of Washington Press.

Wacker, C. (1994). Sustainable development through women's groups: A cultural approach to sustainable development. In *Feminist Perspectives on Sustainable Development*, edited by W. Harcourt. London: Zed Books.

Wilson, D. (1994). Probably as close as you can get to paradise: Tourism and the changing image of the Seychelles. In *Tourism: The State of the Art*, edited by A. V. Seaton. Chichester: Wiley.

Part III

WOMEN IN THE LESS DEVELOPED
TOURIST DESTINATIONS

6

Tourism Behind the Veil of Islam: Women and Development in the Middle East

Sevil Sönmez

In socioeconomic terms, most Middle Eastern countries generally do not fare well when compared with developed nations.[1] The region's socioeconomic underdevelopment has been exacerbated by its well-known problems with religious fundamentalism and social ultraconservatism, political conflict, sporadic wars, and terrorism, which have been serious detriments to both its advancement and its standing in the global community. Further, persistent media reports of political conflict and terrorism in the region, powerful media images of covered women and often repressed citizens, as well as the region's low standards of living have fueled an overall negative image.

Considering the Middle East's low levels of socioeconomic development in light of the region's immensely rich and diverse natural, cultural, and historical resources and attractions, the multiple economic benefits of the international tourism industry make it a very obvious choice as an economic-development tool for the region.[2] In reality, tourist arrivals and receipts are in no way analogous to the Middle East's offerings. From tourism data, it can be simply inferred that the aforementioned challenges and public images have significantly deterred international travelers from going to the region. The problem has other dimensions, however. For religious and cultural reasons, many countries in the region discourage international tourism, others try to limit the activity to citizens of neighboring countries, and still others—while they value the contribution tourism makes to their economies and actively incorporate tourism into their economic-development strategies—are simply ineffective.

Parallels can easily be drawn between levels of socioeconomic development and the social status of women in developing regions. The correlation between the two in the Middle East is the focus of this chapter. The inclusion of women in development goals is essential, not just to insure gender equity, but also to strengthen societal development. In the Middle East, issues of gender equity and women's economic and political contribution to their countries' fates must be viewed in the unique context of an environment characterized by a patriarchal society, Middle Eastern culture, and Islam. This chapter examines socioeconomic development and tourism in the Middle East, how religion and culture influence women's social status, and the role women play in their countries' economic and political spheres and particularly in the production and consumption of tourism.

WOMEN'S ROLE IN ECONOMIC DEVELOPMENT

The level of economic development in the Middle East lags far behind that of European, North American, and several Asian countries. With the exceptions of Israel, Cyprus, and the oil-producing countries of the Arabian Peninsula (Kuwait, UAE, Qatar, and Bahrain), most Middle Eastern countries struggle with low standards of living (Table 6.1).[3] Many countries in the region have very low GDP per capita—$740 in Yemen, $2,400 in Iraq, $2,500 in Syria, and $2,800 in Egypt—which is attributable to several factors, such as international economic sanctions, war, political instability, economic crises, or simply low production and output. Their economic situations are exacerbated by high levels of unemployment (30 percent or higher in Algeria, Iraq, Libya, and Yemen; around 20 to 25 percent in Jordan, Lebanon, and Morocco), high inflation rates (70 percent in Turkey, 24 percent in Iran, 15 to 20 percent in Syria), and significant external debts. Unfortunately, too many countries experiencing economic troubles are also burdened by high annual rates of population growth (Iraq 3.2 percent, Egypt 3.3 percent, Syria 3.1 percent, Jordan 3.1 percent, Libya 2.4 percent, and Algeria 2.1 percent).

Among other issues, economic indicators recount how well or poorly a country is able to utilize its human resources. Despite various attempts (and limited success) to improve estimating women's participation in economic development, it is widely recognized that, especially in developing countries, official statistics fully reflect neither women's eco-

Table 6.1
Economic Indicators in the Middle East

Country	GDP per Capita	Percent of Population Unemployed	Inflation	External Debt ($ billions)
Middle Eastern Countries				
Cyprus	$13,000	3.3	2.3%	$1.56
Iran	$5,000	>30.0	24.0%	$21.9
Iraq	$2,400	N/A	N/A	N/A
Israel	$18,100	8.7	5.4%	$18.7
Jordan	$3,500	25–30.0	4.0%	$ 7.5
Lebanon	$4,500	18.0	5.0%	$ 3.0
Palestinian Authority	N/A	N/A	N/A	N/A
Syria	$2,500	12–15.0	15–20.0%	$22.0
Turkey	$6,600	10.0	70.0%	$93.4
North African Countries				
Algeria	$4,600	30.0	9.0%	$31.4
Egypt	$2,800	10.0	3.6%	$28.0
Libya	$6,700	30.0	24.0%	$ 4.0
Morocco	$3,200	19.0	2–3.0%	$20.9
Tunisia	$5,200	16.0	3.3%	$12.1
Arabian Peninsula Countries				
Bahrain	$13,100	15.0	(-0.2%)	$2.0
Kuwait	$22,700	1.8	1.0%	$ 7.3
Oman	$7,900	N/A	(-0.2%)	$ 3.0
Qatar	$17,100	N/A	7.4%	$11.0
Saudi Arabia	$9,000	N/A	(-0.2%)	N/A
United Arab Emirates	$17,400	N/A	5.0%	$14.0
Yemen	$740	30.0	11.0%	$ 4.9

Source: Central Intelligence Agency, *The World Factbook*, 5 June 2000. Available <http://www.cia.gov/cia/publications/factbook/index.html>.

nomic activities nor their contribution to economic output.[4] The correlation between a country's level of development and the active role (or lack thereof) of women in society should not be overlooked. The social indicators that are the most relevant to women in the Middle East are very revealing.

The role of women in society and as contributors to world development continues to evolve, notwithstanding significant cultural differences around the world. The dominant view of women in the 1960s as
mothers and housewives (Young 1993) began to align itself with the
shift in the 1970s in world development philosophy toward greater
emphasis on issues of equity. The simultaneous growth of the women's
movement facilitated gradual acceptance of women's contributions,
not only to the welfare of the family but also to the economy. In the
1980s—a decade characterized in development literature as a struggle
with global recession, deteriorating economic situations in industrialized nations, and increasing indebtedness in the developing world
(Young 1993)—women played a critical role, especially in those areas
enduring the greatest economic hardships, in mitigating some of the
difficulties through in-home economic management and increased labor-
force participation. In addition, the decade "witnessed mounting evidence of women's wish and capacity to take their problems into their
own hands through organization and action" (Young 1993, 42). By the
time the United Nations Decade for Women (1976–1985) came to a
close, however, the rhetoric on integrating women into global development remained without financial and political backing. The 1990s
ushered in globalization, which is driven primarily by competitive
markets.[5] According to the United Nations (1999), when pressures of
global competition push the market into a dominant position over
social and political outcomes, globalization's benefits spread inequi-
tably. As a result, power and wealth are concentrated in elite groups
of people, nations, and corporations, while others are marginalized.
In the area of women's issues, by monopolizing world attention,
globalization has overshadowed the women's movement.

In this era of globalization, many Middle Eastern and North African countries face marginalization as a result of mounting problems
hindering their economic and social goals (World Bank 1999). With
regard to ethnic, religious, regional, class, gender, and national divisions, development in these nations has been uneven (Jabbra and Jabbra
1992). Even entering the twenty-first century, political uncertainties
as well as socioeconomic problems challenge the region's countries.
Not surprisingly, in the atmosphere of cultural and religious ultraconservatism that defines most of the Middle East, the potential role of
women as active participants in regional economic development is
significantly weakened.

The Middle East, North Africa, and the Arabian Peninsula have not
received needed attention in the body of literature focusing on women
in development. The problem is attributed partly to the difficulty of
obtaining data and partly to the view that women's lives in the region
are influenced more by culture and religion than economic factors

(Moghadam 1994).[6] The common Western stereotypical image of Muslim women is often that of submissive women dressed from head to toe in black. While many women (i.e., in Saudi Arabia, Kuwait, and Afghanistan) lead tightly restricted lives that do not involve working, voting, driving, or traveling without permission, there are many others who lead lives quite close to that of Western women. For example, Egyptian women are becoming increasingly more involved in their country's workforce; Cypriot, Turkish, and Israeli women enjoy high degrees of equality and participation; and the rights movement has placed numerous Palestinian women in prominent roles. Nevertheless, socioeconomic indicators do not always reflect such exceptions. The bleak picture painted by the economic indicators (Table 6.1) of the standard of living in the Middle East is further darkened by the social indicators (Table 6.2), particularly when gender gaps are examined. The indices in Table 6.2, which illustrate the extent of Middle Eastern women's empowerment within the home or outside and ultimately reflect their role in economic development, require closer examination.

Fertility rates, which indicate the level of birth-control technology, are inextricably linked to women's educational levels. In countries where fertility rates are high, women are less likely to be literate and unlikely to work outside the home. For example, the average number of children women bare in Iraq (5.12), Syria (5.37), Saudi Arabia (6.34), and Yemen (7.06) corresponds to women's low literacy rates (45, 56, 50, and 26 percent, respectively) and participation in economic activity.[7] Infant mortality rates and life expectancies indicate general health conditions, including public sanitation, nutrition, and access to medical care. In countries where gender-specific life expectancies indicate shorter lives for women it has been assessed that women do not have equal access to medical care with men. Overall, shorter life expectancies for residents living in Middle Eastern and North African countries is clearly related to the availability of medical care, among other factors. For example, the number of doctors in most of these countries is far lower than numbers in Western societies.[8] Consequently, the rate of infant mortality is extremely high in countries like Iraq (94/1,000), Yemen (76), Morocco (58), and Egypt (54).

Gender differences in literacy rates imply unequal attainment of education, but more important, differences in power and social valuation. It should come as no surprise that uneducated women are more easily controlled because they are unable to find well-paying jobs and remain uninformed of their legal rights. Furthermore, in this vicious cycle uneducated women remain preoccupied with bearing children and thus remain bound to their homes. With only two exceptions (Cyprus and Israel), literacy rates for women in Middle Eastern and North African countries are substantially below those of their coun-

Table 6.2
Social Indicators in the Middle East

Country	Population (millions)	Annual Population Growth Rate	Fertility Rate (number of children per female)	Infant Mortality Rate (per 1,000 live births)	Life Expectancy (years) Women	Men
Middle Eastern Countries						
Cyprus	0.754	0.67	2.00	7.68	79.39	74.91
Iran	65.18	1.07	2.45	29.73	71.16	68.43
Iraq	22.43	3.19	5.12	62.41	67.56	65.54
Israel	5.7	1.81	2.68	7.78	80.60	76.70
Jordan	4.6	3.05	4.64	32.70	75.10	71.20
Lebanon	3.56	1.61	2.25	30.53	73.66	68.34
Palestinian Authority	N/A	N/A	N/A	N/A	N/A	N/A
Syria	17.21	3.15	5.37	36.42	69.48	66.75
Turkey	65.6	1.57	2.41	35.81	75.90	70.80
North African Countries						
Algeria	31.13	2.10	3.27	43.82	70.46	68.07
Egypt	67.27	1.82	3.33	67.46	64.49	60.39
Libya	4.99	2.40	3.79	28.15	77.74	73.81
Morocco	29.66	1.84	3.24	50.96	70.99	66.85
Tunisia	9.51	1.39	2.38	31.38	74.86	71.95
Arabian Peninsula Countries						
Bahrain	0.629	2.00	2.97	14.81	77.96	72.75
Kuwait	1.99	3.88	3.34	10.26	79.30	75.11
Oman	2.45	3.45	6.11	24.71	73.39	69.31
Qatar	0.724	3.62	3.42	17.25	76.90	71.70
Saudi Arabia	21.5	3.39	6.34	38.00	72.50	68.70
United Arab Emirates	2.34	1.78	3.50	14.1	76.72	73.83
Yemen	16.94	3.34	7.06	69.82	61.88	58.17

terparts living in more developed nations, with the least educated women living in Yemen (26 percent), Morocco (31 percent), Egypt (39 percent), Iraq (45 percent), and Algeria (49 percent). Despite such low percentages, Middle Eastern women do receive higher levels of education than women of earlier generations. For example, in Turkey, where urban middle-class and upper-middle-class women have higher levels of education than working-class women, women comprise 50 percent of university students. Lebanese women constituted over 40 percent of the student body of the American University of Beirut even in the early 1980s (*Country Studies* 2000). In Algeria, the 1963 Khemisti Law, and, later, the 1976 National Charter, guaranteed legal equality

Literacy Rate (percentage)		Suffrage		Female Political Participation (percentage in government)	Labor Force		Female Economic Activity Rate (percentage)
					Total (millions)	Women (millions)	
Women	Men	Women	Men				
91	98	18+	18+	5.3	0.3	N/A	37.1
66	78	15+	15+	0.4	15.4	3	15.8
45	71	18+	18+	0	4.4	N/A	10.4
93	97	18+	18+	10.6	2.3	6	34.1
79	93	20+	20+	3.4	1.15	4	13.6
82	91	21+	21+	0	1.0	N/A	19.2
N/A	N/A	N/A	N/A	N/A	N/A	N/A	N/A
56	86	18+	18+	3.9	4.7	N/A	16.3
72	92	18+	18+	5.0	22.7	8	34.9
49	74	18+	18+	4.8	7.8	N/A	16.9
39	64	18+	18+	4.0	17.4	1	22.2
63	88	18+	18+	3.4	1.0	N/A	13.0
31	57	21+	21+	0.9	11.0	N/A	27.1
55	79	20+	20+	7.9	3.3	N/A	24.1
79	89	None	None	0	0.15	N/A	20.7
75	82	None	21	4.9	1.1	N/A	24.8
46	71	None	21	3.6	0.85	N/A	8.7
80	79	None	None	0	0.233	N/A	22.1
50	72	None	None	0	7.0	N/A	10.6
80	79	None	None	0	1.3	N/A	18.9
26	53	18+	18+	0	N/A	N/A	17.8

Source: Central Intelligence Agency, *The World Factbook*, 5 June 2000. Available <http://www.cia.gov/cia/publications/factbook/index.html>.

between the genders and formally recognized women's right to education.[9] Women's access to higher education has thus improved, and today Algerian women represent about 40 percent of university students; unfortunately, most return to the home once their schooling is finished due to societal expectations.

Labor force participation rates do not present a complete picture of women's contribution to their country's economy, mainly because domestic work is not counted and nondomestic work may not be fully reflected.[10] Cultural and religious reasons keep the majority of Middle

Eastern women from achieving economic independence. As a result, women remain reliant on their husbands or other family members. In the region, only Cyprus (37 percent), Israel (34 percent), and Turkey (35 percent) are comparable to Western countries in female participation in economic activity.[11] In other areas, the percentage of women in paid labor outside the home ranges between 9 percent (Oman) and 27 percent (Morocco). Not only is it impossible to make generalizations in the Middle East due to significant variances, a number of surprising contradictions have developed in the region over the years with regard to women's employment, as the following examples demonstrate.

In Cyprus, the number of women in clerical jobs continues to increase, but only one in fifteen work in administrative or managerial positions. On the other hand, many Cypriot women can be found in medicine and teaching (*Country Studies* 2000). Urban middle-class and upper-middle-class Turkish women are primarily employed in teaching, health care, and clerical work, whereas upper-class urban women are often in prestigious professions, such as law, medicine, engineering, academia, and politics (*Country Studies* 2000). In Egypt, between 1978 and 1980 working women doubled from 500,000 to 1 million, with substantial numbers in nonagricultural professions, such as education, engineering, and medicine. Yet most women are employed in low-paying jobs in factories, offices, and service industries. Half of all employed Egyptian women hold jobs as street cleaners, janitors, hotel and domestic servants, and hospital aides (*Country Studies* 2000). In Yemen, despite the prevailing ethic that only severe economic need would push women into factories and offices, women become teachers, medical personnel, civil servants, and factory workers. There is even a visible female minority among lawyers, judges, directors, administrators, and television broadcasters (Carapico 1991). Unlike their Saudi Arabian sisters, Qatari women drive, take advantage of free education (from primary through university levels), and are able to find employment in various professions and work without segregation from men (Curtiss 1996). On the other hand, even though the Algerian government promised the creation of several hundred thousand new jobs for women in the 1980s, their rights to employment, political power, and overall autonomy are curtailed; as a result, the number of women employed outside the home remained low through the 1990s (*Country Studies* 2000). In Iran, the status of women has taken drastic turns over the past three decades. Most professional women from the secular middle class were active participants in the 1979 revolution headed by Ayatollah Khomeini that toppled the shah (*Country Studies* 2000). Following the revolution, because the traditional middle class—which was the main social group to inherit political power—highly valued women's traditional role in a gender-segregated society, women's lives were negatively impacted. In prerevolution Iran women had greater freedoms and opportunities for work. Upper- and middle-class women held professions, while traditional middle- and lower-class women worked outside the home. Although these roles were drastically curtailed immediately following the revolution, the gradual changes in women's roles in the labor force have accelerated under a more moderate government (*Country Studies* 2000).

Finally, political participation rates and suffrage serve as indicators of women's political power. There are a number of inconsistencies in Middle Eastern women's dual role in politics (voting rights and holding political office). With the exceptions of Yemen and Oman—where women are permitted to vote and hold political office, respectively— citizens (male or female) in the monarchies of the Arabian Peninsula do not vote, and women are not represented in government.[12] In dictatorships such as Iraq, Libya, and Syria, votes (by either men or women) are meaningless. For the majority of the Middle East, however, men and women have equal voting rights. The highest percentage of female political participation is seen in Israel (11 percent), Turkey (9 percent), and Tunisia (8 percent) (Waltz 1990).[13]

It is interesting to note that women have not been deprived of their right to vote in Iran under the Islamic Republic, "despite the regime's highly misogynist attitudes which have pushed women out of public life and limited employment in mixed work places" (Graham-Brown 1994, 29). In Algeria, even though male politicians of the Islamic Salvation Front (FIS) have traditionally spoken of women as "subordinates who should not be allowed to work outside the home, let alone participate in politics" (Graham-Brown 1994, 28), after 1976, nine women were elected and women's public participation increased significantly at the local and regional level. By the late 1980s nearly 300 women were serving on communal assemblies, and in 1984 the first Algerian woman cabinet minister was appointed. At the urging of legislators by Mustafa Kemal Atatürk (founder of the Turkish Republic), the *shariah* law was replaced in 1926 with a civil code, abolishing polygamy and granting equal rights to both men and women in inheritance, marriage, and divorce. "In 1934 Turkish women won the right to vote in parliamentary elections—a year later, there were 18 women deputies" (Zak 1994, 53). In the early 1990s Turkey had a female prime minister (Tansu Çiller), and since then has had a number of female ministers of state. Currently, however, only 22 members of the 250-member Turkish parliament are women. In Iran, since the early 1990s the restrictions on women have been relaxing. In fact, as far back as 1992 (in the second round of Majlis elections), 9 of the 268 deputies elected were women (Ramazani 1993).[14] Other examples of Middle Eastern women in politics include Golda Meir (first Israeli ambassador to the USSR, foreign minister, prime minister) and, more recently, Professor Hanan al-Ashrawi (spokesperson for the Palestinian delegation to the peace talks), who conveyed the image of a sophisticated and articulate female participant in regional politics.

With very few exceptions, the social indicators clearly illustrate that women in the Middle East have a long and difficult road to travel to achieve equality, economic and political empowerment, and higher standards of living and quality of life. When women's present-day conditions and achievements are compared to those of the past, certainly the difference is encouraging. When they are compared to those of women living in developed nations, however, it is disheartening. The relationship between Middle Eastern countries' development level and the status of women in society needs to be reevaluated, especially because economic and social indicators clearly indicate that women are not being utilized efficiently or effectively as human resources in their countries. Especially in developing regions such as the Middle East, the "connection between investing in women and improving the welfare of children, households and communities" must be emphasized and human-development goals should be extended to women to assure gender equity and to accelerate societal development (Moghadam and Khoury 1995, 3).

THE INFLUENCE OF ISLAM ON WOMEN'S SOCIAL STATUS

The role of women in Middle Eastern society is primarily defined by culture and religion, and, in many countries, by how strictly Islam is interpreted. Although Islamic life is defined by the interpretation of the Qur'an, the Hadith (sayings of the Prophet Muhammed), *shariah* (Divine Law, laid down in the Qur'an), and *fiqh* (jurisprudential issues), cultural biases often skew individual and collective interpretations, distorting the Qur'an's specifications (Islam-Husain 1997). For example, the Qur'an strictly forbids female infanticide (16:58–59), but most Muslim societies unabashedly favor male children over female.[15] The Qur'an not only advocates equal education and opportunity (4:124), but also equates the attainment of knowledge to *ibadah* (worship of Allah), "even recommending travel to the ends of the Earth to attain knowledge" (Islam-Husain 1997, 77). However, many girls are removed from school while boys are encouraged to continue. Islam permits a woman to work outside the home (provided that she dress modestly and not neglect her family), but the majority of women are forbidden to do so by their men. Further, the Qur'an stresses a woman's right to her earnings, property, and wealth (4:32), but often women who work are expected to directly turn their earnings over to their husbands and fathers. The Qur'an clearly refers to a woman's right to financial security and inheritance (4:7), but too many women are kept from their inheritances and perpetually dependent on their men for financial security.[16] According to the Qur'an, a woman cannot be married against her will—in fact, the marriage is considered null and void if free consent is not given by both parties. However, the majority of Muslim marriages are still arranged, and second wives are often taken.[17] In the event of irreconcilable differences or cruelty, the Qur'an states a woman's right to seek divorce (2:228) and to remarry in case of divorce or death of a spouse. In most Middle Eastern societies, however, divorced women are stigmatized and their behavior strictly scrutinized thereafter.

Although women's inferior social status is legitimized by the misinterpretation of various religious texts, the oppression of women in Arab society preceded the advent of Islam. Therefore, it is not difficult to understand why the rights given to women by the Qur'an nearly fourteen centuries ago are not honored (Islam-Husain 1997). Even though gender-related restrictions have relaxed over the past few decades and a number of countries have laws protecting women's rights, patriarchal Middle Eastern societies repress and oppress women as a result of misguided interpretations of gender relations and misinterpretations of religious dictates.[18] Further, the natural process of change conflicts with the Middle Eastern traditional cultural and religious value system, which controls social behavior.[19] The mainly male-dominated power base, comprised of political and religious leaders, manipulates society's perceptions of the cultural value system to serve its own interests (Seikaly 1994). These leaders' obvious ambivalence toward development can be construed as a perceived contradiction between modernization and cultural and religious traditions. This is most obvious "when it involves social change, especially change of customs considered close to or part of the cultural and ideological value system, such as education and employment, and particularly the status of women and their share in the social transformation of society" (Seikaly 1994, 416). In addition, a wave of sociopolitical conservatism and Islamic fundamentalist thought are believed to dictate limitations to women's social development. Low socioeconomic levels also perpetuate women's dependence on men and continued daily struggle for survival. To make matters worse, the low levels of literacy in these societies in general, and among women in particular, prevent awareness and keep women from exercising their rights. Despite underlying commonalties, Middle Eastern women's experiences differ from one country to the other, with each state in the region having unique economic structures, ethnosocial features, and historical experiences that affect women differently (Seikaly 1994).

Iran provides a noteworthy example of a Muslim society that requires greater scrutiny. Under Khomeini's leadership, clerical leaders "reduced marriageable age for girls, closed day-care centers and family planning clinics, banned abortions and birth control devices, and required *hejab* (modest dress) in public for all women" (Ramazani 1993, 410). In addition, the clerics removed all obstacles to polygamy, segregated universities, barred women from some professions (e.g., prohibiting and removing female judges), and emphasized the importance of motherhood and domesticity. Ironically, in his effort to strengthen his political movement, Khomeini stressed the importance of women's vote and military duty as he simultaneously continued to impose more restrictions on them. As a result, during the lengthy Iran–Iraq war women replaced male government workers in large numbers. Reform issues affecting women found even greater receptivity after Khomeini's 1989 death, when political leaders began to confirm that "in Islam there are no barriers to the education of women in any field" and that "in Islam women enjoy the same rights as men" (Ramazani 1993, 413). Although reforms were "rationalized largely in terms of Islamic norms" (Ramazani 1993, 411), the role of women in Iranian society began to change, coinciding with the waning fervor for the revolution. Today women attend universities, attain graduate education, wear more colorful clothing and relaxed headdresses, and increasingly participate in Iran's political and economic spheres. In addition, the Revolution is credited with triggering an unprecedented literary proliferation in Iran of books by and about women (Ramazani 1993). The revolution, a lengthy war, and serious economic problems created an environment in Iran that made it clear that women were needed and that it was practical to empower them. The clerics then rationalized their integration of women into society as active participants by going back to the Qur'an to echo rights women already had.

Iraq exemplifies another country jolted by hardship into awareness of women's potential contribution. During the Iran–Iraq war, socioeconomic difficulties led Iraq to draw upon the total labor pool and mobilize women (*Country Studies* 2000). In the mid-1980s an overwhelming proportion of employees in ministries were women, and women supervisors were seen on large construction projects, as doctors in hospitals, and in law enforcement. The government sanctioned women's emancipation, as it spent large sums of money to publicize the role of women in helping to win the war. The Iraqi government stated that women would still be encouraged to retain newfound work roles after the war as it simultaneously declared a national determination to increase the birthrate.

In Libya, Qadhafi persisted over the years in trying to involve women in national defense by arguing that Arab women live in a subjugated state and must be liberated from oppression and feudalism (*Country Studies* 2000). Qadhafi stated that regardless of gender, all Libyans should be trained for armed services, and in 1979 established the women's army college to train young women in basic military subjects and in the use of weapons.[20] Algerian women played a significant role in the War of Independence, but once it was over they were expected by the government and society to return to their homes and traditional roles. In 1962, as part of an effort to mobilize society to support socialism, the government created the National Union of Algerian Women. In 1965, 6,000 women participated in its first march to celebrate International Women's Day. More recently, the resurgence of Islamic tradition dealt a blow to the women's movement, which was originally initiated by the French, who pushed for better education and removal of the veil.

For Palestinian women, the fundamentalist movement practically extinguished their increased political and socioeconomic participation in society during the *Intifada*. The fundamentalists "launched a virulent campaign to exclude women from social and political life and relegate them to the household and the home," reinforcing patriarchal traditions ("Reports" 1992, 53). Women are oppressed and threatened by violence into wearing the veil (claimed as a national duty), about forty are victims of "honor killings" each year, they are removed from school at adolescence and forced into marriages, and those who work are forced to relinquish their salaries to their husbands. In 1991, five women in Haifa founded *El Fanar* (the Lighthouse) to help "women organize themselves in an autonomous feminist context" ("Reports" 1992, 53). Despite fundamentalists' attacks on the organization as representing "moral depravity," it continues to mobilize women to claim their rights by carrying the simple message that "there is no contradiction between democracy and feminism" ("Reports" 1992, 54). In light of growing Islamist nationalism, Palestinian feminists are beginning to express their desire for an independent Palestinian state that is "democratic, secular, and supportive of gender equality" (Moghadam 1994, 5).

Conversely, Turkish women, "enjoy freedoms and achievements unparalleled by their Islamic sisters in many countries" (Zak 1994, 53). While polygamy as well as the *chador* (black head-to-toe cover) remains part of Turkish peasant life (although the 1926 civil code abolished both), Turkey's diligent efforts to protect secularism have allowed urban women to move far beyond other Muslim women.[21] Some women exhibit a stronger adherence to religion, whereas others express fear—fueled by Islamists' interference with women's rights—that Turkey will become another Algeria or Iran with regard to their status. The rise of Islamic fundamentalism has been attributed to the too-rapid Westernization of Turkey and the knee-jerk reaction of many by turning toward the more traditional values of the ultra-right-wing Welfare Party (Zak 1994). Counterreaction has been seen in the political mobilization of women and efforts to reclaim secularism as the foundation of Turkey. Recent developments toward Turkey's eventual accession to the European Union are cause for great optimism.[22] Conscious and disciplined efforts to integrate Turkey with the rest of Europe are expected to strengthen Turkey's fight for secularism, improve its socioeconomic development, and encourage greater empowerment of women through more active involvement in labor and politics.

In Cyprus, even though a fledgling feminist movement in the beginning of the 1990s was ridiculed by both sexes, women today are experiencing increasing economic independence. Cypriot women enjoy the same rights to social welfare as men in social security payments, unemployment compensation, and vacation time. However, occupational segregation of the sexes continues and women who work are still expected to fulfill traditional domestic roles of housewife and mother. In a similar fashion, clashing ideologies of gender and economics are believed to cause personal hardships for Egyptian women (MacLeod 1991). Regardless of how mundane, women accept outside employment to add money to household income. However, they are still expected to carry out their household duties. Leaving their children with female relatives, Egyptian women go to work, then return home to cook and clean—having twice as much work as before but without much-needed social support. Other contradictions can be found in Yemen. Although women are constrained by patriarchal social structures and limited in their earning capacities, they play "at least a token role in contemporary political and economic life" and "may be the most 'liberated,' though not the most privileged" in the Arabian Peninsula (Carapico 1991, 15). Although veiling and seclusion are practiced, relatively liberal social legislation allows pregnancy leave, voting, driving, travel, running for office, and property ownership.

While similar in many respects, each country in the Middle East has its own climate and level of tolerance for increased empowerment of women. Cultural and religious characteristics of Middle Eastern society are serious challenges to women's empowerment. Contemporary feminists have stressed the importance of women's networks to their empowerment (Waltz 1990). Predictably, and with few exceptions, such networks differ in the Middle East from those in the West, where professional networks, support groups, and available role models "provide a collective basis for the development of confidence and self-esteem as well as a potential base for political action" (Waltz 1990, 21).[23] Although Middle Eastern women may have found the basis for power and social competence in networks, most feminine circles are believed to educate young women "in conventional rather than innovative behavior and thus have lent support to the patriarchal order" (Waltz 1990, 34). The position and status of contemporary women are often evaluated primarily within the context of religious dictates and traditional norms that govern the female condition in Middle Eastern society (Nga-Longva 1993). There is a "general tendency to assess women's opportunities and constraints in terms of what the Qur'an and Islamic tradition dictate, not in terms of secular and more immediate concerns they may share with the rest of society" (Nga-Longva 1993, 443), which is underscored by the assumption that Muslim women are not part of the societies in which they live, and that in fact their lives remain unaffected by any change occurring around them. Because patriarchal societies often interpret Islam very subjectively, secularism has long been considered the "principal prerequisite for progressive reform in women's social, economic, and political lives" in Muslim societies (Ramazani 1993, 409).

TRAVEL IN ISLAM

Traditional Islamic values as well as Islamic traditions have guided tourism in the Middle East. Islamic doctrine encourages several types of travel. One is the obligation to undertake the pilgrimage to Mecca (*hajj*), a second is to migrate from lands where Islam is constrained to where no such constraints exist (*hijra*), a third involves visits to shrines (*ziyaras*), and a fourth is travel in search of knowledge (*rihla*) (Eickelman and Piscatori 1990). Today, travel motivated by a combination of the foregoing reasons or other reasons (e.g., economic) is widely practiced. Cultural, historical, or archeological forms of tourism fit most appropriately in the category of *rihla* (or "purposeful" travel), because they do not represent idle pleasure. "Muslims are encouraged to travel through the earth so that they appreciate the greatness of God through observing the 'signs' of beauty and bounty of His creations" (Din 1989, 551; Qur'an 3:137, 6:11, 12:109, 16:36, 27:69, 30:42, 47:10). Unlike mass tourism "characterized by hedonism, permissiveness, lavishness" (Din 1989, 551), Islam prohibits "profligate consumption and all forms of excessive indulgence," and, in fact, stresses that the "goal of travel is to help instill the realization of the smallness of man and the greatness of God . . . while the spiritual goal is to reinforce one's submission to the ways of God, the social goal . . . is to encourage and strengthen the bond of Muslim fraternity among the Muslim community" (Din 1989, 552). Travel is also considered to be a difficult endeavor as well as a test of one's patience and perseverance (Din 1989). To ease the traveler's difficulties, Muslims are encouraged to always help the traveler, and travelers are exempted from many religious duties during their trips (e.g., no fasting during Ramadan, shorter or combined daily prayers, permission to drink or eat otherwise prohibited food and drink under life-threatening conditions). Middle Eastern hospitality is deeply rooted in Islam, as religious doctrine stresses the need to accommodate the traveler, offer the best possible food, show compassion and provide assistance to the traveler, and never cheat or exploit him or her. Crucial host–guest relations are also guided by Islam, which, for example, forbids both from excessive displays of wealth through dress and material possessions. Through examples, stories of the Prophet Muhammed's travels also stress respect for local customs and traditions, tolerance for differences, and "genuine, equitable, and reciprocal cross-cultural communication" (Din 1989, 554).

For millions of Middle Easterners, domestic tourism (primarily to seaside resorts or summer homes), tourism among countries of the region, and the annual *hajj* pilgrimage to Mecca comprise the most common and acceptable forms of travel. This is not to say, of course, that Middle Easterners do not travel to destinations that the rest of the international traveling public enjoy or that their travel activities and host behaviors are always guided by Islamic doctrine.[24] This is not only because such doctrine is often subject to cultural or political interpretations and different societies adhere to religious doctrine to varying degrees, but also due to socioeconomic factors permitting or hindering travel. For example, in Turkey, Cyprus, and Israel, leisure travel (whether domestic or international) is actively practiced. This is also the case for citizens of the oil-producing countries of the Arabian Peninsula, who have discretionary time and money to travel (not necessarily always with religious motives), often with wives, children, parents, and servants. In fact, according to the Economic Intelligence Unit (EIU) (1985), three of the most popular destinations for outgoing tourists from the Arabian Peninsula are the United States, India, and Thailand, and "the Arab traveler [to Thailand] is typically a young man . . . in his mid-twenties, often intent on having a good time" (p. 56, quoted in Din 1989, 549). Further, opulent trips are "frequently undertaken by the rich Muslims from the Middle East to Europe" or other international destinations (Din 1989, 559). Citizens of other countries, on the other hand, with political or economic constraints, may find their travel activities limited to the types encouraged by religious doctrine or limited experiences within their own countries.[25]

TOURISM AS AN
ECONOMIC DEVELOPMENT TOOL

In light of the low levels of socioeconomic development throughout most of the Middle East—demonstrated by low per capita GDP, high levels of unemployment and inflation, external debt, high population growth rates, and low literacy rates—the international tourism industry is an obvious choice as an economic-development tool. Yet in many Middle Eastern countries the travel industry is treated in one of three general manners. "Tourism is either discouraged, treated with a *laissez faire* attitude, or is subject to certain accommodationist control in which case the popular approach is to isolate it from the mainstream livelihood of the host community" (Din 1989, 555). As a result, international tourist activity in the region is not analogous to its immensely rich and diverse natural, cultural, and historical resources and attractions.

The discrepancy is attributable to several factors. First, the Middle East has experienced significant political upheavals over the past three decades. In the recent past, many countries in the region (e.g., Afghanistan, Lebanon, Syria, Libya, Iran, Iraq) have experienced war. In addition, the rest of the world is familiar with the lengthy Iran–Iraq war, the U.S.–Libya conflict, the Gulf War, ongoing conflict between Israel and her neighbors, tension between Turkey and Greece over Cyprus, and terrorism associated with Algeria, Egypt, Iraq, Israel, Lebanon, Syria, and southeastern Turkey. These events have tainted the region's image so much that tourist arrivals and earnings have fluctuated significantly in some cases (e.g., Egypt, Turkey), virtually stopped in others (e.g., Iran, Iraq, Libya, Lebanon), and are conspicuously low in some countries (e.g., Algeria, Kuwait) that are perceived as unsafe and therefore eliminated as possible destination alternatives by travelers. Algeria, Cyprus, Egypt, Morocco, and Tunisia are specific examples of countries that depend heavily on tourism-based earnings and are, as a result, highly vulnerable to fluctuations in travel flows.

Second, perceptions of the traveling public have also been negatively affected by the increase in religious fundamentalism in the region. Muslims are often perceived by Westerners as not only ultraconservative but also anti-Western. Regardless of the degree of truth in this view, the appeal of Muslim countries to Western tourists is closely linked to tourist perceptions.[26] While these views might represent stereotypes, the views and actions of some Muslims confirm them (Din 1989). Among other things, negative images related to Iran's religious revolution and the growing fundamentalism in Egypt and Algeria have deterred incoming travelers. In addition, "there are—and this is perhaps unique in the world—a number of Islamic countries having high touristic potential that are frankly not interested in having non-Islamic visitors" (Ritter 1975, 59). Some of the more conservative countries have little tolerance for sexual permissiveness, gambling, and consumption of pork and alcohol, which can be easily found in contemporary Western tourist styles (Din 1989). Terrorist attacks on international tourists in Egypt in the past decade have been tragic demonstrations of such intolerance. In some countries, inbound international tourism is actively discouraged (e.g., Libya). In others, "purposeful" types of travel are actively supported: "Islam, both as bearer of its stereotypes and as a source of policy precepts, does have influence on the mode of tourism development in Muslim countries" (Din 1989, 543).

Third, the region's environment of poverty is anything but attractive to international tourists. "Poverty not only tends to breed beggars, criminals, touts, and hustlers, it also means that there is little private capital available for the development of adequate tourism facilities and attractions" (Din 1989, 546). Downward slopes in tourist arrivals and earnings resulting from various negative events are, in turn, potentially negative influences on the economies of the region's countries that do not have well-diversified industries. And fourth, inadequate promotions by the region's countries conveying clear and positive touristic images translate to a lack of awareness on the part of international travelers. For example, Western travelers may find it difficult not only to distinguish between Algeria, Tunisia, and Morocco (as well as many other countries in the region), but also to eliminate long-held negative stereotypes of Muslim countries, especially in the absence of counterpromotional efforts (Din 1989). Such unsuccessful marketing and public-relations efforts lead to low visitation and earnings. In order to compete with other international tourist destinations and eliminate negative images, it is crucial for countries to identify and convey positive images through active and effective promotion.

Despite the aforementioned challenges, all the countries in the region have some level of tourist activity. Turkey, Tunisia, Saudi Arabia, Morocco, Egypt, United Arab Emirates, Cyprus, and Israel record the highest tourist arrivals and receipts.[27] Seven countries (Cyprus, Egypt, Morocco, Saudi Arabia, Tunisia, Turkey, and the UAE) constitute 76 percent of total arrivals and 71 percent of total tourist receipts for the twenty-one countries, and Turkey by itself represents 24 percent of total arrivals and 31 percent of receipts for the region. It is important to keep these figures in perspective through comparisons with other popular tourist destinations in Europe and North America. For example, in 1999 France alone received 34.3 million international travelers and earned $31.7 million (World Tourism Organization 2000), a comparison in which Middle Eastern countries do not fare well. It is difficult to accurately determine individual countries' attitudes toward utilizing tourism as a tool of economic development. Notwithstanding the conservative views of most Middle Eastern countries toward tourism, nearly all Muslim countries are members of the World Tourism Organization, and most Arab countries are also members of the Arab Tourism Union, implying a desire to promote tourism professionally (Din 1989). While some countries (e.g., Yemen, UAE) have taken an active—albeit late—interest in tourism development, others (e.g., Turkey, Cyprus, Israel, Egypt, Morocco, Tunisia, Jordan) have long viewed tourism as part of their economic development (Table 6.3).

Table 6.3
Tourism Indicators in the Middle East

Country	Rank in International Tourist Arrivals	International Tourist Arrivals	Rank in International Tourism Receipts	International Tourism Receipts (millions)
Middle Eastern Countries				
Cyprus	2	2,223,000	3	$1,671
Iran	6	1,008,000	7	$477
Iraq	N/A	N/A	N/A	N/A
Israel	3	1,942,000	2	$2,656
Jordan	5	1,256,000	6	$853
Lebanon	7	631,000	4	$1,285
Palestinian Authority	N/A	N/A	N/A	N/A
Syria	4	1,267,000	5	$1,190
Turkey	1	8,960,000	1	$7,809
TOTAL		17,287,000		$15,941
North African Countries				
Algeria	N/A	N/A	4	$20
Egypt	3	3,213,000	1	$2,264
Libya	4	32,000	5	$18
Morocco	2	3,243,000	2	$1,745
Tunisia	1	4,718,000	3	$1,557
TOTAL		11,206,000		$5,604
Arabian Peninsula Countries				
Bahrain	3	1,750,000	3	$366
Kuwait[1]	7	79,000	4	$188
Oman[1]	5	375,000	5	$108
Qatar[1]	4	435,000	N/A	N/A
Saudi Arabia[2]	1	3,325,000	1	$2,050
United Arab Emirates[1]	2	2,476,000	2	$813
Yemen	6	88,000	6	$84
TOTAL		8,528,000		$3,609
OVERALL TOTAL		37,021,000		$25,154

Source: World Tourism Organization, *World Tourism Statistics*, 6 April 2000. Available
<http://www.world-tourism.org/esta/database.htm>.

[1]1997 figures.

[2]1995 figures.

WOMEN AS TOURISM
PRODUCERS AND CONSUMERS

Tourism employment is considered to be overtly gender biased, "reflecting local and trans-national norms of 'women's work'" (Kinnaird, Kothari, and Hall 1994, 17–18). Women generally fill the ranks of tourism workers as low-paid subjugated domestics, service employees, handicraft producers, clerks, cooks, servers, and even commercial sex workers (Enloe 1989; Swain 1995, 1993). Along these lines, even in more developed nations tourism employment is compared to a pyramid, with many women located in seasonal, part-time, lower-skilled, and lower-paying jobs at the bottom, and few with access to well-paid, skilled, and managerial positions (Jordan 1997; Richter 1994). Further, there is evidence that women's employment in tourism is both horizontally and vertically segregated (Jordan 1997), with the majority of female workers in positions subordinate to males in an occupational hierarchy (again at lower levels of pay) (Stockdale 1991). Men's overall control of power and decision making has a direct bearing on the exploitation of women in the tourism workplace. Horizontal segregation in the tourism organization is at times rationalized in relation to the industry's unique nature-specific work requirements: "Employers believe that the exploitation of perceived feminine characteristics and domestic skills is justified by commercial needs"(Jordan 1997, 532). Traditional gender distinctions, which have promoted the image of men as travelers and women as hostesses (Leontidou 1994), have also fueled the social construction that "has enabled national governments and tourist organizations to portray women in a service role" (Jordan 1997, 528). "Women's choices with regard to tourism employment are circumscribed both by their individual qualifications and experience, and by the social and cultural pressures which apply to women working in the leisure field" (Scott 1997, 66).

Information that illustrates the role of Middle Eastern women as tourism producers is anecdotal at best. Considering societal perceptions of women in the region, however, one can surmise that Middle Eastern women's role in tourism production is highly limited. Women are likely to work as cleaners, tour guides, receptionists, secretaries, accountants, travel agents, shopkeepers, managers, and administrators in the tourism industries of some of the more open societies (e.g., Cyprus, Israel, Turkey), or in those countries where the tourism industry has become established and accepted (e.g., Egypt). In Turkey, for example, many vocational schools prepare young women to work in the tourism industry as entry-level employees in hotels and restaurants, tour guides, and translators. Turkish women are also involved in the tourism industry in higher capacities as managers, consultants, and entrepreneurs and, in the recent past, Turkey has had several female ministers of tourism. Further, many women are involved in family businesses, such as pensions, bed and breakfasts, and restaurants, in Turkey as well as other more open countries, while in the more conservative societies any contact between Muslim women and male strangers would be unthinkable. In some countries, female migrant workers "do those jobs, particularly in the entertainment field, which are socially and culturally unacceptable" to local women (Scott 1997, 71). For example, women from Eastern Europe, Russia, and Romania accept jobs that Turkish Cypriot women would be unwilling to take or would be unacceptable to their families. Comparatively speaking, for Greek Cypriot women there are fewer restrictions on their involvement in the production of tourism services.

It would be highly desirable for Middle Eastern women to initiate efforts to take advantage of tourism's wage-earning opportunities in order to gain more independence as women do in other parts of the world.[28] Such endeavors would have to be within the context of work and behavior deemed acceptable for women in Muslim societies. Keeping in mind Middle Eastern views on male honor and female virtue, tourism employment bringing women in contact with strangers is likely to be viewed as anywhere between unappealing to strongly objectionable.

MUSLIM WOMEN TRAVELERS

Differences in the traditional definitions of the roles of women and men in society are echoed by their travel behaviors. In many societies, "being feminine has been defined as sticking close to home," while masculinity, by contrast, "has been the passport for travel" (Enloe 1989, 21). Feminist geographers and ethnographers have chronicled a principal difference between women and men in numerous societies as "the license to travel away from a place thought of as 'home.' . . . A woman who travels away from the ideological protection of 'home' and without the protection of an acceptable male escort is likely to be tarred with the brush of 'unrespectability'" (Enloe 1989, 21). Despite the fact that this perspective seems dated today, it lingers on in the traditional societies of the Middle East.

According to the Hadith of the Prophet Muhammed, a woman is not permitted to travel alone for more than twenty-four hours unless accompanied by a *mahram* (a nonmarriageable companion). Muslim women's movements outside their homes are often in the forms of visits to other women's homes (alone or in groups), family trips, and visits to religious sites and shrines, including pilgrimages, often without male family members (Tapper 1990). These types of "travel" are generally construed positively; however, their extent, frequency, and societal emphasis are likely to vary, primarily due to differing ideological constructions of relationships between the sexes (Tapper 1990). If, for example, men and women believe that the sexes are different and men are superior to women, "women's theoretical equality with men as Muslims becomes paradoxical and problematic, particularly for the women themselves" (Tapper 1990, 250). If men and women believe that the sexes are different but complementary (or similar human natures), then their equality as Muslims does not become an issue. In such cases, women are likely to travel outside their homes as men's equals. It has been suggested that Muslim women "accumulated leisure through restriction or enforced idleness" (Rimmawi and Ibrahim 1992, 94), as social constraints forced women to avoid contact with strangers and stay home to take care of their families.

Actual accounts of Middle Eastern women travelers or data representing their travel behavior are virtually nonexistent. One can only surmise that women's travel is quite restricted, at best, with very few exceptions. In fact, it would be inconceivable for women in highly restricted societies (e.g., Algeria, Bahrain, Kuwait, Iran, Oman, Saudi Arabia, Yemen) to undertake pleasure travel without the protection and approval of their families. For example, Saudis often travel in groups and as extended families, especially during long trips, in order to share costs, for safety reasons, and to minimize boredom. As a result, for Saudi women travel is restricted to family activity. Even in more open societies, such as Northern Cyprus, traveling around is perceived as primarily a male activity that combines socializing, information circulation, and networking opportunities: Women travel only with their families. On the other hand, travel behaviors of Greek Cypriot women are much less restricted than that of their counterparts in the North. In Turkey, depending on the region of the country, women travel either with their families or with other female companions, but not, for the most part, without the knowledge of their menfolk. Those living in major urban centers, such as Istanbul, Ankara, and Izmir, are able to enjoy greater freedoms (not only with regard to their travel behavior but many aspects of their lives) than their sisters living in rural areas. In addition, younger generations of women enjoy greater freedoms than their mothers and grandmothers. Many young Turkish women travel within or outside their country on their annual vacations without significant social restrictions, and participate in activities that include dancing, drinking, and recreational activities.

The lack of available information on Middle Eastern women's travel behavior makes it very difficult to give specific examples of how (or even if) women consume tourism services in the region. It can be speculated, however, that women's travel behaviors are largely determined by their societies, culture, and how strictly Islam is interpreted. Therefore, it would not be frivolous to assume that, with few exceptions (e.g., Cyprus, Israel, Turkey), Middle Eastern women travel (domestically or internationally) primarily with their families and in special cases with female or acceptable male companions.

CONCLUSION

Demographic growth, the spread of knowledge, and struggles over resources (e.g., oil and water) are believed to be the primary predictors of the course of the Middle East in the twenty-first century (Maynes 1998), and some forecasts of the region's future are rather bleak. Globally, Muslims accounted for 18 percent of the global population in 1980 and are expected to represent 30 percent by 2025. This growth is expected to be particularly rapid in the Middle East, with Egypt, Saudi Arabia, Syria, Iraq, Iran, and Afghanistan doubling or tripling their populations by the middle of this century (Maynes 1998). Without doubt, this will stretch the already limited resources of many countries in the region. Especially due to arid climates and growing population, "water is perhaps the only resource over which any country facing severe shortages will fight" (Maynes 1998, 15). With regional conflicts expected to erupt over issues of oil and water and the region's growing political consciousness, there are worries that the non-Muslim world will be threatened through terrorism and even with weapons of mass destruction (Maynes 1998). These risks are serious potential threats to regional socioeconomic development, and they, in turn, are likely to be exacerbated by the stagnation of such development.

While in the next century much of the world will be involved in internal development and the expansion of human capital in the effort to participate in the global economy, the Middle East is expected to remain in the struggle over external security and resources (Maynes 1998). In addition, the technological gap between the Middle East (excluding some of the more advanced countries) and the developed world is expected to widen (Maynes 1998), leaving the region lagging behind the rest of the world. In light of these predictions, it becomes more difficult to hope for significant improvements to the status of Middle Eastern women. Just as "feminism lost ground to the environment as a global issue" in the 1980s (Jabbra and Jabbra 1992), globalization and the information superhighway have monopolized global attention in the 1990s, overshadowing women's issues. Regardless of how challenging it might be, it is very important to keep women's issues at the forefront of the development discussion in the coming years. The growth of women's rights and opportunities can be viewed as a function of the speed and extent of societal change as a "push" effect, complemented by the "pull" of the undeniable need for women's participation in socioeconomic development (Peterson 1989). Further, it is significantly influenced by changing attitudes, representing not only men's tolerance for the expanding role of women but also women's determination to expand their roles (Peterson 1989). Women's issues in the Middle East are not only in constant danger of being eclipsed by growing religious fundamentalism, they are often the first casualties of this religious revolution.

It is highly important for Middle Eastern countries to modify their views toward tourism development and to improve their efforts to incorporate the tourism industry into their economic-development strategies. With proper planning and management, tourism has the potential to invigorate the economies of the less developed countries in the region and also—through opportunities for cross-cultural contact between countries of the region and citizens of other countries—holds the potential to improve the Middle East's standing in the international community. If the tourism industry is to be successfully integrated into the region's economic development, it is also very important that human resources—regardless of gender—be utilized effectively. Societal restrictions impeding women's full participation in determining the future of their countries is a very significant barrier to the achievement of socioeconomic goals. Undeniably, the gradual relaxation of religious codes affecting women's role in Iranian society is an encouraging example; however, it must be remembered that this relaxation has been both limited and very slow in coming, considering the revolution occurred over twenty years ago. Just as various countries (e.g., Iran, Iraq, Libya) have drawn from the pool of women in difficult times, whether economic downturn or war, countries of the region would benefit immensely from the recognition that tourism is an important economic-development tool, and one that requires better utilization of human resources, regardless of gender. As an issue of principal as much as practicality, it is imperative for Middle Eastern countries to reexamine their practices and policies with regard to women's issues so that more women can participate in determining the economic and political fate of the region. At the start of the third millennium, the time is more than ripe for Middle Eastern countries to recognize their economic and political problems as an opportunity to fully integrate women into their societies in order to meet such challenges successfully and become productive members of the global community. Middle Eastern countries simply cannot afford to continue utilizing only half of their population.

NOTES

1. Strictly speaking in geographical terms, as a region the Middle East includes Cyprus, Iran, Iraq, Israel, Jordan, Lebanon, the Palestinian Authority, Syria, and Turkey. For cultural or religious reasons other countries in North Africa (e.g., Algeria, Egypt, Libya, Morocco, and Tunisia) and the Arabian Peninsula (e.g., Bahrain, Kuwait, Oman, Qatar, Saudi Arabia, United Arab Emirates, and Yemen) are often included in the loosely used term "Middle East." Although Afghanistan does not technically belong to the Middle East, due to increasing awareness of the oppression of women as a result of Islamic fundamentalism it deserves mention from time to time in this chapter.

2. Although the Middle East is predominantly Muslim—with the exception of Israel and minority populations of other regions—the region is exceptionally diverse in ethnic composition and natural resources.

3. It should be noted that much of the wealth in the wealthy countries is concentrated in the hands of the elite minority, while the majority live in conditions very similar to those in poor Muslim states (Din 1989).

4. International definitions of economic activity essentially focus on the production of goods and services that are exchanged on the market, whereas much of women's work in developing countries would not fit that description. It has been argued that "women's participation was often underestimated because common methods of enumeration often omitted seasonal and part-time work, ignored unpaid family workers on family farms or in small family businesses, and did not usually take into account the production (such as food preservation or the production of clothing) which took place within the household" (Papps 1992, 597). These activities are often typical of women's work in developing countries.

5. Globalization has been described as the increasing interdependence of the world's people in terms of culture, technology, and governance, in addition to economy (United Nations 1997).

6. For example, Arab nations have tried to maintain the family system of domesticated and secluded women by importing large amounts of foreign male labor. As a result of cultural and religious restrictions, women are discouraged from working outside the home, and thus female labor levels in the region are consistently low.

7. The World Fertility Survey of 1978–1982 (United Nations 1983) showed the causal relationship between women's increased education levels and lower fertility rates. In Afghanistan (not shown in Table 6.2), the fertility rate is close to six children per female and the literacy rate is 15 percent. Further, there are no data to indicate women occupy a place in the labor force. To the contrary, reports have been published to indicate that the Taliban forbids women from attending school or working outside the home.

8. If the United States can be taken as an example, with 245 doctors per 100,000 people, the corresponding numbers in the Middle East are well below 200. Discounting a few exceptions, such as Israel (459 doctors), Cyprus (231), and Egypt (202), a number of countries are alarmingly low: for example, Bahrain (11), Iraq (51), Tunisia (67), and Algeria (83). One particularly disturb-

ing example of the lack of access to medical care is Afghanistan, where Taliban decrees have had devastating impacts on women's health especially. Because male doctors are not permitted to examine women´and female physicians' freedom to practice is restricted, women do not receive medical care (which also explains the infant mortality rate of 140 out of every 1,000 births) (Walt 2000).

9. The law was drafted by Fatima Khemisti (wife of the former foreign minister), and presented to the government to raise the minimum age of marriage (to nineteen) in order to facilitate more education. Finally the age was raised to sixteen (*Country Studies* 2000).

10. In the most highly developed countries of North America and Western and Northern Europe, women are fully active participants in economic and political life.

11. In addition to their participation in the labor force, Israeli women comprise 15 percent of the Israel police (although primarily in clerical and traffic control positions, rather than patrol), and are also active in the Israel Defense Forces (*Country Studies* 2000).

12. In Kuwait, only males over twenty-one vote, although Article 29 of the constitution—which states, "People are equal in human dignity and under the law in public rights and duties, and should not be discriminated against because of sex, origin, language or religion"—contradicts the practice (Glubb 1997, 16). Hopes for greater political participation for women were raised in May 1998, when Sheikh Jaber al-Ahmad al-Sabah, Kuwait's leader, issued an Emiri decree to give women the right to vote and to be candidates as of the 2003 elections. When the bill was presented to the Kuwaiti National Council in December 1999, however, the decree was voted down when the majority of parliament refused to give women the right to vote (ArabicNews.com 2000; Glubb 1997).

13. In Israel, although Jewish religious law does not view husbands and wives as equal partners and stresses gender differentiation as well as women's dependence on their husbands (Berkovitch 1996), there are no legal obstacles to women's full political participation. Israel's Declaration of Independence states that the State of Israel will ensure "complete equality of social and political rights to all its inhabitants, irrespective of religion, race or sex" (Hermann and Kurtz 1995, 450). In addition, the 1951 Women's Equal Rights Law declared any official discrimination against women to be illegal. Despite these safeguards and the belief that the socialist branch of the Zionist movement gave women equal opportunities to participate in the creation and operation of the new Israeli society, Hermann and Kurtz (1995) suggest that there is an "equality myth." The myth is described as serving as a "smoke screen hiding the unequal role of Israeli women, who, even in the early pioneering days, were excluded from positions of power" (p. 450). They point to the exceptional political career of Golda Meir as having reinforced the myth of equality.

14. Women serving in the parliament often hold degrees in philosophy and Islamic law, Islamic culture, French language and literature, midwifery, and medicine.

15. In traditional Arab society, the birth of a boy is an occasion for great celebration, while that of a girl is not necessarily observed. Further, failure to produce sons may be used as grounds for divorce or for taking a second wife.

16. This may be related to a widely held view in Arab societies that women are weaker than men in mind, body, and spirit and therefore need male protection.

17. In some Arab societies, such as Syria, endogamy (marriage of members within a religious or ethnic group; in fact, one's first cousin is considered as the most appropriate mate) is highly preferred and encouraged, as it is viewed as a practical bond between families and as a deterrent to divorce. As a result and because marriage is viewed as a familial matter, it is customarily arranged (*Country Studies* 2000). Islamic intentions behind polygamy are to protect women and children rather than satisfy male sensuality. The only passage in the Qur'an on the topic restricts its practice: "If you fear that you shall not be able to deal justly with the orphans, marry women of your choice, two or three or four: but if you fear that you shall not be able to deal justly with them, then only one" (4:3). The passage was revealed after the battle of Uhud (A.D. 625), which left dozens of Muslims martyred (leaving behind their orphans and widows). Its implication for continued permissibility is to deal with contingencies that may arise—providing a moral, practical, and humane solution to problems of widows and orphans, who in the absence of a father figure would suffer in economic terms. Islam also stipulates that a woman may specify in a prenuptial contract that her husband will practice monogamy, and in the event he violates that contract she can seek divorce with associated financial rights. Despite these rights, many women (especially in villages and rural areas) do not have a say in their husbands' decisions to take additional wives.

18. In Iraq the 1959 Law of Personal Status liberalized provisions affecting women's status. The judiciary tends to be conservative, however, in applying provisions of the law (*Country Studies* 2000). In 1985 Cypriot women benefited from special protective legislation providing them with marriage and maternity grants. In the same year, the Republic of Cyprus ratified the U.N. Convention on the Elimination of all Forms of Discrimination Against Women (*Country Studies* 2000). However, legislation guaranteeing women the right to equal pay for equal work and rights to the same employment opportunities as men has been late in coming.

19. Male honor (easily damaged, nearly irreparable) depends on the conduct of women. Wives, sisters, and daughters are expected to be modest, to keep their virtue above reproach, and to meet expectations of virginity before and fidelity after marriage.

20. Even though 7,000 students graduated from the academy by 1983, the notion of women as soldiers remained unpopular and it closed.

21. In urban areas and among middle- and upper-class women it is very common to see Turkish women wear the most recent Western dress, including short skirts, jeans, and shorts.

22. The Customs Union, facilitating free trade between Turkey and EU member countries, entered into force in December 1995. More recently, the Helsinki European Council of December 10–11, 1999, designated Turkey as a candidate country for EU membership.

23. In the United Arab Emirates, in the early 1990s Shaykh Zayid ibn Sultan Al Nuhayyan acknowledged the validity of women participating in the workforce. The president's wife, Shaykha Fatima, headed the Women's Fed-

eration and promoted training, education, and advancement of status of women. In the early 1990s, five women's societies successfully promoted various issues of importance to women, including health and literacy (*Country Studies* 2000).

24. Din (1989) offers a critical and thought-provoking analysis of how distant today's reality—with regard to host–guest relationships and travel behaviors of Muslims—is from the teachings of Islam.

25. Data on domestic tourism in the region are virtually nonexistent.

26. "Muslim countries" refers to those where the majority of the population are Muslims. The proportion of Muslims in each country discussed in this chapter ranges between a low of 75 percent (Lebanon) to 100 percent (Bahrain), with the rest somewhere between 90 and 99 percent. The only two exceptions are Cyprus (18 percent) and Israel (11 percent).

27. For Saudi Arabia, incoming travelers represent primarily Muslim pilgrims entering the country for the annual *hajj*.

28. In Greece women have gained more independence than their mothers and grandmothers enjoyed—despite insecurities due to their work's seasonal nature and disruption of traditional lifestyles—through agrotourism cooperatives owned and controlled by Greek women. Such enterprises have also offered them an alternative to their previous peripheral role in the context of "Greek male host/foreign female guest" (Leontidou 1994).

REFERENCES

ArabicNews.com. (2000). Kuwaiti parliament refuses to give women the right to vote. 26 July. Available <http://www.arabicnews.com/ansub/Daily/Day/991201/1999120117.html>.

Berkovitch, N. (1996). Women and the women's equal rights law in Israel. *Middle East Report* 26 (1): 19–21.

Carapico, S. (1991). Women and public participation in Yemen. *Middle East Report* 21 (6): 15.

Country Studies. (2000). Library of Congress. 8 May. Available <http://rs6.loc.gov/frd/cs/>.

Curtiss, R. H. (1996). For Qatari educators, women are both the problem and the solution. *Washington Report on Middle East Affairs* 15 (1): 84.

Din, K. H. (1989). Islam and tourism: Patterns, issues, and options. *Annals of Tourism Research* 16: 542–563.

Economic Intelligence Unit. (1985). Arabian Peninsula: Saudi Arabia, Kuwait, UAE, Oman, Bahrain, Qatar, North Yemen, South Yemen. *International Tourism Report* 4: 50–57.

Eickelman, D. F., and J. Piscatori, eds. (1990). *Muslim Travellers: Pilgrimage, Migration, and the Religious Imagination.* Berkeley and Los Angeles: University of California Press.

Enloe, C. (1989). *Bananas, Beaches, and Bases: Making Feminist Sense of International Politics.* Berkeley and Los Angeles: University of California Press.

Glubb, F. (1997). Kuwait: Towards votes for women. *Middle East International* 543: 15–16.

Graham-Brown, S. (1994). Women and politics in the Middle East. *Women in Action* 1: 28–31.

Hermann, T., and G. Kurtz. (1995). Prospects for democratizing foreign policymaking: The gradual empowerment of Israeli women. *Middle East Journal* 49: 447–466.

Islam-Husain, M. (1997). It's up to Muslim women to reclaim our God-given rights. *Washington Report on Middle East Affairs* 16 (1): 77–78.

Jabbra, N. W., and J. G. Jabbra. (1992). Introduction: Women and development in the Middle East and North Africa. In *Women and Development in the Middle East and North Africa*, edited by J. G. Jabbra and N. W. Jabbra. New York: E. J. Brill.

Jordan, F. (1997). An occupational hazard? Sex segregation in tourism employment. *Tourism Management* 18 (8): 525–534.

Kinnaird, V., U. Kothari, and D. Hall. (1994). Tourism: Gender perspectives. In *Tourism: A Gender Analysis*, edited by V. Kinnaird and D. Hall. Chichester: Wiley.

Leontidou, L. (1994). Gender dimensions of tourism sub-cultures and restructuring. In *Tourism: A Gender Analysis*, edited by V. Kinnaird and D. Hall. Chichester: Wiley.

MacLeod, A. E. (1991). *Accommodating Protest: Working Women. The New Veiling, and Change in Cairo*. New York: Columbia University Press.

Maynes, C. W. (1998). The Middle East in the twenty-first century. *Middle East Journal* 52: 9–16.

Moghadam, V. M. (1994). Introduction and overview: Gender dynamics of nationalism, revolution and Islamization. In *Gender and National Identity: Women and Politics in Muslim Societies*, edited by V. M. Moghadam. London: Zed Books.

Moghadam, V. M., and N. F. Khoury, eds. (1995). *Gender and Development in the Arab World*. Tokyo: U.N. University Press.

Nga-Longva, A. (1993). Kuwaiti women at a crossroads: Privileged development and the constraints of ethnic stratification. *International Journal of Middle East Studies* 25: 443–456.

Papps, I. (1992). Women, work and well-being in the Middle East: An outline of the relevant literature. *Journal of Development Studies* 28 (4): 595–615.

Peterson, J. E. (1989). The political status of women in the Arab Gulf states. *Middle East Journal* 43: 34–50

Ramazani, N. (1993). Women in Iran: The revolutionary ebb and flow. *Middle East Journal* 47: 409–428.

Reports from around the world: Middle East. (1992). *Women's International Network News* 18 (1): 53–54.

Richter, L. (1994). Exploring the political role of gender in tourism research. In *Global Tourism in the Next Decade*, edited by W. F. Theobald. Oxford: Butterworth Heinemann.

Rimmawi, H. S., and A. A. Ibrahim. (1992). Culture and tourism in Saudi Arabia. *Journal of Cultural Geography* 12 (2): 93–98.

Ritter, W. (1975). Recreation and tourism in the Islamic countries. *Ekistics* 40: 149–152.

Scott, J. (1997). Women and tourism in northern Cyprus. In *Gender, Work and Tourism*, edited by M. T. Sinclair. London: Routledge.

Seikaly, M. (1994). Women and social change in Bahrain. *International Journal of Middle East Studies* 26: 415–426.

Stockdale, J. E. (1991). Sexual harassment at work. In *Women at Work: Psychological and Organizational Perspectives*, edited by J. Firth-Cozens and M. A. West. Philadelphia: Open University Press.

Swain, M. B. (1993). Women producers of ethnic arts. *Annals of Tourism Research* 20: 32–51.

Swain, M. B. (1995). Gender in tourism. *Annals of Tourism Research* 22: 247–266.

Tapper, N. (1990). *Ziyeret*: Gender, movement, and exchange in a Turkish community. In *Muslim Travellers: Pilgrimage, Migration, and the Religious Imagination*, edited by D. F. Eickelman and J. Piscatori. Berkeley and Los Angeles: University of California Press.

United Nations. (1983). *Human Development*. Oxford: Oxford University Press.

United Nations. (1997). *Globalization and Liberalization: Effects of International Economic Relations and Poverty*. New York: Oxford University Press

United Nations. (1999). *United Nations Human Development Report 1999*. New York: Oxford University Press.

Walt, V. (2000). Life under cover. *Working Woman*, December/January, 62–68.

Waltz, S. E. (1990). Another view of feminine networks: Tunisian women and the development of political eficacy. *International Journal of Middle East Studies* 22: 21–36.

World Bank. (1999). *The World Bank Annual Report 1999*. 7 February. Available <http://www.worldbank.org/html/extpb/annrep/index.htm>.

World Tourism Organization. (2000). *WTO Tourism Statistics*. 6 April. Available <http://www.world-tourism.org>.

Young, K. (1993). *Planning Development with Women, Making a World of Difference*. London: MacMillan.

Zak, S. (1994). Turkish women offer mixed reviews on Islamist party's victories. *Washington Report on Middle East Affairs* 13 (2) :53–91.

7

Gender, Tourism, and Development in Latin America

Antònia Casellas and Briavel Holcomb

In comparison to other regions of the developing world, tourism in Latin America is not well developed outside of the Caribbean region and there is little existing literature on the topic. Meyer-Arendt (1992) attributed the paucity of literature partly to the fact that tourism research is concentrated where English is the native language, but also to the relative remoteness of the continent. Virtually none of the extant work addresses the question of gender and tourism. Consequently, this chapter brings together issues relevant to an examination of gender and tourism in the context of Latin America, but uses as primary data only informal observations from one author's (Holcomb) visits as a tourist to Brazil, Venezuela, Mexico, and Peru, as well as marketing brochures aimed at the consumers of tourism in the United States and Spain. In various places in the chapter we make comparisons between tourism in Latin America and the Caribbean, since, despite their proximity and some historical and cultural similarities, their tourist industries are quite disparate.

The main goal of this chapter is to explore the intersection of gender and tourism in Latin America in various contexts. Primary consideration is given to the differential economic impacts of tourism for men and women, including the gendered roles played by each. It is argued that tourism can enlarge economic opportunity for women, though it often increases their work burden at the same time. To provide context for this discussion, conventional gender roles and recent trends in the Latin American economy are summarized. Examples illustrate how tourism has the potential to change gender roles and cultural expectations, but can also contribute to cultural preservation.

One of the fastest growing segments of the tourism industry, particularly in Latin America, is ecotourism. While there is no consensus on exactly what constitutes ecotourism, and some view it as an oxymoron, we explore the connections between perspectives of ecotourism supporters with those of ecofeminism. Both make claims of harmony with nature and support of indigenous peoples, and there is some evidence to suggest that ecotourism is more "feminist" than mass tourism.

Turning our attention to the consumers of tourism, we examine some marketing materials, especially brochures, designed for potential tourists from North America and Spain. This reveals the generally stereotypical depictions of local women (even more so than men), images often far from the real lives of women in the region. Consideration is given to the ways in which marketing materials are designed to appeal to men versus women in the tourism source countries. The chapter concludes with a discussion of the possibilities of the tourism industry having a significant repercussion on women's lives in Latin America during the next century.

GENDER ROLES IN LATIN AMERICA

Prior to considering the tourism industry, it is useful to summarize some characteristics of conventional gender roles in Latin America. This is not to imply they are monolithic throughout the continent—obviously there are significant urban/rural and cultural variations—but some generalizations are possible. Gender relations in Latin American are usually assumed to be based upon the notions of female "motherhood" connected to the Catholic theme of Marianismo, and Spanish male "machismo" (Preston 1996; Chassen-Lopez 1997). Marianismo implies the idea that women are spirituality superior to men. The Virgin Mary as a symbol of what a woman should be exemplifies self-sacrifice for the good of family and community. Male virility and honor represent the counterpart. Under the machismo stereotype, men are unfaithful by nature, while women are monogamous by nature (Fisher 1993). In this framework, a woman's role is strongly linked to family obligations and the private sphere, while men dominate in the public sphere.

The complexity and hybridized character of Latin American cultures complicate these stereotyped gender patterns. Variations on gender roles depending on social classes, the rising number of female households, and the political and social struggles of Latin American women during the 1980s and 1990s have modified male–female roles and relationships (Preston 1996). While women have long contributed to household economies in Latin America in both rural and urban settings, they are increasingly entering the paid labor force as well as the informal economy (French and James 1997). Unlike Africa, where more men than women migrate to cities from rural areas in search of employment, in Latin America a disproportionate number of women have migrated to cities to work as domestics and in other sectors. "Domestic service is a major gender-segregated sector for women, with about a quarter of Latin America's working women here; for example, 25.5 percent of Bogota's female labor force and 32 percent of Brazil's" (Preston 1996, 156). The average income of domestic employees is lower than any other employment category, averaging only 1.4 times the poverty line in urban areas (see Table 7.1).

Although women are likely to be disproportionately employed in the lower-wage sectors, wages provide a degree of economic security and lessen dependence on men. Meanwhile, various feminist groups and women's movements have begun the movement toward greater gender equity and have empowered women in numerous contexts, ranging from legislatures to households.

Latin American women's movements started in the mid- and late-1970s and evolved through the ensuing decades. Jaquette (1994) asserts that four factors have influenced Latin American women's activism. The first factor was the impact of structural adjustment programs (SAPs). Under the new economic conditions characterized by high levels of inflation and cuts in basic social services, urban women organized themselves to provide food and other basic services collectively at the same time they actively protested the economic programs of their countries (Benton 1993). One of the best examples of women's mobilization at that level was the communal kitchens organized by women in several Latin American countries (Scarpaci 1993). A second factor that contributed to Latin American women's activism was their mobilization as a response to the political repression that took place in countries such as Chile and Argentina after the military coups (Roxborough 1997). In this context, and in an indirect way, women's role as mothers made them active players in the political sphere. The best example is the Argentine Mothers of the Plaza de Mayo. Their quiet weekly gatherings in Mayo Square in Buenos Aires to protest for their missing children and husbands captured global mass media interest and helped them to become key political actors in the democratization process of Argentina. A third factor was the emergence of a feminist movement among middle-class professional women that opened the debate on gender issues and pushed women's interests into the agenda of leftist

Table 7.1
Income and Occupational Categories for Twelve Latin American
Countries, Urban Areas (1994)

Occupation	Average Monthly Income in Multiples of the Poverty Line
Domestic employees	1.4
Private-sector wage earners in firms employing five or less persons	2.5
Unskilled own-account workers	3.2
Private-sector wage earners in firms employing more than five persons	3.6
Public-sector employees	5.1
Professional and technical workers	7.4
Employers in firms employing up to five persons	10.4
Employers in firms employing more than five persons	27.3

Source: United Nations Economic Commission for Latin America and the Caribbean
(ECLAC), *CEPAL News* (New York: Author, June 1997).

parties. Finally, the opposition to military governments created a de-
cisive space where women could debate alternative political and social models with large audiences. In addition to these urban-based
phenomena, Latin American women's organizations have flourished
in rural areas. An example is the Bolivian women's farmer movement,
which in the mid-1980s was organized under "La Federación Nacional
de Mujeres Campesinas de Bolivia Bartolina Sisa" and brought their
agenda into Bolivian national unions (Barbieri and Oliveira 1989).

In the 1990s new political and economic contexts brought new challenges for Latin American women. The emerging democracies changed
the political and social context in which women's movements operate. In
a study of gender movements in Brazil, Alvarez (1994) points out that
Brazilian feminists are less visible than in previous decades, but that
new forms of organization, strategies, and strands are proliferating.
From the growing number of women's nongovernmental organizations (NGOs) and working-class women's movements to expanding
black-feminist organizations, Brazilian women's organizations remain
alive and socially and politically active.

Simultaneous with political changes, new regional economic inte-
grations such as Mercosur and NAFTA also affect women's access to
jobs. Between 1980 and the year 2000, jobs in the *maquila* industries in
Mexico were predicted to grow from 100,000 to 1,000,000, constituting
one-third of the total manufacturing labor force in Mexico. This type

of employment is characterized by poor working conditions, with most jobs held by young women (Zermeño 1997). Women continue to bear the triple burden of household, employment, and community work. Furthermore, some aspects of the modernizing economy have reduced women's opportunities as mechanization replaces handmade production. Nevertheless, gender relations in Latin America are, as in other parts of the world, in a state of flux.

ECONOMIC CHANGE IN LATIN AMERICA AND ITS IMPACTS ON LATIN AMERICAN WOMEN

As in much of the developing world, the economies of Latin America have suffered a strong recession since the late 1980s. Macroeconomic indicators show that in the period from 1990 to 1996 the average growth was only about 3 percent. This percentage is lower than the average 5.5 percent for the period from 1945 to 1980, and it represents only half of the output growth that the United Nations Commission for Latin America and the Caribbean (ECLAC) considers necessary in order to catch up in technological and social development. In addition, growth has been unstable, changing from a 5.3-percent average growth rate in 1994 to 0.3 percent in 1995 (ECLAC 1997a). In 1996 and 1997 Latin American countries enjoyed some relative economic expansion due to the decline of inflation, the increase of capital inflows, and domestic investment. In 1997 unemployment fell for the first time since 1989, especially in Mexico and Argentina. However, toward the end of 1997 the financial crisis that began in Southeast Asia extended to Latin America (Inter-American Development Bank 1997). Stock market turbulence, currency instability, inflation, and falling prices of primary products threatened the economies of the region. Oil prices dropped from an average of $20 barrel in November 1997 to less than $13 in early 1999. This situation posed a particular threat to the economies of Venezuela (where 70 percent of the fiscal revenues came from oil) and Mexico (where oil represents 35 percent of fiscal revenues). In addition, Chile's exports to Asia represented 30 percent of its total exports, half being copper. The drop in copper prices in 1997 nearly halved Chile's annual growth for 1998 (Gualdoni 1998). In light of the effects of external factors together with recent macroeconomic policies adopted to reduce inflation, the most likely scenario for the immediate future is a return to the lower rates of growth of the beginning of the 1990s (ECLAC 1998).

Most of the employment created in the 1990s in Latin America was in the informal sector. The International Labor Organization (ILO) estimates that for the period from 1990 to 1995, out of every 100 new jobs, 84 were in the informal sector. While workers employed in skilled work have enjoyed large wage increases, informal workers earn on average half the amount paid to workers in the formal sector (ECLAC 1997b). In this context, low-productivity and low-paid jobs are the ones that expanded the most. In thirteen of seventeen Latin American countries the real minimum wage was lower in 1995 than in 1980. Only in a few countries, such as Brazil and Chile, did real wages grow for the period from 1990 to 1995. In the majority of countries real wages grew very little or, as in the case of Venezuela, they declined significantly. Productivity decreased in Bolivia, Brazil, Honduras, Mexico, Panama, Paraguay, and Venezuela (see Table 7.2).

Latin American economies have been greatly affected by the structural adjustment programs implemented by the Wold Bank and the International Monetary Fund (IMF) starting in the 1980s. The SAPs were designed to reduce consumption and to redirect resources to exports for the repayment of debt. These policies directly affected women's economic and social conditions in Latin America. Bolivia (1985), Chile (1975), and Mexico (1985–1986) were the first countries in Latin America to adopt SAP policies. They were followed by Costa Rica (1988) and Uruguay (1987–1988). A third round included Argentina (1990–1991), Brazil (1991), Colombia (1990–1991), El Salvador (1989–1990), Guatemala (1992), Honduras (1990), Nicaragua (1990), Panama (1992), Peru (1991), and Venezuela (1989) (Edwards 1995). Structural adjustment policies have, in some cases, been "successful" in restoring a country's ability to compete in the global economy and to meet the conditions required for continued international funding from the World Bank and investment from multinational corporations. However, their effects have been socially regressive, and drastic cuts in social expenditures in Latin America, especially in health and education, have heavily affected the more needy groups in society, among them women. It is ironic that the International Decade of Women (1976–1985) coincided with the implementation of structural adjustment policies that often worked to further immiserate many women in the developing world (Daines and Seddon 1993; Vickers 1991). While the negative effects of structural adjustment policies have been somewhat offset more recently with social programs funded by the IMF, there remain millions of people, disproportionately female, living in conditions of poverty in Latin America.[1]

Due in part to the increasing insecurity of men's work and to cuts in social services, in order to maintain their households Latin American women have increased their labor-force participation in recent decades. During the period from 1950 to 1970 women made up around 26 percent of the total labor force (Preston 1996). By 1997 women's participation had increased to one-third of the workforce. In urban areas

Table 7.2
Growth and Performance of Latin American Labor Markets (1990–
1995 annual growth rates)

Country	GDP	Employment	Real Wages	Productivity
Argentina	5.2	1.0	0.2	4.1
Bolivia	4.0	4.0	1.6	-0.1
Brazil	2.5	2.6	5.1	-0.1
Colombia	4.5	3.7	1.5	0.8
Costa Rica	4.4	4.0	0.4	0.4
Chile	7.2	3.7	4.4	3.3
Honduras	3.4	5.8	0.1	-2.3
Mexico	0.8	3.1	0.8	-2.2
Panama	5.0	7.3	—	-2.1
Paraguay	3.0	5.8	-0.3	-2.7
Uruguay	3.6	4.0	0.8	2.1
Venezuela	3.2	4.0	-7.5	-0.8

Source: United Nations Economic Commission for Latin America and the
Caribbean (ECLAC), *CEPAL News* (New York: Author, June 1997).

women's workforce participation increased from 37 percent in 1980 to
45 percent in 1994. Women's participation in the formal workforce increases with amount of education, such that 71 percent of women with
thirteen or more years of schooling are employed. In 1994 women contributed between 28 and 38 percent of total household income. In the
current situation, without women's income the number of households
officially classified as poor would rise between 10 and 20 percent
(ECLAC 1997c). As in other parts of the world, women have increasingly entered the paid workforce for economic and other reasons, but
motivations are more likely to be economic than social in Latin America.

Despite the increasing presence of women in the workforce in Latin
America, as in the United States, income inequality between men and
women remains high. A series of studies of income inequality in Latin
American countries show that there are five different explanatory variables to determine levels of inequality: education, age, sector of employment, type of employment, and gender (Cardoso, Barros, and
Urani 1993, cited in Edwards 1995). The studies provide evidence that
level of education is the most significant determinant and that the probability of being at the bottom of the distribution scale is higher for

females than for males (Edwards 1995). In the early 1990s women's earnings averaged 72 percent of men's. Employment for women is concentrated in small- and medium-size businesses. Poor women tend to work in the informal economy and in the service sector, particularly in domestic service and commerce (ECLAC 1997c). Women have also been recruited by international corporations seeking a nonunionized, low-cost workforce (Preston 1996). As can be seen in Table 7.3, in the urban areas of Latin America women are frequently household heads such that in Argentina, Colombia, Costa Rica, Honduras, Panama, Paraguay, Uruguay, and Venezuela a quarter of all urban households have female heads. As in most parts of the world, female-headed households are much more likely to be in poverty than other household types. As indicated in Table 7.3, in Costa Rica, Panama, Paraguay, and Venezuela over 60 percent of female-headed households are poor. Despite the expansion of family planning, fertility rates remain high in the region. In Bolivia, Guatemala, Honduras, and Nicaragua fertility rates exceed five children per mother (Edwards 1995).

THE TOURIST INDUSTRY IN LATIN AMERICA

Before turning to the more specific issues related to gender and tourism in Latin America, a short summary of the state of the industry in this region is appropriate. The World Tourism Organization asserts that tourism is one of the world's most durable and dynamic economic sectors. In 1996 international tourist arrivals and revenues reached a new record. Globally, nearly 593 million international tourists generated $423 billion in spending, excluding airfares. By the year 2010 the WTO forecasts that international tourist arrivals will reach 1 billion and will generate $1.55 trillion in revenues annually, nearly four times more than current earnings (World Tourism Organization 1997).

The tourist industry is, however, very unevenly distributed, with most international tourism originating in developed countries. In the early 1990s, 80 percent of international travel involved people from only twenty countries, and 50 percent of all international tourists came from just five countries (Germany, United States, Britain, Japan, and France). In 1996 Mexico was the only Latin American country to rank in the top twenty-five destinations globally for international arrivals; it ranked seventh. However, in tourism receipts for the same year Mexico ranked only sixteenth, with $6.9 billion in receipts, while Argentina ranked twenty-third, with $4.6 billion (Crossette 1998). Thus, while tourism is growing in most countries of Latin America, compared to Europe or North America the numbers are still small. In 1996, for example, North America received nearly 84 million tourist arrivals, while South America received only 14 million and Central America 2.5 million. The Caribbean received

Table 7.3
Female-Headed Households in
Urban Areas (1994 percentages)

Country	Total	Poor
Argentina	24	42
Bolivia	18	37
Brazil	22	44
Colombia	24	48
Costa Rica	24	69
Chile	22	48
Honduras	25	53
Mexico	17	27
Panama	25	60
Paraguay	25	60
Uruguay	27	44
Venezuela	25	64

Source: United Nations Economic Com-
mission for Latin America and the
Caribbean (ECLAC), *CEPAL News*
(New York: Author, December 1997).

Note: Brazil percentages for 1993; Paraguay percentages for 1992.

300,000 more than South America (World Tourism Organization 1997).
Table 7.4 shows tourism arrivals and receipts for 1996 for selected destinations in Latin America and for the United States and Cuba for purposes of comparison. As can be seen from this table, Mexico is the
only country with a significant number of arrivals. Mexico is the leading destination for U.S. tourists, receiving 20 percent of all international tourists from the United States. No other Latin American country
ranks in the top ten of the destinations of the top six countries whose
tourists spend the most on international tourism (United States, Germany, Japan, Britain, France, and Italy) (Crossette 1998). The tourist
industry is the leading source of foreign exchange in Mexico, and since
the 1970s Mexico has devoted considerable resources to planning and
developing the tourism infrastructure, especially on its Caribbean and
Pacific coasts (Schluter 1993). However, considering receipts per tourist, with an average expenditure in 1995 of $317 per tourist, Mexico

Table 7.4
Tourism Arrivals and Receipts (1996)

Countries	Tourism Arrivals (in thousands)	Tourism Receipts (in $ millions)	Receipts per Tourist (in $)
Cuba	865	1,375	1,590
United States	44,791	64,373	1,437
Venezuela	621	846	1,362
Argentina	4,285	4,560	1,064
Peru	515	535	1,039
Brazil	2,386	2,353	986
Chile	1,508	928	877
Costa Rica	779	654	840
Colombia	1,450	864	596
Guatemala	521	290	557
Ecuador	482	253	525
Mexico	21,732	6,898	317
Honduras	257	81	315
Uruguay	2,209	617	279

Source: Data compiled from the World Tourism Organization, *Tourism Highlights–1996* (Madrid: Author, 1997), and United Nations Economic Commission for Latin America and the Caribbean, *Statistical Yearbook for Latin America and the Caribbean 1996* (Santiago, Chile: Author, 1997), xiv.

ranks in the third lowest position, above only Honduras and Uruguay. In contrast, in 1996, with an average of $1,590 per tourist, tourists visiting Cuba spent five times more than those who visited Mexico. After Cuba, and closer to Unites States ($1,437), Venezuela, Argentina, and Peru received more than $1,000 per tourist. In absolute terms, however, Venezuela, with $846 million, and Peru, with $535 million, contrast with Argentina, which had $4,560 in tourism receipts (Table 7.4).

In most Latin American countries a relatively small portion of total value of exports of goods and services comes from travel (see Table 7.5). For the data in Table 7.5 travel "includes good and services—including those related to health and education—acquired from an economy by nonresident travelers (including excursionists) for business purposes and personal use during their visits (or less than one year) in that economy. Travel excludes international passenger ser-

Table 7.5
Countries Ranked by Proportion
of Exports from Travel Income
(1995 percentages)

Country	Travel Income
Paraguay	26.8
Costa Rica	19.2
Uruguay	18.6
Guatemala	7.6
Peru	7.4
Mexico	6.9
Nicaragua	6.9
Colombia	6.2
Bolivia	5.8
El Salvador	5.7
Honduras	5.6
Ecuador	4.9
Argentina	4.4
Chile	4.4
Panama	4.0
Suriname	3.1
Venezuela	2.3
Brazil	1.8

Source: United Nations Economic Com-
mission for Latin America and the
Caribbean, *Statistical Yearbook for
Latin America and the Caribbean 1996*
(Santiago, Chile: Author, 1997), xiv.

Note: Suriname percentage for 1993.

vices, which are included in transportation" (United Nations Economic
Division for Latin America and the Caribbean 1997, xiv). Only in Paraguay, Costa Rica, and Uruguay do more than 10 percent of exports
come from travel (in contrast with some Caribbean destinations, such
as the 64 percent in 1993 in Barbados, 60 percent in 1994 in the Bahamas, or 45 percent in the Dominican Republic).

An analysis of the ratio of the number of visitors to the population of the countries of Latin America provides an indication of the relative impact of tourism on local society (see Table 7.6). In Brazil or Panama, for example, the numbers of tourists is very small in relation to the overall population, while in Uruguay, Costa Rica, and Belize the ratio of host to guest is more equal. In fact, Belize is the only Latin

Table 7.6
Latin America Destinations Ranked by Host-to-Guest Ratio (1994)

Destination	Population (in thousands)	Tourist Arrivals (in thousands)	Host-to-Guest Ratio
Brazil	155,300	1,612	96.34:1
Panama	2,500	342	73.10:1
Peru	22,900	386	59.33:1
Venezuela	21,300	428	49.77:1
Colombia	35,000	1,047	33.43:1
El Salvador	5,200	181	28.73:1
Bolivia	8,200	319	25.70:1
Suriname	400	18	22.22:1
Ecuador	10,600	481	22.03:1
Guatemala	10,300	537	19.18:1
Honduras	5,300	290	18.27:1
Nicaragua	4,300	237	18.14:1
Paraguay	4,800	406	11.82:1
Argentina	33,900	3,866	8.77:1
Chile	14,000	1,622	8.63:1
Guayana	800	112	7.14:1
Mexico	91,800	17,113	5.36:1
Costa Rica	3,200	761	4.20:1
Uruguay	3,200	2,175	1.47:1
Belize	200	357	0.56:1

Source: Population Reference Bureau Fact-Sheet 1994 and United Nations Economic Commission for Latin America and the Caribbean, *Statistical Yearbook for Latin America and the Caribbean 1996* (Santiago, Chile: Author, 1997).

American country to have more visitors than there are residents, in contrast to some Caribbean island countries, some of which (e.g., the Bahamas) receive many times the number of guests than the local population total. Just as tourism is unevenly distributed between countries, it is usually concentrated within countries. In Peru, for example, the major destinations for international tourists are the World Heritage sites of Machu Picchu and Cuzco, while northern Peru receives few international travelers, and indeed the Amazon selva is relatively inaccessible to all but the most intrepid traveler. Likewise, the old colonial town of Salvador de Bahia, also a World Heritage site, is visited by many North American and European tourists, some of whom stay in the luxury hotels lining the seafront, while most towns and villages of the interior of Bahia, Brazil, have no tourist accommodations and receive no international visitors. Meisch (1995) reports heavy visitation to Otavalo, Ecuador, of Americans and Europeans, while nearby Chimborazo, which is among the country's poorest provinces, has no equivalent "tourism scene."

It will be noted that the discussion has focused on international tourism, mainly because the data are more accessible. Data on domestic tourism in Latin America are scarce, but it can be assumed that it constitutes an important portion of tourism consumption and expenditures there, as in other parts of the world. Domestic tourism may be of significant economic importance to individual men and women who provide goods and services to their compatriots, but is of less importance nationally, since it does not earn foreign exchange. Moreover, the social and cultural implications are presumably different, although not necessarily less severe. In El Salvador, for example, though international visitors are still few in number, prostitution has escalated since the war ended and attitudes "liberalized," with many clients, especially of child prostitutes, being Salvadorean (Cerna 1998). We have no data on the proportion of Latin American international tourists who originate in another Latin American country, but we assume that the numbers are high, especially in Southern South American countries such as Uruguay or Paraguay, which are distant from all major sending areas and have few sites or sights with international reputations. In summary, tourism is a significant part of the economy in only a few locations in Latin America, so its role in, for example, changing gender roles or providing economic opportunities for women is relatively minor compared to other parts of the world.

WOMEN AND TOURISM IN LATIN AMERICA

As noted earlier, the literature on gender and women and tourism in Latin America is scant. Two recent volumes on gender and tourism include very little discussion of Latin America. Kinnaird and Hall's (1994) book includes a chapter on the Caribbean by Momsen (1994), and some of her observations of the Caribbean would apply to other parts of Latin America. But as seen earlier, tourism is more dominant in the economies of most Caribbean nations, so its impacts are greater than on the rest of the continent. Sinclair's (1997) volume on gender, work, and tourism includes a chapter by Chant (1997), in which she discusses women's employment in tourism in Mexico. She finds that women's income from tourism-related employment supplements their husbands' earnings, while men tend to retain dominance in the household.

Periodical literature on gender and tourism in Latin America includes the following. Meisch (1995) discussed the romantic and sexual relations between young female tourists and local men in Otavalo, Ecuador, and while she reflected the liberation from traditional values of both visiting women and to a lesser extent local men, she also noted the greater pressure on local women to conform to traditional expectations (such as the avoidance of the appearance of premarital sex) and their lesser opportunities for foreign travel than their male peers. Swain's (1993) study of ethnic-arts production among the Kuna of Panama recounts how women make *molas* (traditional dresses) both for local and tourist consumption, which empowers them at the household level. However, their "empowerment at the community level is individually possible, but [it is] more problematic as gender and ethnicity ideologies intertwine" (p. 49). Nash (1992) showed how women's pottery production in highland Chiapas, Mexico, contributed to the maintenance of traditional methods but also led to the creation of new designs for the tourist market. The construction of the Pan American Highway brought tourists to previously remote villages from which men had taken the pottery on horseback to towns and usually exchanged the pots for corn or other products. With the advent of tourists, women could sell their wares directly to tourists without the middleman.

This entry of the outside world into what had been a closed world encouraged women to use Spanish and open their houses to tourists. Some women, particularly those who were active in the cooperative before its demise, have even moved out of town to live in the departmental capital. Young women who can support themselves and their children with the earnings from pottery are now avoiding marriage, since many see it as an abusive and often exploitative institution (Nash 1992, 16).

Cone (1995) also studied craftswomen in Chiapas, comparing and contrasting the lives of two women, one a potter and the other a weaver. While their relationships with tourists were similar, their cultural identification with their communities differed. This review of extant literature, while not exhaustive, is indicative of the paucity of previous work in this area.

WOMEN AS TOURISM PRODUCERS: PERUVIAN EXAMPLES

Observations by one of the authors (Holcomb) in the Peruvian Andes in the summer of 1998 suggest the many ways in which females of all ages are involved in the tourist industry. Young Quecha girls dressed in traditional clothing and carrying their small siblings in blankets on their backs roam the plazas of Cuzco and Pisac posing for photos for which tourists pay them a *sole*. Old women wearing tall felt hats and brilliantly colored full skirts spin lama wool or lead alpacas through the streets and on ancient Incan stone temples, offering similar photogenic possibilities for a price. (Men wearing traditional dress are similarly colorful, but although tourists may take photos, men seldom request payment, at least not from the female author!) People of all ages and both genders are street and market vendors of the richly patterned woolen and alpaca clothing, beadwork, leather goods, weaving, and musical instruments, most handmade in the region. Frequently, such vendors live in rural areas quite distant from town and travel by *collectivo*, starting early in the morning and leaving late at night. One woman (from whom I purchased a sweater) was probably reasonably representative. In her thirties, she has five children whom she left with her mother in a village several hours from Cuzco while she carried a large bundle of sweaters and woven belts made by her family and herself. Her husband was working in the fields that day. Her cash income for the day (which she could not estimate or predict) would exceed that of her husband (who is essentially a subsistence farmer) and enable her to purchase such desirable commodities as coffee and sugar. She is bilingual (Quecha and Spanish), calculates quickly, and, one gathered, is bright and enterprising. While the possibilities for her future are clearly restricted, tourism has probably widened them.

Many women are employed in the hospitality industry in those parts of Peru that attract tourists. They are employed as cleaners, waitresses, housekeepers, maids, and even occasionally as managers. Other jobs, such as night manager, hotel security guard, *maitre d'hotel*, and porter seem to be largely occupied by men. Smaller hostels, especially in small towns such as Pisac or Ollotaytambo, are often family run, with the wife usually serving as receptionist and the husband chief "troubleshooter" when the plumbing or electricity fails. Similar kinds of division of labor are visible in other tourist settings. In museums and galleries women may staff the admission desk, but the guards are invariably male. When hikers on the Inca Trail hire porters and guides, they are invariably male, even though Quecha women are expert at carrying large, heavy bundles. Presumably this is partly traditional, but it is also likely that tourists of either sex from North America or Europe would feel uncomfortable walking empty-handed while a woman carried their gear. The ferryboats on Lake Titicaca, which take tourists from Puno to the floating reed islands of the Uros Indians, are invariably "manned" by male sailors, but women vendors sell their wares on arrival at the islands. Further away, on the larger (nonfloating) islands of Taquile and Amantani, women carry huge bundles of al-paca woven and knitted goods up and down the steep hillsides, some-times with men walking empty-handed beside them. On these islands there is no electricity or hotel accommodations, but visitors are wel-comed in private homes, where women cook meals for their (paying) guests. The train between Cuzco and Puno follows a scenic route over the continental divide above 14,000 feet, stopping at numerous small towns and villages whose inhabitants eke out a precarious living in the mountains. At each stop the train is boarded by women and chil-dren selling sweaters and chicha (corn beer), hats of rabbit fur, and *papas a la huancaina* (potatoes with cheese sauce). The vendors are oc-casionally male, but usually female.

In summary, Peru may be typical of other Latin American destina-tions in that women play an important part in tourism production, though their roles are more often in the informal and lower-paid sec-tors. For every Peruvian woman who is employed in better-paid jobs such as a flight attendant or accountant at a five-star hotel, there are undoubtedly a hundred who knit and sell alpaca hats or launder tour-ists clothes by hand in the back courtyards of their Cuzco homes. Most indigenous handicrafts in Peru are the product of women's work, and tourism has obviously expanded the demand for such products. While women sustain culture by reproducing traditional designs, as in other contexts, these designs are also modified and new tourist-oriented products are added to the mix. In this way, women can be seen as both guardians and innovators of indigenous cultures.

ECOTOURISM, SUSTAINABILITY, AND GENDER IN LATIN AMERICA

With a short tradition in the promotion of mass tourism, and with rich natural, historical, and cultural resources, some Latin American countries are finding a tourism niche in the promotion of ecotourism. Strongly linked to the concept of sustainability, ecotourism is promoted as a new type of relationship between the environment and the host communities based on the respect and appreciation of natural richness and local culture. Tourism as a sustainable development activity is an activity "developed and maintained in an area (community environment) in such a manner and at such a scale that it remains viable over an indefinite period and does not degrade or alter the environment (human or physical) in which it exists to such a degree that it prohibits the successful development and well-being of other activities and processes" (Butler 1993, 29).

The principles of sustainable tourism and ecotourism present interesting similarities with ecofeminist principles. The term "ecofeminism" was introduced by the French writer Françoise d'Eaubonne in 1974. The term refers to women's potential for fomenting an ecological revolution to ensure human survival on the earth. This revolution would entail new gender relations between women and men and between humans and nature (Merchant 1990). Linking gender issues with sustainability, ecofeminist writers as diverse as Irene Diamond and Gloria Feman Orenstein (1990), Riane Eisler (1990), Ynestra King (1990), Carolyn Merchant (1990), Gloria Feman Orenstein (1990), Lee Quinby (1990), Vandana Shiva (1994), and Charlene Spretnak (1990) assert that today feminism is facing a double challenge. On the one hand there is a need to transform the patriarchal dominant values characterized by the dichotomy of mind–body, economic value–ecological contribution, and culture–nature; and on the other hand there is the challenge of ecological disruption. Ecofeminist theories and ecotourism principles coincide in recognizing the intrinsic value of nature. They assume that human life is dependent on the well-being of earth. Ecotourism claims to be nurturing of "Mother Earth" and to be enabling its consumers to get closer to nature. It also claims the need to respect local communities' cultures and interests.

Since the 1980s government organizations and NGOs have increasingly directed attention to the potentials of ecotourism as a development strategy for Latin American countries. The Agenda 21 resulting from the United Nations Conference on the Environment and Development (UNCED), held in Rio de Janeiro in June 1992, asserts that an effective strategy against poverty should consider development and the environment simultaneously. To achieve this goal the report points out the need for education, support for the rights of women, and enhanced roles for youth and indigenous peoples. The World Bank, the Inter-American Development Bank, and the European Union have also encouraged the development of ecotourism in Latin America through grants and special credit lines.

Costa Rica, Guatemala, and Belize were among the first countries in promoting ecotourism as a national strategy for economic development. More recently, other Latin American countries, such as Ecuador, Peru, Brazil, Venezuela, Argentina, and Chile, have also turned to ecotourism to capture tourism revenues (Collinson 1997). However, contrary to the positive expectations of governmental and nongovernmental organizations, after almost a decade of practicing ecotourism the cases of Belize and Costa Rica provide evidence of the limitations of ecotourism as a form of sustainable development.

In Belize, despite government efforts to restrict foreign ownership of land, 90 percent of all coastal development was foreign owned and the designation of large national parks took 30 percent of the land out of agriculture. A 1996 study (Lindberg, Enriquez, and Sproule 1996) revealed that the ecotourism industry did not provide sufficient revenues to manage protected areas, and since foreign interests controlled the most successful tourist facilities, it is difficult to escape the impression that Belize is little more than a piece of real estate (Mowforth and Munt 1998). In Costa Rica, where 11 percent of land is in national parks, the "success" of ecotourism has led to overvisitation, habitat loss, and demand for real estate development in parks. Both Belize and Costa Rica may have reached the saturation point in ecolodges.

Despite the limitations of the ecotourism model, recent programs of tourism development sponsored by the Inter-American Development Bank—the Infrastructure Program for Tourism Development Areas in Mexico (1993), the Northeast Tourism Development Program in Brazil (1994), and the Program of Cooperation for Tourism in Bolivia (1995)—reiterate the concept of sustainability and ecotourism. With the support of the Inter-American Development Bank, these programs, which range in cost from $6 million (Bolivia) to $400 million (Brazil), pursue the objectives of improving Latin American countries' shares of the world tourism market through diversifying and planning tourism incorporating the development of ethno- and ecotourism.

Although ecotourism is closer than mass tourism to the principles of ecofeminism, in practice it can be argued that in Latin America ecotourism has ambivalent consequences for women producers. McCormick (1994) has shown how ecotourism disrupts traditional social and economic relations, particularly in remote areas such as the Amazon. While such disruptions may offer possibilities to women (e.g., to sell craft items to tourists), the advent of cash economies and the curtailing of traditional gathering practices require women to adapt to new, not necessarily welcome, ways of life.

Women in the conventional tourism industry tend to be more peripheral than core workers. They often undertake tasks similar to household tasks: serving meals, working in kitchens, and making beds (Shaw and Williams 1994). Ecotourism emphasizes small-scale economic enterprises. At this scale, women may have a greater influence than in the traditional tourism industry. However, as the cases of Belize and Costa Rica suggest, the ecotourism industry in Latin America seems to be increasingly dominated by much larger-scale organizations than the household unit. In this sense, women's role in the industry can be relegated to tasks similar to those in traditional tourism. A study that examines the compliance behavior of ecotourism operators with ecotourism principles suggests, however, that gender plays a role in the compliance of the ecotourism principles. The sample of the research consisted of 298 U.S., 19 Ecuadorian, and 9 Canadian ecotour operators. The study found that being a women ecotour operator significantly increased compliance with the Ecotourism Society's ecotourism guidelines (Sirakaya 1997).

GENDER AND TOURISM MARKETING OF LATIN AMERICA

For an exploration of the ways in which women are depicted as both producers and consumers of tourism in Latin America, we collected marketing materials that are intended to attract tourists for vacations in Latin America—primarily brochures—in both Spain and the United States. We obtained material from commercial outlets, such as travel agents and airlines, and from official country tourist boards and offices. Our focus was on the illustrations rather than the text of these materials.

Contrasting especially with the neighboring Caribbean, which is marketed more often as a mass tourism destination of sea, sand, sun, and sex, Latin American destinations are marketed to a more upscale and independent visitor. Cultural sites and natural wonders are depicted much more frequently than beaches or luxurious resort hotels. The emphasis is on adventure rather than relaxation.

With striking frequency, local people are depicted wearing traditional dress. Almost every woman and all children are adorned in colorful "native" dress, while in reality most residents of Cuzco, Caracas, or Mexico City wear contemporary Western dress indistinguishable from their peers in Milwaukee, Madrid, or Miami. While it is true that some indigenous people continue to wear traditional dress for everyday purposes, and those catering to tourists often don traditional dress for "authenticity," they are vastly overrepresented in the tourism-marketing materials. In contrast, visitors are often depicted wearing either sports clothes or evening wear. In the brochures it is easy to say who is a guest and who is a host. On the streets of Salvador de Bahia or Lima it is more difficult, especially if relying on clothing clues.

In brochures, local women are frequently depicted either alone or with other women and children in a market, sitting in the plaza, or making handicrafts. Rarely are local couples depicted. In contrast, visitors appear frequently as (heterosexual) couples, though perhaps not with the same inevitability as in Caribbean brochures, where virtually every tourist in some brochures is depicted hand-in-hand on the strand or romantically embracing at sunset (see Holcomb 1992). Visitors are often seen engaged in adventurous pursuits on horseback, mountain climbing, and scuba diving.

It could be noted that the depictions of servility—so pervasive in the Caribbean promotional material, where white-gloved black waiters serve bejeweled blondes and resorts offer "girl Fridays" to pamper you and take care of your every need—are rare in Latin American materials. Whether this is explicable as a legacy of slavery or as a desire on the part of mass tourists to be "waited on" and treated as higher in the social hierarchy than at home, or perhaps even as conscious policy, it is conspicuous that there are relatively few scenes of hosts providing personal services to guests in the Latin American brochures, while they are frequent in Caribbean equivalents.

In the traditional tourism advertisement, waiters, cleaners, attendants, hostesses, and reception staff are presented as a key part of the tourism experience. In fact, scholars point out that for many tourists it is the fact of being served for the holiday's period that is a most appealing aspect of the trip (Burns and Holden 1995). In contrast, ecotourism advertisements typically do not portray workers at all. The image of fresh fruit ready for breakfast or a clean bedroom seems to be more a magic gift of nature than the work of humans. The only local person portrayed is usually the guide. The consumers of ecotourism as represented in promotional materials are both male and female (though rarely children or elderly); the producer is often only visible as "Mother Earth."

CONCLUSION

In summary, though tourism is not a major part of the economy in Latin America, it is seen as an avenue to development and has both positive and negative consequences for women. In providing employment and other opportunities in the informal sector for economic gain, tourism improves women's economic position (often marginally), though often by increasing workloads. Similarly, through contact with visitors and the "demonstration effect," traditional expectations of women's roles are changing and opening new possibilities for women. On the other hand, the exploitation of women's labor (and bodies) continues as women are disproportionately engaged in low-wage work and prostitution increases. Women of all ages continue to carry heavy burdens of household responsibilities, to which the labor required for the tourist industry is added. This is not to suggest that men's work responsibilities have lessened (indeed, many men have work in the tourist industry, often in addition to other economic roles), but that the major tasks of household management usually fall to women.

As consumers of tourism in Latin America, it could be argued that both men and women have similar roles, and it may be that their interaction in gender-role norms from their countries of origin has "demonstration effects" in changing gender relations in Latin America, although we have no evidence of this. Neither do we suggest that there are gender differences in the consumers in their sensitivity to local cultures, their patterns of consumption and expenditure, or their propensity to engage in certain kinds of behaviors as tourists in Latin America, though such differences may exist. In terms of affecting Latin American society, the role of affluent Latin American tourists to destinations in the developed world may be as strong or stronger than those of tourists to that continent. Affluent Latin American tourists visiting New York may easily take back to their countries material culture and changed value systems. Local culture and identities have, however, a capability to resist global trends by their particular way of decodifying external values and the exclusion or adaptation of them into their specific cultures. In this context, the extent to which Latin American women can benefit from the increasing tourist presence on that continent will depend on the capability of the tourist industry to empower Latin American women, both economically and socially. Tourism practices that value women's production and encourage guest–host interaction have the capability to influence Latin American women's conditions. Cultural tourism and ecotourism, two of the fastest growing tourism sectors with high potentiality in Latin America, may play an important role in this direction.

NOTE

1. In contrast with the 1980s, social expenditure has recently begun to increase. Most Latin American countries now have social funds (Fondos de Inversion Social) that come primarily from loans from the World Bank and the Inter-American Development Bank (Zuvekas 1997). These funds were established after strong popular unrest provoked by the negative effects of structural adjustment programs on poor groups. Between 1990 and 1995 the greatest increase in social expenditures took place in education, social security, and health (CEPAL 1997a). Nevertheless, women remained part of the more vulnerable working groups, suffering wage discrimination and lack of opportunity for education and training. Women's working and social situations are likely to worsen gradually after the announcement in summer 1998 that Brazil, Argentina, Chile, and Mexico will cut public expenditures in response to the recent economic crisis (Gualdoni 1998). However, it is still too early to see manifestations of this change.

REFERENCES

Alvarez, S. (1994). The (trans)formation of feminism(s) and gender politics in democratizing Brazil. In *The Women's Movement in Latin America: Participation and Democracy*, edited by J. Jaquette. Boulder, Colo.: Westview Press.

Barbieri de, T., and O. Oliveira de. (1989). *Mujeres en América Latina, análisis de una década de crisis*. Madrid: IEPALA Editorial.

Benton, J. (1993). The role of women's organization and groups in community development. In *Different Places, Different Voices: Gender and Development in Africa, Asia, and Latin America*, edited by J. Momsen and V. Kinnaird. London: Routledge.

Burns, P., and A. Holden. (1995). *Tourism, a New Perspective*. London: Prentice Hall.

Butler, R. (1993). Tourism and evolutionary perspective. In *Tourism and Sustainable Development: Monitoring, Planning, Managing*, edited by J. Nelson, R. Butler, and G. Wale. Waterloo, Ohio: University of Waterloo, Department of Geography.

Cardoso, E., R. Barros, and A. Urani. (1993). Inflation and unemployment as determinants of inequality in Brazil: The 1980s. In *Stabilization, Economic Reform and Growth Conference*, edited by R. Dornbusch and S. Edwards. Cambridge: National Bureau of Economic Research.

Cerna, F. (1998). Personal communication with author.

Chant, S. (1997). Gender and tourism employment in Mexico and the Philippines. In *Gender, Work and Tourism*, edited by T. Sinclair. London: Routledge.

Chassen-Lopez, F. R. (1997). From casa to calle: Latin American women transforming patriarchal spaces. *Journal of Women's History* 9: 174–191.

Collinson, H., ed. (1997). *Green Guerrillas: Environmental Conflicts and Initiatives in Latin America and the Caribbean*. Montreal: Black Rose Books.

Cone, C. (1995). Crafting selves: The lives of two Mayan women. *Annals of Tourism Research* 22: 314–327.

Crosette, B. (1998). Surprises in the global tourism boom. *New York Times*, 12 April, 5.

Daines, V., and D. Seddon. (1993). Confronting austerity: Women's responses to economic reform. In *Women's Lives and Public Policy: The International Experience*, edited by M. Turshen and B. Holcomb. Westport, Conn.: Praeger.

Diamond, I., and G. F. Orenstein, eds. (1990). *Reweaving the World: The Emergence of Ecofeminism*. San Francisco: Sierra Club Books.

ECLAC. (1997a) *CEPAL News*. April ed. New York: United Nations Economic Commission for Latin America and the Caribbean.

ECLAC. (1997b). *CEPAL News*. June ed. New York: United Nations Economic Commission for Latin America and the Caribbean.

ECLAC. (1997c). *CEPAL News*. December ed. United Nations Economic Commission for Latin America and the Caribbean.

ECLAC. (1998). *CEPAL News*. January ed. United Nations Economic Commission for Latin America and the Caribbean.

Edwards, S. (1995). *Crisis and Reform in Latin America.* Oxford: Oxford University Press.

Eisler, R. (1990). The Gaia tradition and the partnership future: An ecofeminism manifesto. In *Reweaving the World: The Emergence of Ecofeminism,* edited by I. Diamond and G. F. Orenstein. San Francisco: Sierra Club Books.

Fisher, J. (1993). *Out of the Shadows: Women, Resistance and Politics in South America.* London: Latin America Bureau.

French, J. D., and D. James, eds. (1997). *The Gendered Worlds of Latin American Women Workers.* Durham, N.C.: Duke University Press.

Gualdoni, F. (1998). Las claves de la crisis en América Latina. *El País,* 26 August.

Holcomb, B. (1992). Re-imaging the Caribbean for tourism. Paper presented at the Congress of Latin American Geographers, September, Santo Domingo.

Inter-America Development Bank. (1997). Annual report. Available <http://www.iadb.org/exr/pub/areport/index.htm>.

Jaquette, J., ed. (1994). *The Women's Movement in Latin America: Participation and Democracy.* Boulder, Colo.: Westview Press.

King, Y. (1990). Healing the wounds: Feminism, ecology, and the nature/culture dualism. In *Reweaving the World: The Emergence of Ecofeminism,* edited by I. Diamond and G. F. Orenstein. San Francisco: Sierra Club Books.

Kinnaird, V., and D. Hall, eds. (1994). *Tourism: A Gender Analysis.* Chichester: Wiley.

Lindberg, K., J. Enriquez, and B. Sproule. (1996). Ecotourism questioned: Case studies from Belize. *Annals of Tourism Research* 23: 543–562.

McCormick, K. (1994). Manuel Antonio National Park, in Costa Rica: Victim of its own popularity. *Rainforest Action Network.* Available <http://www.emf.net/~cheetham/gracrk-1.html>.

Meisch, L. (1995). Gringas and Otavalenos: Changing tourist relations. *Annals of Tourism Research* 22: 441–462.

Merchant, C. (1990). Ecofeminism and feminist theory. In *Reweaving the World: The Emergence of Ecofeminism,* edited by I. Diamond and G. F. Orenstein. San Francisco: Sierra Club Books.

Meyer-Arendt, K. J. (1992). Geographic research on tourism in Latin America, 1980–1990. *Yearbook of the Association of Latin Americanist Geographers* 17: 199–207.

Momsen, J. H. (1994). Tourism, gender and development in the Caribbean. In *Tourism: A Gender Analysis,* edited by V. Kinnaird and D. Hall. Chichester: Wiley.

Mowforth, M., and I. Munt. (1998). *Tourism and Sustainability: New Tourism in the Third World.* London: Routledge.

Nash, J. (1992). One thousand years of pottery in Highland Chiapas. Paper presented at Rutgers University Center for Historical Analysis, October, New Brunswick, New Jersey.

Orenstein, G. F. (1990). Artists as healers: Envisioning life-giving culture. In *Reweaving the World: The Emergence of Ecofeminism,* edited by I. Diamond and G. F. Orenstein. San Francisco: Sierra Club Books.

Preston, D., ed. (1996). *Latin American Development: Geographical Perspectives.* 2d ed. Essex, U.K.: Longman.

Quinby, L. (1990). Ecofeminism and the politics of resistance. In *Reweaving the World: The Emergence of Ecofeminism*, edited by I. Diamond and G. F. Orenstein. San Francisco: Sierra Club Books.

Roxborough, I. (1997). Citizenship and social movements under neoliberalism. In *Politics, Social Change and Economic Restructuring in Latin America*, edited by W. C. Smith and R. P. Korzeniewics. Boulder, Colo.: North–South Center Press.

Scarpaci, J. (1993). Empowerment strategies of poor urban women under the Chilean dictatorship. In *Women's Lives and Public Policy: The International Experience*, edited by M. Turshen and B. Holcomb. Westport, Conn.: Praeger.

Schluter, R. (1993). Tourism and development in Latin America. *Annals of Tourism Research* 20: 364–367.

Shaw, G., and A. Williams. (1994). *Critical Issues in Tourism*. Oxford: Blackwell.

Shiva, V., ed. (1994). *Close to Home: Women Reconnect Ecology, Health and Development*. Philadelphia: New Society Publishers.

Sinclair, M. T., ed. (1997). *Gender, Work and Tourism*. London: Routledge.

Sirakaya, E. (1997). Attitudinal compliance with ecotourism guidelines. *Annals of Tourism Research* 24: 919–950.

Spretnak, C. (1990). Ecofeminism: Our roots and flowering. In *Reweaving the World: The Emergence of Ecofeminism*, edited by I. Diamond and G. F. Orenstein. San Francisco: Sierra Club Books.

Swain, M. B. (1993). Women producers of ethnic arts. *Annals of Tourism Research* 20: 32–51.

United Nations Economic Division for Latin America and the Caribbean. (1997). *Statistical Yearbook for Latin America and the Caribbean, 1996*. Santiago, Chile: Author.

Vickers, J. (1991). *Women and the World Economic Crisis*. London: Zed Books.

World Tourism Organization. (1997). *Tourism Highlights—1996*. Madrid: Author.

Zermeño, S. (1997). State, society and development neoliberalism in Mexico: The case of the Chiapas uprising. In *Politics, Social Change and Economic Restructuring in Latin America*, edited by W. C. Smith and R. P. Korzeniewics. Boulder, Colo.: North–South Center Press.

Zukevas, C. (1997). Latin America's struggle for economic adjustment. *Latin American Research Review* 32 (2): 152–169.

8

The Forgotten Giant: Women's Role in Africa's Delayed Tourism Development

Peter U. C. Dieke

This chapter examines the proposition that African women are important in the tourism sector in the region. It presents the general trends and problems in Africa's development, sets out the situation in the tourism industry, identifies and examines the problems, and considers the role of gender in these contexts. The chapter concludes by suggesting measures to enhance African women's participation in tourism development and draws from the analysis implications for other tourism destinations. Although the theme of this book is women as producers and consumers of tourism, in this chapter the focus is on African women as producers of tourism development. For reasons that will become obvious later on, the aspect of women as tourism consumers is completely excluded from consideration.

The proposition emanates from several gender issues, broadly "defined by problems, by the processes which generate them, or by the interventions which solve them" (Collier 1988, 1). Thus, in the context of this chapter gender perspectives refer to issues and problems of concern to African women by taking into account the relations between men and women, how they arise, and the policy measures to overcome them. It could be that women in society are either materially disadvantaged or that their potential contribution to the development process is not recognized by society at large. This lack of recognition vis-à-vis the men's world tends to manifest itself in the achievement of a lower human development index (HDI) of literacy level, health, and decent living standards (see United Nations Development Programme 1999). The result may be a loss of self-worth and therefore low status in the world of economic decision making.

There may be several explanations for this situation, including societal, institutional, or even legal structures that may be operating at two distinct levels. The first of these is in the household, where women's role is satisfied through the reproduction process of childbearing. There is also the issue of discrimination against women in the workplace. Attempts to reverse the imbalances through the process of redistribution in benefits sharing might invariably yield mixed results. One could likewise argue that the policy interventions to redress the imbalance may be too late in coming or perhaps too little to merit any significant impact. This state of affairs will therefore prompt the following questions: Can these problems be overcome? What has been done to encourage women's participation in the process of development? What more needs to be done? These questions are central to this chapter.

In relation to African women, the United Nations Economic Commission for Africa (ECA) is explicit:

African women have made tremendous progress over the four decades. Awareness of the rights of women has been awakened by global mechanisms such as the Beijing Platform for Action and the Convention on the Elimination of All Forms of Discrimination Against Women, ratified by some 160 states worldwide. However, there is still a large gap between rhetoric and action to maintain the momentum of this progress in Africa. Economic and legal barriers, as well as social discrimination, continue to prevent women in Africa from improving their status and productivity and achieving their full potential. These barriers include low investment in women's education and health and poor access to services and assets, as well as legal and regulatory barriers that restrict women's options and impede their full participation in and contribution to the continent's development. (Economic Commission for Africa 1999b, 25; see also United Nations 1995)

Tourism as an economic activity is similarly not immune from the criticisms of exploitation and abuse of women. However, it has been suggested that tourism has indeed offered many opportunities for women's productive participation in the sector through various means, including suggestions to do more:

In many countries women have been entrepreneurially very active and have created for themselves new economic and social opportunities. Every effort should be made to encourage this trend through affirmative action programme, training and education, and appropriate support measures. Much has been achieved in this area over the last decade but more has to be done. There are already in existence a wide range of organisations at the national and international level which pursue specific agendas for women. Stakeholders in the tourism sector should recognise the contribution that women have made to tourism and can continue to [make] in the future. (Jenkins 1997, 19)

Thus, this chapter focuses on these issues and examines how gender is, arguably, absent from much development thinking in Africa. It also shows the implications, both for understanding and for policy development, of incorporating gender into the development of tourism in Africa, and considers whether such an effort would be a major improvement on the current situation.

GENDER ISSUES IN AFRICA'S DEVELOPMENT

In this section the prime emphasis will be on two areas: a brief overview of the development indicators and changes in Africa, and a look at the role that gender plays in that development. The whole purpose is to provide a context within which to appreciate the current situation in the tourism sector in Africa and, in particular, the role that women play in it.

General Context of Africa's Development

Africa, like the other developing-world economies (e.g., Asia), is a region of considerable economic, political, social, and cultural diversity. Part of this variation has to do with differences in colonial experience, among other things, although it can be said at the outset that such diversity holds immense potential for tourism development. Today the continent is comprised of fifty-three countries categorized into five geographical subregions: Central, Eastern, Northern, Southern, and Western (Table 8.1). In a land area of 478,841 square miles (1,240,192 square kilometers) and with a population estimated at 800 million in 1998 (Economic Commission for Africa 1999a, 51–52), Africa has a population density of 9.3 per square mile, arguably one of the highest in any developing region.

The economies are overall undiversified, with services the dominant sector (see Table 8.1). In the 1960s, when most countries in the region were gaining political independence, their economies were (judged by the countries' relative stage of development) generally good. However, in the late 1970s and early 1980s the economies of most of the countries were in steep decline. For instance, as a World Bank report (1990) notes, the growth rate of real per capita GDP fell

Table 8.1
Sectoral Distribution of GDP (percentages)

	Agriculture		Industry		Manufacturing		Services	
	1997	1980	1997	1980	1997	1980	1997	1980
North Africa	18.3	13.5	27.1		14.1		54.6	38.0
Algeria	6.4	8.3	49.9	59.0	11.0	7.8	43.7	32.7
Egypt	18.6	19.3	26.8	41.5	8.4	13.6	54.6	39.2
Libya	9.2	2.5	53.9	64.5	10.7	3.0	36.9	33.0
Mauritania	29.9	24.3	25.1	29.2	8.0	6.3	45.0	46.5
Morocco	20.1	18.3	28.3	34.3	17.2	19.3	57.6	47.5
Sudan	36.1	36.9	15.9	15.9	9.4	7.8	48.0	47.1
Tunisia	20.1	15.6	34.6	36.6	18.4	13.6	45.3	47.8
West Africa	**30.7**	**25.9**	**32.2**	**35.4**	**8.5**	**6.4**	**37.1**	**36.7**
Benin	38.4	47.9	17.1	13.8	4.6	6.1	44.5	38.2
Burkina Faso	36.6	46.9	33.9	14.7	13.6	11.9	29.5	38.4
Cape Verde	20.6	20.5	30.9	27.3	7.1	5.5	48.5	52.1
Cote d'Ivoire	24.8	35.4	21.6	20.8	14.0	11.2	53.6	43.8
The Gambia	23.9	25.4	13.5	17.4	5.8	6.7	62.6	57.1
Ghana	51.9	46.8	17.6	12.7	9.8	7.6	30.5	40.5
Guinea	22.7	45.8	34.8	21.5	4.7	3.2	42.5	32.7
Guinea-Bissau	52.3	51.0	4.6	6.0	1.2	1.7	43.1	42.9
Liberia	42.9	15.7	31.4	33.6	12.5	9.1	44.6	50.7
Mali	56.0	61.2	15.3	10.0	8.8	3.7	28.7	28.7
Niger	44.6	44.5	15.7	19.0	3.9	3.7	39.7	36.5
Nigeria	32.5	20.6	38.5	41.7	3.9	5.7	29.0	37.6
Senegal	21.2	21.1	31.9	27.7	19.6	17.2	46.9	51.1
Sierra Leone	50.0	31.9	22.3	19.5	5.7	4.5	27.7	48.6
Togo	28.1	30.5	26.5	23.4	6.8	4.9	45.4	46.1
Central Africa	**21.9**	**28.9**	**36.9**	**32.7**	**10.7**	**6.8**	**41.2**	**38.4**
Cameroon	23.2	30.3	34.1	28.0	13.4	8.4	42.7	41.7
Central Afr. Rep.	44.6	39.6	11.2	19.2	9.1	7.5	39.2	41.2
Chad	40.4	41.7	16.3	12.2	8.7	8.8	48.3	46.1
Congo Rep.	12.5	9.5	26.2	49.3	8.1	6.6	45.3	41.2
Equatorial Guinea	46.2	41.5	8.1	11.9	0.4	5.1	45.7	46.6
Gabon	9.3	6.1	53.8	64.7	4.5	6.4	36.9	29.3
Sao Tome and Principe	22.8	37.1	20.6	22.0	9.5	8.4	44.4	40.9

from 0.4 percent per year during the 1970s to –1.2 percent in the 1980s. GDP per capita fell by 15 percent from 1977 to 1985. The economic decline was exacerbated by military coups and civil conflicts. All this had an adverse effect on domestic budgets, export earnings, and political stability.

In the mid-1980s, against this difficult background, twenty-nine African countries implemented (with varying degrees of commitment

Table 8.1 (*continued*)

	Agriculture		Industry		Manufacturing		Services	
	1997	1980	1997	1980	1997	1980	1997	1980
East Africa	**36.7**		**17.6**		**8.1**		**45.7**	
Burundi	47.9	61.1	18.9	13.5	12.2	8.2	33.2	25.3
Comoros	44.0	46.3	13.7	16.5	5.6	5.7	42.3	37.1
Congo Dem. Rep.	33.7	34.0	29.5	25.3	1.2	2.8	36.8	40.6
Djibouti	2.0	4.6	21.7	21.1	3.0	10.1	76.3	74.4
Eritrea	——	——	——	——	——	——	—	——
Ethiopia	46.1	50.3	10.7	15.5	5.7	10.7	43.2	34.2
Kenya	26.2	32.4	18.1	21.7	11.8	12.7	55.7	45.9
Madagascar	31.9	42.6	15.0	18.0	11.3	11.5	53.1	39.3
Rwanda	42.1	44.8	19.7	19.4	12.2	14.2	38.2	35.8
Seychelles	4.8	7.8	25.9	20.4	18.8	10.5	69.5	71.8
Somalia	62.2	38.7	9.4	19.6	3.3	8.2	28.4	41.7
Tanzania	54.8	46.3	19.9	15.6	8.8	10.2	25.3	38.1
Uganda	44.3	73.8	16.4	5.2	8.1	4.4	39.4	20.9
Southern Africa	**10.0**		**39.8**		**21.7**		**50.2**	
Angola	40.0	42.4	25.7	30.5	2.9	2.6	34.2	27.1
Botswana	3.5	13.8	52.7	46.6	4.7	6.9	43.8	39.6
Lesotho	10.9	22.6	54.5	22.7	15.5	6.0	34.6	54.7
Malawi	40.6	38.1	16.5	21.8	10.2	13.9	42.9	40.1
Mauritius	9.9	14.3	33.3	24.7	24.4	15.7	57.6	60.9
Mozambique	49.8	42.8	29.6	16.6	14.1	8.8	20.8	40.6
Namibia	12.7	——	34.6	——	7.6	——	52.7	——
South Africa	5.4	——	41.6	——	24.6	——	52.7	——
Swaziland	9.3	24.8	44.7	31.8	37.5	22.0	45.9	43.3
Zambia	28.8	14.3	39.3	34.9	29.9	17.7	31.8	50.8
Zimbabwe	17.8	16.0	29.8	36.5	20.9	25.1	52.4	47.5
TOTAL	19.4	22.3	31.9	39.0	12.7	8.7	48.7	38.7

Source: Economic Commission for Africa, *Economic Report on Africa 1999: The Challenge of Poverty Reduction and Sustainability* (Addis Ababa, Ethiopia: Author, 1999), 53–54.

and external pressures) International Monetary Fund and World Bank–inspired economic recovery programs, usually known as structural adjustment programs (see World Bank 1994a). The overriding objective was to return Africa to a sound economic-development path in order for the region's members to become viable members of the global system.

There are signs today that the economies are slowly but surely recovering, explicitly stated in the *Economic Report on Africa 1999* (Economic Commission for Africa 1999a). In summary, the suggestion is that "for the fourth consecutive year, gross domestic product (GDP) in

Africa grew faster than population, contrasting markedly with a decade and a half of declining per capita. The 3.3 percent GDP growth of 1998, compared with 2.9 percent growth in 1997, was the highest among regions of the world" (Economic Commission for Africa 1999a, ix). That said, some development challenges lie ahead, including inter alia poverty reduction, sustainability of the economies, and an improvement in the state of well-being.

Given this macroeconomic framework, two broad conclusions may be appropriate: First, there is a need to diversify export earnings. Second, there is a need to broaden participation in development efforts, with women playing a significant role.

Gender Roles in Africa's Development: Issues and Constraints

The literature on economic and social development is replete with the description of an imbalance in the relationship between men and women in many African countries (Baden, Green, Otoo-Oyortey, and Peasgood 1994; Economic Commission for Africa/World Bank n.d., 6; Saito, Mekonem, and Spurling 1994; World Bank 1995). In essence, gender disparities are in access to productive assets and social services, namely in education and employment, among other things. In education, for instance, a recent study (UNICEF 1995) on a number of African countries (e.g., Côte d'Ivoire, Malawi, Mali, South Africa, and Uganda) showed that more than 50 percent of the women over twenty-five vis-à-vis the men in the study areas are illiterate. There are a number of reasons for this (Economic Commission for Africa/World Bank n.d., 9), ranging from the perception that education does little to help women in their traditional roles of child care and household chores as these functions will be the opportunity cost of educating women, to the higher direct costs to be incurred because of providing more resources for school clothes. There is also the problem of poor access or long distances to a school, in which case a girl needs to be accompanied, itself the result of social customs requiring that boys and girls be taught in separate schools. In some cases, probably because of poverty levels, parents are attracted by the prospects of "bride price," and so they give their daughters in early marriage. Finally, the widespread belief that once a woman leaves she becomes part of the husband's family does not encourage parents, who may feel that they do not stand to gain in an educational program for their daughters.

It is unfortunate if these reasons are accepted without questioning, as some writers have noted. Moock's (1976) study on women in the agricultural sector in Kenya, for instance, has concluded that education has a strong, sustained impact on female productivity. Moock's view is that if all women received just one year of primary schooling, women's yields would increase by 24 percent, a position to which Summers (1994) and an earlier United Nations (1987) study have subscribed. In the main, Africa's fertility rates fall with women's schooling and Africa's child mortality rates equally decrease with increased education.

The second and related area of gender gap is employment, because of the difference in education levels between men and women (Appleton, Collier, and Horsnell 1993). The major problem here is that women are highly concentrated in the informal sectors. In the case of Côte d'Ivoire (World Bank 1992) it was found that two-thirds of those active in the informal sector of the country's economy are female. This particular sector is characterized by few income-generating opportunities, unsafe labor conditions, and the absence of coverage by labor laws. Female position in the formal sector is not better either, because the nature of this sector's employment denies African women the opportunity to lead more independent lives (World Bank 1994b).

Women who do manage to secure employment in the formal sector do not receive adequate compensation, especially in comparison with men's wages (Martin and Hashi 1992). This is not necessarily because of wage differentials for the same work—many countries do have equal-opportunity and equal-wages legislation. It is often because of job segregation by gender, with women in lower-paid professions, such as teaching and nursing, and men in managerial posts. But there are other much more fundamental reasons for the imbalances. Other factors pertain to time constraints stemming from childbearing and rearing and household management, which limit women's ability to secure regular employment. Some writers working in Kenya, Nigeria, Burkina Faso, and Zambia (Saito, Mekonem, and Spurling 1994) have found out that African women work much longer hours than men.

Women also face other challenges, including their traditional responsibilities and social taboos that prevent them from traveling or migrating in search of employment, as men are able to do. Women have little access to vocational training and apprenticeships, except in "traditional" stereotyped spheres, such as secretarial work, hairdressing, and tailoring. Women's other handicaps are low access to credit that stifles entrepreneurship and legal restrictions that promote the perception that women's labor is more costly than men's. As Martin and Hashi (1992) have claimed, in some African countries women are barred from working at night.

Policy makers in Africa face a number of challenges, including equalizing opportunities for men and women, building the institutional and technical structures of governments to design and implement gender-sensitive policies and programs, and also reversing the historic marginalization of women in decision making (Economic Commission for

Africa 1999a). In addition to democratizing the process so as to equalize women's citizenship rights with men's, all these measures will enhance women's representation in political structures in order to permit their voices to be heard in policy formulation. These are issues for further development and, in the next section, this chapter will examine how the general principles here have relevance to the tourism sector in Africa.

In essence, the major gender issues and constraints in Africa can be summarized as follows: (1) limited access to productive resources, particularly good land, credit, and other agricultural inputs such as farm equipment; (2) relatively lower levels of educational attainment and more limited training opportunities than their male counterparts; (3) the heavy burden of high fertility, exacerbated by poor maternal health and nutritional status; (4) prevailing attitudes of society concerning women's abilities and socioeconomic role, which reduce their status and mobility; and (5) women's perception of themselves, combined with a lack of knowledge concerning both their rights and the resources potentially available to them.

Women in the Labor Market

The female labor force in Africa was estimated to be about 73 million in 1990, representing 38 percent of the total labor force (International Labor Organization/Jobs and Skills Programme for Africa 1990, 65). In the 1970s it was estimated at 40 percent; a decline continued in the 1980s, reflecting economic crisis, restructuring policies, and high enrollment rates in schools, as well as high fertility rates that necessitate that women defer employment in favor of child- and domestic-related nonmarket activities. The decline occurred in spite of the fact that the female population increased from 47 percent in 1976 to 50 percent in 1990. During this period, the economically active female population not only dropped from 16 to 14 percent, but the female activity rates in the overall economic activity dropped from 27 to 23 percent. Table 8.2 confirms this trend, particularly relating to the ratio of men and women in the labor market between 1970 and 1990 in the five subregions of Africa.

The situation has been explained mostly by the decline of the subsistence sector, where most active women were concentrated, and the growth of the industrial sector. Sources (ILO/JASPA 1990) hinted that between 1970 and 1985 the modern sector of the African economies created only 3 million jobs for women, while the agricultural female labor force declined by as much as 5.5 million people. During the same period, more women than men enrolled in schools, thus delaying entry into the labor market. Equally important is the high demographic

Table 8.2
Percentage Distribution and Ratio (Women to Men) of Economically
Active Population by Sector and by Sex

Subregion		Agriculture			Industries			Services		
		1970	1980	1990	1970	1980	1990	1970	1980	1990
North Africa	F	54.0	44.8	37.6	14.0	20.5	23.7	32.0	34.8	38.8
	M	56.7	47.9	39.8	16.0	20.7	24.2	27.3	31.3	36.1
Ratio (F/M%)		95.2	93.5	94.5	99.0	97.9	117.2	117.2	111.2	107.5
West Africa	F	77.1	73.8	69.9	5.4	6.0	7.2	17.5	20.1	23.0
	M	74.3	69.8	65.4	10.9	12.5	14.2	14.8	17.6	20.4
Ratio (F/M%)		103.8	105.7	106.9	49.5	48.0	50.7	118.2	114.2	112.7
Central Africa	F	95.5	91.2	89.1	1.0	1.7	2.1	3.5	7.1	9.0
	M	74.5	66.1	59.8	11.3	13.8	16.9	14.2	19.4	23.4
Ratio (F/M%)		128.2	138.0	150.0	12.3	12.3	12.4	24.6	36.6	38.5
East and South Africa	F	85.2	80.3	76.0	3.1	4.6	6.1	11.7	15.0	17.9
	M	71.8	66.6	61.6	12.7	14.9	16.4	15.2	18.6	22.1
Ratio (F/M%)		118.7	120.6	123.4	24.4	30.9	37.2	77.0	15.0	17.9
Total Africa	F	82.3	77.2	72.4	4.1	5.7	7.2	13.6	71.1	20.0
	M	69.6	63.5	57.8	12.9	15.1	17.6	17.4	21.2	24.5
Ratio (F/M%)		118.2	121.6	125.3	31.8	37.7	40.9	40.9	80.7	81.6

Source: Economic Commission for Africa, *African Women Report 1995* (Addis Ababa,
Ethiopia: Author, 1996), 21.

growth rates, which kept women occupied in the nonmarket services
related to child care and domestic services.

As Table 8.2 shows, the number of economically active women in
agriculture dropped in all the subregions during the period in focus,
even though the agriculture sector continued to absorb the highest
number of women. It should be noted, however, that the number of
women absorbed in industries and services increased, especially in
services where the ratio of women to men practically doubled. In fact,
the ratio of women to men increased in all sectors despite the drop in
absolute numbers in the agricultural sector. That said, the overall rates
of women in the labor force remained lower that they were in the 1970s.

Despite these difficulties, women contribute substantially to the
economy and to the well-being of their families and communities in
many ways. As entrepreneurs, they are very active in the informal
sector, comprising the majority of the self-employed workers. For instance, in the urban areas they are engaged in such enterprises as retail marketing of fresh produce, small-restaurant services, textile dying,
and tailoring (for both the domestic and tourist markets). In the rural
areas their activities are limited to crafts production, the marketing of
surplus vegetables and fruits, and in the farming system.

AFRICAN WOMEN'S ROLE IN
TOURISM DEVELOPMENT

It has been noted that African women are producers of tourism development and not consumers of the activity. An explanation of why this description pertains must be sought. Theoretically, tourism consumption is a demand-led phenomenon usually associated with developed tourist-generating countries (e.g., France, Germany, the United Kingdom, the United States, and so on). The demand determinants include economic factors (e.g., sufficient disposable income, price level, and so forth) and noneconomic considerations (e.g., leisure-time availability, image, and such). These factors are exogenous (i.e., external) to the tourist host country, and it has no control over them. Tourism production, on the other hand, relates to the supply factors, generally defined to embrace attractions, amenities, services, and so on, which are internal to the tourist-receiving countries and over which they have control. In short, these are the resources that attract tourists in the first place to vacation in a destination. Providers of such resources might include individuals, organizations, governments, and so on.

In terms of women tourism consumers in Africa, it has been suggested, though in a different context, that most arguments have turned either to aspects of the culture of African society or to certain economic realities (Dieke 1998). Much of the debate is that indigenous Africans (including women) are not leisure minded. This implies that the values of African society do profoundly influence holiday-taking behavior in the sense that leisure travel is not integral to the lifestyle of an average African. It further means that the traditions of African family life prevent Africans from participating in recreational tourism. Demand is constrained partly by Africans' low income per capita and partly as a consequence of extended-family commitments and obligations. The effect of all this on Africa might be to depress demand for leisure travel. Since, by implication, African women are not leisure minded but they participate in the supply or provision of services to tourists, the connotation must be that they are not consumers of tourism but rather producers of the activity. If any single idea could sum up the tourism production–consumption divide, it must be that African women's emphasis is placed on the provision of "basic needs" for their families. In this sense their consumption of tourism can be seen as an economic absurdity—it is an industry targeted to the rich.

Against this background, this chapter goes on to examine the place of African women in the tourism sector. This is followed by an analysis of critical issues and some perspectives, and the chapter ends by presenting Zambia as a case study.

Tourism in Africa: The Current Situation

The World Tourism Organization (1999) has estimated the extent and impact of international tourism in 1998. The estimate is that 625 million tourists traveled worldwide in 1998, generating about $445 billion (excluding transport). Africa received nearly 8 percent of the global tourist trips (25 million arrivals), an increase over the 1997 level of 6.1 percent (23 million tourists). Similar increases were achieved in tourist arrivals, and the region's share rose from 3.3 percent ($9 million) in 1997 to 5.9 percent ($10 million) in 1998. Within Africa, the Northern subregion had the highest share of traffic (34.6 percent) and revenue (33 percent), followed in descending order by Southern Africa, Eastern Africa, Western Africa, and Middle (or Central) Africa. Also in 1998, almost 40 percent of all visits to Africa originated in the region, with Europe accounting for about 36 percent of total arrivals.

Tables 8.3 and 8.4 indicate the most visited destinations and top earners in Africa in 1998, respectively. In terms of arrivals, of the twenty countries profiled here, South Africa was the most favored destination, taking 24 percent of total traffic, followed by two Northern countries, Tunisia (18 percent) and Morocco (13 percent), and two Eastern countries, Zimbabwe (6.4 percent) and Kenya (4.3 percent).[1] The pattern of receipts is similar (as shown in Table 8.4), with South Africa the leading earner (24.8 percent), followed by Tunisia and Morocco. However, although Zimbabwe and Kenya attracted considerable numbers of tourists, Mauritius and Tanzania were able to earn more from tourism.

This brief background demonstrates the extent of international tourism in Africa and the economic importance of the tourism sector in some countries in the region, which is clearly influenced by the wider nature of economic development. For the purposes of this chapter, the analysis provides a context within which to consider the scope of women as producers of tourism development on the continent.

Women's Presence in the Tourism Sector

Women's involvement in the tourism sector in Africa, according to an Economic Commission for Africa survey (1989c), has been identified as falling into two main areas: tourism proper and tourism-related activities. In the first of these, women are engaged in the hotel subsector, in independent catering services, in entertainment and travel agencies, and as tour organizers. In the hotel subsector, women perform the so-called traditional females jobs, such as receptionist, housekeeper, chambermaid, linen maid, clerk, restaurant and bar attendant, kitchen assistant, secretary, various administrative positions, accountant, and

Table 8.3
Top Twenty Tourism Destinations in Africa (1998 international tourist arrivals, in thousands)

Rank 1990	Rank 1995	Rank 1998	Country	Estimated Figures up to 11 January 1999	Figures Received after 11 January 1999	Percentage Change 1997 to 1998	Percentage of Total 1998
4	1	1	South Africa	5,981	5,981	10.0	24.0
2	2	2	Tunisia	4,700	4,471	10.7	18.9
1	3	3	Morocco	3,241	3,243	5.6	13.0
6	4	4	Zimbabwe	1,600	1,600	7.0	6.4
5	5	5	Kenya	1,062	951	-5.0	4.3
7	7	6	Botswana	740	740	0.8	3.0
3	8	7	Algeria	648	678	6.8	2.6
13	6	8	Nigeria	640	640	4.7	2.6
8	9	9	Mauritius	570	558	4.1	2.3
—	10	10	Namibia	510	560	11.6	2.0
15	15	11	Tanzania	447	447	28.8	1.8
—	11	12	Eritrea	414	414	1.0	1.7
17	20	13	Zambia	382	362	6.2	1.5
11	12	14	Réunion	377	377	1.9	1.5
16	14	15	Ghana	335	335	3.1	1.3
9	13	16	Swaziland	325	325	0.9	1.3
10	16	17	Sénégal	309	332	6.1	1.2
12	18	18	Côte d'Ivoire	302	301	9.9	1.2
30	18	19	Uganda	238	238	4.8	1.0
18	17	20	Malawi	215	205	5.7	0.9
				23,036	—	7.6	92.5
				24,903	—	7.5	100.0

Source: World Tourism Organization, *Tourism Market Trends: Africa, 1989–1998* (Madrid: WTO, 1999), 32–33.

Table 8.4
Top Twenty Tourism Earners in Africa (1998 international tourism receipts, in $ millions)

Rank 1990	Rank 1995	Rank 1998	Country	Estimated Figures up to 11 January 1999	Figures Received after 11 January 1999	Percentage Change 1997 to 1998	Percentage of Total 1998
2	1	1	South Africa	2,366	2,366	3.0	24.8
1	3	2	Morocco	1,600	1,600	10.9	16.8
3	2	3	Tunisia	1,550	1,550	8.9	16.2
5	4	4	Mauritius	502	503	3.7	5.3
11	7	5	Tanzania	431	431	9.9	4.5
4	5	6	Kenya	400	358	5.0	4.2
9	6	7	Namibia	339	339	0.9	3.5
10	8	8	Ghana	274	274	3.0	2.9
—	9	9	Réunion	250	250	0.4	2.6
13	11	10	Zimbabwe	246	246	7.0	2.6
8	10	11	Botswana	185	185	0.5	1.9
6	12	12	Sénégal	165	161	5.2	1.7
33	14	13	Uganda	142	142	5.2	1.5
25	19	14	Nigeria	124	124	5.1	1.3
7	13	15	Seychelles	120	111	-9.0	1.3
16	15	16	Côte d'Ivoire	97	97	10.2	1.0
18	21	17	Zambia	90	75	0.0	0.9
—	17	18	Eritria	75	75	0.0	0.8
19	16	19	Madagascar	74	74	1.4	0.8
20	18	20	Sierra Leone	57	57	0.0	0.6
			TOTAL	9,087	—	5.9	95.1
			TOTAL AFRICA	9,551	—	5.9	100.1

Source: World Tourism Organization, *Tourism Market Trends: Africa, 1989–1998* (Madrid: WTO, 1999), 32–33.

179

various other duties broadly allied to public relations. In the independent catering-services areas, women are employed as manager or proprietor, host, head waitress, dining room bar clerk, chef and chef's assistant, linen maid, or in various categories related to cleaning. In entertainment (especially in bars, night clubs, and so forth), they may be employed as manager, barmaid or hostess, disc-jockey, or various categories of performing artists. Finally, in the travel trade, which includes tour operation, travel agency, and transportation businesses, women act as tour organizer, manager or proprietor, sales agent, tour guide, and hosts. They also participate in all transport activities (e.g., as flight attendants, playing a vital role in creating a distinctive image of the intended tourism destination).

The Profile of African Women in Tourism: Some Issues and Perspectives

There are a number of observations one can make based on the preceding categorization of the presence of African women in the tourism sector. The comments will also take into account the earlier background analysis focusing on the general profile of women in Africa's development. First, there has often been a tendency to confuse the behavior of some marginal elements involved in tourism as being typical of the entire tourism industry. This attitude has projected and continues to project a tarnished image of women employment in the tourism sector.

Second, situations that are considered as strictly female roles are often subordinate positions: chambermaids, kitchen assistants, restaurant and bar attendants, dancers, dance hostesses, cashiers, and so forth. In fairness, these are very difficult jobs both physically (involving long hours standing, pressure on the vertebral colon, hectic pace of work) and morally (confinement indoors for long hours, mental pressure, client relations, stress), for which the salaries paid are not the most motivating.

Third, professional training in this sector is often at a low level, if not totally nonexistent. Men and women engaged in the lower echelons of tourism careers have attained at most only a secondary school education. In Africa some of these employees are semi-illiterate. The few qualified staff represent the new generation of hotel employees. Most of them work in services that only rarely offer prospects for advancement to supervisory and managerial positions within the enterprise. Finally, it should be pointed out that the development of tourism and the shortage of employment have given rise to careers in private enterprise. Women are now proprietors of restaurants, bars, and even hotels. However, in view of the impossibility of having access to bank credits, these women often operate small enterprises or simply become subcontractors.

With regard to the informal sector, it is necessary to underscore the shortage of professionally trained staff in catering services and beverage distribution. Cottage industries and agricultural enterprises involving women are characterized in most cases by the low level of technology and supervision of their employees. Often enough, the informal sector makes use of family members and the notion of human resources costs and productivity is totally unknown.

Given this state of affairs, the challenge, of course, is to consider the problems of professional training for women involved in the informal sector of tourism. It is therefore necessary that national and subregional programs are established for the purpose of improving the level of technology and management of small enterprises that contribute to the development of tourism.

The majority of women, whether they operate in the formal or informal sectors, are in a state of dependence. The point at issue here is why women cannot increase their incomes by acquiring additional skills, by increasing the size of their enterprises, or by making use of new technologies. Arguments that could be advanced include, among others, socioeconomic constraints (in some countries women have no access to land ownership) and sociocultural constraints (low level of education, household responsibilities, division of work on a sexual basis, restrictions on women's mobility, and so on).

Another critical issue to be addressed is why, in spite of all these constraints, more and more women are embarking on careers in tourism. One of the reasons is that the division of work traditionally assigns certain production activities to women. Most careers in the hotel and catering subsectors consist of functions that are traditionally assigned to the "housewife." Any intervening changes are in terms of quantity and quality, but the psychological reasoning remains unchanged. The mere fact that as of now women who have attained high professional standards have not embarked on careers in tourism, or hesitate to do so, makes it imperative to conjure up the reasons for this or the preconceived view held of women in the tourism sector.

However, subsequent to the growth in population, the possibilities of improving living conditions motivate more and more women to strive for socioeconomic independence by embarking on remunerative activity. This is one of the reasons that motivate women to become proprietors and not employees of tourism enterprises. Being the proprietor of a hotel or a restaurant commands respect socially. Owning real estate is a symbol of success socially, even for men. Thus, many

African women seek ways and means of propelling themselves to the topmost echelons of society, while keeping within the confines of professions that are classified socially as female careers.

This current revolution has brought about changes in African women's mentality, and they realize that the sector is not a guarantee in itself. The activities of these women serve as stimulis to other women who have not yet gained access to the necessary financial and cultural emancipation. Thus, in some African countries there has been an accelerated increase in the number of tourism enterprises managed by women (hotels, various restaurants, retail stores, and enterprises dealing with producing and processing agricultural commodities and animal husbandry).

In conclusion, it can be said that if the image of African women as agents for the development of tourism has for too long been tarnished by prejudices due to the marginal behavior of certain elements, or by the low level of responsibility assigned to women employed in the formal sector of tourism, the situation is changing rapidly, with the intervention of female entrepreneurs who, through their success and moral conduct, have demystified the traditional image of women as agents of tourism development. Sociocultural changes that have swept through the continent and a certain degree of women's emancipation are the factors that brought about this revolution. On account of their lack of professionalism or access to credit facilities, independent female entrepreneurs in the tourism sector are still confined to subordinate positions, and often to operating small-scale enterprises.

Case Study of Zambia

In this section one short case study of African women's tourism-production activities in the informal sector is presented. As used here, the informal-sector concept simply embraces microenterprises and businesses that operate outside the framework of national accounts and statistics, from where they derive their informality. The concept has its genesis in the dualistic model of traditional (i.e., rural) and modern (i.e., urban) economic-sector dichotomies of poor countries (see Lewis 1954). In Africa the concept did not gain wide currency until the International Labor Organization Employment Mission to Kenya in 1972 (see International Labor Organization 1972), because small-scale enterprises and businesses have been a dominant feature of African economic structures. The mission drew attention to the apparent ability of such enterprises to accommodate the growing army of unemployed workers, especially in African urban centers.

The country selected is significant because it exemplifies variations in terms of the levels, the nature, and the activities of women's involvement in the tourism sector. It also highlights problems that can be found in many of the countries in the region, situations that are themselves influenced by the stage of economic development. Zambia has limited tourism development, with considerable potential, but now has established a tourism development strategy.

In presenting the case for Zambia, emphasis will be on three areas: some background on the country itself, an analysis of women's participation in informal tourism-sector activities, and the policy environment and its effects on informal-sector women's tourism production enterprises.

General Background

Zambia is a land-locked Southern African country, bordered by the Democratic Republic of Congo (north), Tanzania (northeast), Malawi and Mozambique (east), Zimbabwe, Botswana, and Namibia (south), and Angola (west). It has an area of 752,614 square kilometers (290,584 square miles), making it the sixteenth largest country in Africa. With an estimated population of about 9 million in 1998, between 1988 and 1998, it grew at an annual rate of 3.6 percent per annum (Economic Commission for Africa 1999a, 52). A former British territory, the country is currently a democracy and multiparty politics are permitted.

Zambia's economy is dependent almost entirely on its mineral wealth (notably copper, of which it is one of the world's leading producers, and cobalt). In the mid-1980s copper prices were in steep decline and this had a devastating effect not only on export earnings and employment in the country, but also on the poor in general and women in particular, a point acknowledged by the ILO Director-General: "The burden of declining living standards has fallen most heavily on the poor, that is, on precisely those groups that could least afford it, given their already wretched levels of income" (International Labor Organization 1989, 30). The government began to seek ways of diversifying earnings and employment away from almost total dependence on copper. Agriculture as an export sector was based on sugar, with other crops (e.g., corn, beans, peanuts, and so forth) being used for domestic consumption. Manufacturing, mainly of textiles and clothing, was limited. A potential sector was tourism. This was the background that encouraged the government to approach the European Union with a request to assist it with formulating a tourism-development strategy (see Republic of Zambia 1995).

Tourism and Women's Informal-Sector Activities

The tourist product of Zambia is largely based on its wildlife attractions, which include a walking safari, a safari by canoe, and a hunting safari. It could be said none of these features are in themselves unique, because they are available to a greater or lesser extent in neighboring countries. In 1998 it was estimated that there were 362,000 international visitors arriving in Zambia, with over 58 percent of the visitors coming from three countries: Zimbabwe, South Africa, and Tanzania (World Tourism Organization 1999, 110). It was further noted that visitors from Europe comprised approximately 15 percent of the total arrivals (33,755), with the majority coming from the United Kingdom.

These statistics show that Zambia has a low-volume tourist industry that is very reliant on regional markets and with a heavy dependency on one non-African market, the United Kingdom. But the forecast in 2000 is that visitor arrivals will increase, as will receipts.

The role played by women in Africa's tourism development has been noted. In relation to Zambia, a relatively recent study (Economic Commission for Africa 1989b) provided insight into the structure of women's informal-sector activities in this country. It is argued that most of the female operators are migrants and poor, are (on the average) between the ages of twenty-five and forty-five, have little education, and lack access to essential support structures. In addition, between 25 and 30 percent are heads of households, with all the attendant difficulties this entails. What is implied here is that women's participation in the informal sector in Zambia seems to follow a similar pattern to those found elsewhere in Africa. For example the street-food retail trade dominates the informal sector (49 percent), with fishing, basket making, pottery, and personal services equally important. In this way they are supplying products or providing services required to serve tourists.

Zambian women entrepreneurs have the least access to production resources (e.g., capital). They also form a significant proportion of unpaid family labor, and their incomes are frequently below that required to live beyond primary poverty. That said, in the words of the Economic Commission for Africa (1989b), "If one were to look more closely, one would discover that the really successful female entrepreneurs, either in the small-scale enterprise sector or in the informal sector spectrum, have either been assisted by relatives or are simply fronting for them" (p. 22). While this raises important issues pertaining to female subordination and continued dependence on men, it seems a "better" alternative to being penurious and dependent.

Policy Environment for and Effects on the Informal Sector

The Zambian situation is representative of many Eastern and Southern African countries in the sense that the informal sector is not exactly popular with government authorities (Economic Commission for Africa 1989b). The fact that most of the by-laws currently used to deal with the informal sector have their antecedents in, and derive their legitimacy from, a colonial legacy is an indication of the prevailing attitudes toward the sector. Indeed, where colonial laws were found to be disagreeable or antithetical to national interests or development, they were rapidly changed. In other words, that many of these by-laws are still extant (many years after independence), and in view of the fact that they continue to constitute tremendous bottlenecks that informal-sector operators continually grapple with cannot, in itself, be a coincidence. They are, in essence, an explicit policy toward the informal sector. It needs to be stated at this juncture that these colonial and similar by-laws have undoubtedly outlived their usefulness and should be replaced by laws that take cognizance of the country's current sociopolitical and economic milieu.

In terms of impact, it is difficult to overemphasise the degree of sociopsychological and economic insecurity created for women entrepreneurs by a hostile policy environment. Reference has been made to the problems, especially those pertaining to the question of capital formation and other production resources. When, for instance, the question of legality is applied rigidly, as it is in Zambia, it has the effect of defining a large and important business sector—in this case, the informal tourism sector—as illegal or, in Zambian local parlance, as "black-market":

Black-marketeers belong to the urban informal sector. Within this group we can distinguish sellers of essential commodities: street sellers of groundnuts, sweet potatoes and vegetables, and different types of artefacts etc. The members of the informal sector do not hold licences authorising them to sell or make the various goods. In this broad sense they can all be described as engaged in illegal activity . . . police moves against the black-market are aimed at the sellers of essential commodities although during such swoops even the poor woman selling groundnuts . . . ends up being arrested. (Economic Commission for Africa 1989b, 30)

It seems obvious that informal-sector women entrepreneurs live in perpetual fear of being arrested, which must be a major constraining factor to their business operations. It further raises questions about their contribution to the tourism economy in the country. For instance, where a woman is forced by necessity to display and sell handicrafts that are not primarily Zambian made, one could suppose she may be at odds with the law, which stipulates that the content of such commodities must comprise more than 75 percent Zambian content to be considered a Zambian product. Such a regulation further impacts negatively on the women who may wish to venture into a line of business because of, among other things, the intense competition that is characteristic of retail trade.

Conclusion

The combination of continuing disequilibria in the Zambian economy and a hostile policy environment have combined to retard growth and development of female informal-sector tourism production. As Anderson (1989) points out, "The sector [in Zambia] has so far not shown any tendency towards viable economic growth, neither as a sector nor for its individual participants. Prone to lateral expansion and involuntary growth, particularly in petty services activities, the tendency has been for real incomes to decline as more sellers attempt to capture the shrinking informal sector demand" (p. 46). In summary, it can be said that while a favorable policy environment may not transform this sector, there can be no doubt that a removal of some of the negative laws and regulations would be an important and welcome intervention.

ENHANCING AFRICAN WOMEN'S PARTICIPATION IN TOURISM

It is important, first and foremost, to base any future strategy on factual knowledge of the problems. Such knowledge should relate not only to professional practice, but also its effects on the economy and society as well as on the cultural behavior of those concerned and their environment. Women should be closely associated with surveys to be carried out. They should take their problems in hand and play an active part in finding solutions to them. The challenge, as ever, is to indicate certain guidelines for research and scientific methods of approach in order to lay the basis for future projects and programs of action.

Enhancing the contribution of African women toward the development of tourism should also entail upgrading careers in tourism. Indeed, apart from certain sociocultural attitudes currently undergoing changes, one of the constraints is still the reputation of tourism in Africa. Consequently, training programs designed to help tourism agents acquire the right skills and attitudes should be closely associated with mass-education programs on the socioeconomic, cultural, and political functions of tourism.

The focus should be on measures to be undertaken to eliminate the major constraints. The responsibility of implementing these programs will be assigned in such a way as to prevail on states and citizens alike to play a major role. The intervention of intergovernmental or international organizations will only serve as added support for the activities being undertaken at the national level.

Before concluding, it is worth noting that female entrepreneurs are required to play a leading role in the development of intra-African and domestic tourism. Furthermore, particular attention should be given to training and motivating them. This should be one of the conditions for implementing the Kinshasa Declaration on Tourism in Africa (see Economic Commission for Africa 1987), as well as for developing intra-African tourism as a major contributor toward implementing the decisions reached by African heads of state and government with regard to the integration of the continent.

CONCLUSION

Tourism has been recognized as a major economic force in Africa's development, and the role of women in this process, albeit as producers, has been identified. As argued in this chapter, tourism's importance lies in the occupational choices it provides for women outside of the traditional home-based opportunities of childbearing. Tourism also provides African women with employment opportunities that, although in the informal sector, are significant because of the autonomy and independence they provide for women.

Women's full potential is inhibited by a number of gender disparities, themselves a consequence of educational, institutional, legal, and other societal structures, including limited access to capital. These imbalances are reflected in the household, where women's role is satisfied, as noted, through the reproduction processes of childbearing, and in discrimination against women in the workplace. Policy interventions have gone a long way toward mitigating the situation, but much more needs to be done. To actualize this ideal, the actions and attitudes of African society and men in particular must change. Men must learn to accept women as equal partners, in general development terms and in tourism in particular. Finally, there is a need to devise strategies to eliminate gender gaps, and strategic policies ought to be flexible and amenable to a variety of situations within which women operate. The support of the Economic Commission for Africa is particularly welcome, especially their current response measures to raising gender awareness in the region in such issues as promoting economic and legal policies, monitoring and supporting implementation of the Beijing agenda, fostering economic empowerment of women, and so forth.

Essentially, tourism development in Africa would immensely benefit from a sustained program aimed at eliminating the major barriers to realizing women's full potential. It needs to be stressed, however, that if African women are to participate in and benefit equally from tourism development, national policies and strategies for women have to take into account male–female dynamics in African society as well as make attempts to ensure that males and females work as partners on equal terms. In effect, women's position in African society cannot be changed without transforming existing gender relations. For the integration of women into the development of tourism to reflect the concerns of most African women, a strategy has to be on the terms of the majority of the women. That is, it should serve as a basis for all categories of women to define what is important in their lives, and within this framework participate in the process of transforming the society.

In the final analysis, it is pertinent to mention the need for developing regions like Africa to refine and clarify the concept of development and its relevance to the tourism sector. This involves moving beyond the conceptualization of development primarily in economic terms, and redefining development to recognize and remunerate the roles of women for tourists as the source of the human resource element in the development of tourism and, therefore, the need to transform all structures and ideologies that constrain their role in tourism-development policy initiatives. This transformation implies making conscious attempts to redress the sexual division of labor and gender relations to make these less biased against women.

NOTE

1. The World Tourism Organization's regional classification of countries does not always coincide with that adopted by the United Nations. Thus, according to the World Tourism Organization the Northern African countries do not include Egypt, which is regarded as part of the Middle Eastern region.

REFERENCES

Anderson, K. (1989). *Mineral Dependence, Goal Attainment and Equality: Zambia's Experience with Structural Adjustment in the 1980s.* Goteborg, Sweden: Department of Economics and Legal Science, University of Goteborg.

Appleton, S., P. Collier, and P. Horsnell. (1993). Gender, education and employment in Côte d'Ivoire, social dimensions of adjustment in Sub-Saharan Africa. Working paper, World Bank, Washington, D.C.

Baden, S., C. Green, N. Otoo-Oyortey, and T. Peasgood. (1994). Background paper on gender issues in Ghana: Briefings on development and gender. Institute of Development Studies, University of Sussex, United Kingdom.

Collier, P. (1988). Women in development: Defining the issues. Working paper 129, World Bank, Washington, D.C.

Dieke, P.U.C. (1998). Regional tourism in Africa: Scope and critical issues. In *Embracing and Managing Change in Tourism: International Case Studies*, edited by E. Laws, B. Faulkner, and G. Moscardo. London: Routledge.

Economic Commission for Africa. (1987). *Kinshasa Declaration on Tourism in Africa.* Presented at the conference of African Ministers of Tourism, 22 November, Addis Ababa, Ethiopia.

Economic Commission for Africa. (1988). *Study on the Status of Women Entre-preneurs in the Informal Sector.* Addis Ababa, Ethiopia: Author.

Economic Commission for Africa. (1989a). *Abuja Declaration on Participatory Development: The Role of Women in Africa in the 1990s.* Addis Ababa, Ethiopia: Author.

Economic Commission for Africa. (1989b). *Improving the Role of African Women in Informal Sector Production and Management: The Case of Zambia.* Addis Ababa, Ethiopia: Author.

Economic Commission for Africa. (1989c). Women's participation in the development of tourism in Africa. Presentation at the Seminar on Hotel Management and Women's Participation in the Development of Tourism, 18–25 September, Addis Ababa, Ethiopia.

Economic Commission for Africa. (1995). Economic empowerment of women. Paper presented at the Sixteenth Meeting of the Technical 30th Session of the Commission, 24–28 April and 1–4 May, Addis Ababa, Ethiopia.

Economic Commission for Africa. (1996). *African Women Report 1995.* Addis Ababa, Ethiopia: Author.

Economic Commission for Africa. (1998). Report of the International Conference on African Women and Economic Development: Investing in Our Future. Held on the occasion of the Fortieth Anniversary of the Economic Commission for Africa, 28 April–1 May, Addis Ababa, Ethiopia.

Economic Commission for Africa. (1999a). *Economic Report on Africa 1999: The Challenge of Poverty Reduction and Sustainability.* Addis Ababa, Ethiopia: Author.

Economic Commission for Africa. (1999b). *The ECA and Africa: Accelerating a Continent's Development.* Addis Ababa, Ethiopia: Author.

Economic Commission for Africa. (n.d.). *The African Centre for Women (ACW).* Addis Ababa, Ethiopia: Author.

Economic Commission for Africa/World Bank. (n.d.). *Gender in Africa: The Issues, Facts.* Addis Ababa, Ethiopia: Author.

International Labor Organization. (1972). *Employment Incomes and Equality in Kenya: A Strategy for Increasing Employment in Kenya.* Geneva: Author.

International Labor Organization. (1989). *Recovery and Employment: Report of the Director-General.* Geneva: Author.

International Labor Organization/Jobs and Skills Programme for Africa. (1990). *African Employment Report 1990.* Addis Ababa, Ethiopia: Author.

Jenkins, C. L. (1991). Tourism policies in developing countries. In *Managing Tourism,* edited by S. Medlik. Oxford: Butterworth Heinemann.

Jenkins, C. L. (1997). Social impacts of tourism. Background paper presented to the World Tourism Leaders' Meeting on Social Impacts of Tourism, 22–23 May, Manila, Philippines.

Johnson-Sirleaf, E. (1998). Developing African economies: The role of women. Paper presented at the International Conference on African Women and Economic Development, 28 April, Addis Ababa, Ethiopia.

Lewis, W. A. (1954). Economic development with unlimited supplies of labor. *The Manchester School* 22: 139–191.

Martin, D. M., and F. O. Hashi. (1992). Women in development: The legal issues in Sub-Saharan Africa today. Working paper, World Bank, Africa Technical Department, Washington, D.C.

Moock, P. R. (1976). The efficiency of women as farm managers: Kenya. *American Journal of Agricultural Economics* 58 (5): 831–835.

Oleko, T., and D. Shapiro. (1991). *Employment, Education and Fertility Behaviour: Evidence from Kinshasa.* Kinshasa, Democratic Republic of the Congo: University of Kinshasa.

Republic of Zambia. (1995). *Medium-Term National Tourism Strategy and Action Plan for Zambia.* Lusaka: Government of Zambia.

Saito, K., H. Mekonem, and D. Spurling. (1994). Raising the productivity of women farmers in Sub-Saharan Africa. Discussion paper, World Bank, Washington, D.C.

Summers, L. (1994). *Investing in All People: Educating Women in Developing Countries.* Washington, D.C.: World Bank.

United Nations. (1987). *Fertility in the Context of Development: Evidence from the World Fertility Survey.* New York: Author.

United Nations. (1995). Platform for action and the Beijing declaration. Fourth Conference on Women, 4–15 September, Beijing, China.

United Nations. (1996). *The World's Women 1995.* New York: Author.

United Nations Children's Fund. (1992). *The State of the World's Children.* Oxford: Oxford University Press.

United Nations Children's Fund. (1995). *The State of the World's Children.* Oxford: Oxford University Press.

United Nations Development Programme. (1999). *Human Development Report.* New York: Oxford University Press.

World Bank. (1990). *Trends in Developing Economies.* Washington, D.C.: Author.

World Bank. (1992). *Côte d'Ivoire: Gender Issues, Information Sheet.* Washington, D.C.: Author.

World Bank. (1994a). *Adjustment in Africa—Reforms, Results, and the Road Ahead.* New York: Oxford University Press.

World Bank. (1994b). *World Development Report.* Washington, D.C.: Author.

World Bank. (1995). *Social Indicators of Development.* Washington, D.C.: Author.

World Tourism Organization. (1999). *Tourism Market Trends: Africa, 1989–1998.* Madrid: WTO.

9

From the "Iron Curtain" to the "Dollar Curtain": Women and Tourism in Eastern Europe

Derek R. Hall

This chapter discusses women as producers and consumers of tourism in the former communist societies of Central and Eastern Europe (CEE). The existing literature covering material for this chapter is not extensive. Indeed, as recently as September 1997, Weiner (1997, 473) could argue that in general there had been relatively little discussion of women's and men's productive and reproductive roles in post-communist CEE. Although the level of debate in and concerning the restructuring economies has generally improved, sources on women's production and consumption of tourism in the region remain scant. Major academic collections of gender-aware evaluations of tourism (e.g., Kinnaird and Hall 1994; Swain 1995) do not embrace empirical material from, nor theoretical perspectives explicitly relating to, gender dimensions of tourism in CEE. There is opportunity for both good empirical studies to be undertaken in the region and for establishing an appropriate culturally sensitive theoretical framework within which to evaluate gendered dimensions of tourism in the region.

The degree to which restructuring has adversely or positively affected women in the region is a matter of some debate. Ners (1992), for example, has argued that the processes of stabilization and structural adjustment are particularly "socially painful" for women. Weiner (1997) points to the growing research on the effects of these policies for marginalizing and/or excluding women through reductions in state-funded services such as health care, child care, family planning, education, and sectoral restructuring with heavy reductions in the administrative employment positions that women tended to find (e.g., Beneria and Feldman 1992). This removal of state support for social services has been interpreted as a means of undermining the identity of women as workers—and indeed of leisure consumers—and of reinforcing the ideology of viewing women as wives and mothers (Pearson 1991; Einhorn 1993).

In trying to summarize a wide range of (essentially nontourism-related) empirical material, Aslanbeigui, Pressman, and Summerfield (1994) suggest a number of overall themes concerning the impact of restructuring on the region's women: (1) negative employment trends arising from discrimination in hiring, limited opportunities available outside low-paying sectors, and overrepresentation among the unemployed; (2) women have traditionally had little money and few assets, and are less likely than men to have accumulated capital or to have the collateral necessary for obtaining a loan (such lack of credit prevents women from taking advantage of the new opportunities created by restructuring); (3) meager financial resources can be linked to the inferior position of women within the household—they may be forced to work longer and harder in the workforce, but not gain any additional goods and services to make their lives easier; (4) bargaining power within the household arises at least in part from cultural norms (within the region traditions of male dominance and discrimination against women, often reinforced by organized religion, have been reinvigorated and reasserted themselves in the post-communist period); and (5) as a consequence, women do not have a strong political voice and lack political representation and power. One consequence is that when budgets are cut, the first programs to go are those that tend to benefit women: governments have failed to prevent women from being marginalized on the assumption that reforms are gender neutral.

Fodor (1997) is more optimistic, and argues, in comparing Hungary, Poland, and Slovakia, that (1) only in Poland are women directly discriminated against; (2) there are often country- and transition-specific reasons for observed gender differences in levels of unemployment—women lack, or are unable to capitalize upon, certain resources that are useful for retaining employment, such as party membership in the case of Slovakia or self-employment in Hungary and Poland; and (3) there are specific assets that women are more likely to hold than men, such as high levels of education and experience and positions in the service sector, which can be mobilized to women's advantage to help retain employment. Fodor's approach certainly tends to be more optimistic than most other evaluations of women's experience of "transition."

TOURISM EVOLUTION IN CENTRAL
AND EASTERN EUROPE

Tourism grew in popularity in the region during the first half of this century, especially in upland areas and spa towns. The postwar adoption of variations on the Soviet model of political, economic, and social development, however, replaced previous patterns of organization and attractions with a new context and roles for recreational activity.

Tourism could support a number of "socialist" objectives: redistributing employment opportunities, promoting positive regional and national images, and convincing visitors of the superiority of the socialist system (Hall 1984). But the structural characteristics of state socialism—centralized bureaucratic organization, inflexibility and antipathy towards individualism and entrepreneurialism—tended to limit the success of international tourist programs except within the decentralised Yugoslav system. Further, alleged fear of Western ideological contagion and social corruption were early constraints on the region's governments' pursuing international tourism, such that its economic impact on the region remained relatively small, certainly by comparison with Western Europe. (Hall 1991)

Under communism, domestic recreation was subsidized to provide inexpensive accommodation and transport for (usually urban industrial) workers and their families to take a holiday at least once every two years. But this labor-union- and enterprise-supported activity tended to exclude a substantial element of the rural population, rendering them unsubsidized and relatively immobile. Despite the human rights clauses of the 1975 Helsinki agreement, most of the region's nationals found it difficult to travel Westward: currency inconvertibility, restricted access to hard currency, and stringent vetting and exit-visa policies proscribed most forms of extrabloc tourism. Thus, cross-border tourism movement tended to be dominated by exchanges of "friendship groups" between like-minded countries. The political and bureaucratic elite—the *nomenklatura*—with access to convertible currency was, however, able to travel to the capitalist world. There were thus several levels of a tourism and recreation underclass arising out of prevailing social, economic, and political relations, although gender appeared not to be a significant variable in this structural inequality.

By 1997 the gross output from travel and tourism in CEE was estimated to be worth $162 billion, and to be employing 16.1 million people, some 8.7 percent of the region's total employment. A 37-percent growth to almost 22 million employees was projected for the year 2007 (World Travel and Tourism Council/Wharton Economic Forecasting Associates 1997). The conceptualization of tourism within transitional development is not well developed (e.g., Debbage and Daniels 1998), and the political-economy literature on post-communism (e.g., Holmes 1997) has rarely addressed questions relating to tourism. A wide range of tourism-related empirical material now exists, but rarely is a gender dimension addressed.

Three dynamic contexts have been recognized as important in molding CEE's evolving post-communist tourism industry (Johnson 1997). These involve changes in (1) individual countries' political economies; (2) a country's pattern of external relationships, including tourism patterns; and (3) the world tourism industry itself. A symbiotic relationship between tourism development and processes of economic, political, and social restructuring has embraced issues of price liberalization, encouragement of entrepreneurial activity, large- and small-scale privatization, deregulation, divestment, changing circumstances for personal mobility, enhanced and reoriented foreign trade and investment, and currency convertibility.

The role of tourism as an important means of gaining hard currency has been somewhat modified since 1989. Achievement of currency convertibility has become one symbol of the fiscal maturity of post-communist states and of their integration into the global economy. While some Central European states have achieved convertibility, the currencies of others remain inconvertible and thus a pejorative indicator of economic status. Post-communist economic programs, whether of the "shock therapy" or more gradual (and uncertain) variety, have needed to respond to a range of previously unknown economic circumstances: a loss of Eastern markets, high levels of industrial closure and unemployment, price inflation, and diminishing living standards. In attempting to combat these circumstances, the improvement of trade balances has been a common government objective, although the acknowledgment of tourism's role in this process has varied markedly between countries.

By encouraging greater and closer interaction between formerly restricted host populations and the outside world, both inbound and outbound tourism may be seen as catalysts of change and as positive educational forces stimulating a thirst for knowledge of the outside world, encouraging entrepreneurial activity, providing supplementary incomes, generating new forms of employment, and creating new patterns of travel; or in setting up potentially negative demonstration effects, modifying cultures, and generating major economic leakages through transnational involvement. The integration of CEE into the global economy, and in particular in preparation for individual countries' possible accession to the European Union, has been a prime foreign-policy driving force, especially of the more advanced economies of Central Europe.

THE POSITION OF WOMEN IN
CENTRAL AND EASTERN EUROPE

Life expectancy for women in the CEE countries is about 75 years. Slovenia has the longest expectancy at 77.4 years. Mortality is highest in the Baltic countries and in Hungary. The birth rate is highest in Slovakia (14.9/1,000). Average family size ranges from 2.6 in the Czech Republic to 4.0 in Estonia and 4.8 in Albania. In rural areas families are slightly larger. Marrying age is over 20 years in all the CEE countries except the Czech Republic, where the median age for women is 18 years. Divorce rates are highest in the Baltic countries, in the Czech Republic, and in Hungary (Siiskonen 1996). Migration of young, educated, single women from rural to urban areas is a common trend in most countries of the region, although young men are also eager to move out of rural areas. There is little internal migration in the Baltic countries. In Bulgaria, Hungary, Lithuania, Croatia, and Slovakia, migration from the cities to rural areas is more common than from villages to urban areas, and men migrate from rural areas more often than women.

Restructuring has brought about profound impacts on the region's women. There has been a reevaluation of the question as to whether a woman's right to work, as guaranteed under communist law and ideology, was indeed a form of emancipation or simply one more aspect of state exploitation. Women often felt forced to work outside of the home (in addition to the inevitable domestic chores), and were likely to be treated at the workplace within the confines of sexual stereotypes. Yet an early report by the United Nations Commission on the Status of Women and the Committee on the Elimination of Discrimination Against Women confirmed that restructuring was eroding any economic and social advantages that women had gained under the Communists (Einhorn 1991). The role of women in post-communist political life has also tended to diminish (Weyr 1992), reflecting both structural constraints and a reaction against the manipulation of women as political representatives under communism.

National patterns have tended to be replicated locally. For example, Graham and Regulska (1997) found, through three case studies in Poland, that women were unsuccessful in their attempts to influence local public policy decisions through community organization. Although women's ability to participate on the political arena has been somewhat discredited, Siklova (1994) argues that in the case of the Czech Republic at least, while women appear to have deliberately withdrawn from formal politics, by early 1994 they comprised more than three-quarters of those who had registered some 24,000 nongovernment and nonprofit organizations. This "third sector," which barely existed under communism, is viewed as the grassroots of democracy by aiding and supporting social transformation. The United Nations (1992) has viewed this sector at a global level as an important nontraditional means for women to gain access to power and leadership.

While longer-term freedoms of contraception, mobility, and employment and the inevitable onslaught of Western modernity on traditional values may assist in improving the social position of women, there are clearly other factors ready to diminish it (Corrin 1992; Edmundson 1992). "Freedom" is bringing rising levels of crime against people— not least rape—as well as the more obvious crimes against property. Pornography has become a common phenomenon sold on the streets of most major centers. Rapid growth among younger people in the use of and dealing in narcotics has adversely impacted on family life.

ACCESS TO TOURISM PRODUCTION

In particular, women have been unable to take advantage of new economic opportunities as readily as men. In the former East Germany, for example, the labor market has developed in such a way that many easterners now need to travel westward to work, yet 80 percent of such commuters are male, reflecting women's limited ability to commute long distances because of family obligations (Rudolph, Appelbaum, and Maier 1994). Exhausted by the double burden of work inside and outside the home, women are reluctant to take jobs with private firms that demand even more working hours and do not guarantee maternity leave or child-care benefits. In the early years of "transition," at least, most newly founded or privatized firms were being run by former male managers of state-owned enterprises (Fischer and Standing 1993).

The result is that women have the same double burden as before, but this is now augmented by new economic difficulties (Kotowska 1995). As unemployment has risen, women have been expected to be the first to be displaced (Szalai 1991; Williamson 1992), and discrimination is often overt in, for example, newspaper job advertisements for foreign joint ventures (Fong and Paull 1993). In tourism, acting as guides, hostesses, and the like in newly privatized or new companies often means being paid a poor basic wage and having to depend on tips and other favors to sustain an adequate income. A marginalization of women has been identified in tourism-related production, such as crafts and folk arts, just as in other economic spheres (Buckley 1997).

Women have been found to typically have only limited participation in higher-wage sectors, and have been negatively impacted by increasing salary differentials: in Romania, for example, the sectors with the greatest differentials—health care and education—are the most asymmetrically female (Bacon and Pol 1994). Numbers of unemployed women have exceeded those of men, a characteristic that, ironically, does not accord with the global trend of increasing female labor-force participation (Standing 1989). Within the first two or three years of restructuring, women made up 56 percent of the unemployed in Czechoslovakia, 60 percent in Bulgaria and Albania, and 58 percent in Poland. More recently it was reported that in Ukraine 80 percent of the jobless were women and in Russia the figure was nearly 63 percent (Lakhova 1998). In the latter case women suffered job losses at about ten times the rate of men, as they became the first targets of the scaling down of large-plant employment. The probability of obtaining new employment in CEE was calculated at being three times more likely for a man than for a woman (Einhorn 1993; Fong and Paull 1993).

For entrepreneurial women, a way out of this situation is to start their own businesses, despite the difficulties of obtaining credit and the risks of trying to survive alongside the gray economy, particularly when they often do not have the all-important connections. Business incubators—large facilities that can provide low-rent office space; access to computers, fax, and photocopying machines; and business training advice and courses—have been developed with Western financial support in most countries of the region. In Russia, women have received nearly half of the loans made to small businesses by a $300-million fund of the European Bank for Reconstruction and Development. In Hungary about 40 percent of new business are being started by women (Medvedev 1998).

But tourism-related employment opportunities for local women are often typified by a predominance of unskilled, low-paid jobs. The gendered horizontal segregation of occupations is particularly noticeable in semiskilled, domestic, and service-type occupations (Kinnaird and Hall 1994, 1996), especially where they mirror functions carried out in the home. This is reinforced by assumptions that if the best jobs and highest rewards are linked to an accumulation of human capital, women are inevitably disadvantaged because their process of accumulation is interrupted by marriage, birth, and child rearing (Coppock, Haydon, and Richter 1995).

Gender stereotyping is evident and sex segregation at different levels of employment activity is apparent within the hotel and catering industry, for example. Women work as unskilled, low-paid counter and kitchen staff, domestics, and cleaners, while men work as porters and stewards, but a high proportion of men employed in the industry are in professional, managerial, or supervisory positions (Rees and Fielder 1992). Certainly, in the southern fringes of the region much of women's work lies outside the realm of wage labor in forms of work that include homeworking, unpaid domestic and caring labor, family help, and/or informal work in tourism or personal services. Stratigaki and Vaiou (1994) argue that the bulk of women's work cannot therefore be adequately appreciated and evaluated by looking exclusively at formal employment categories in officially recorded statistical data.

Early advocates of tourism as a strategy of modernization viewed tourism employment as a positive way of integrating underprivileged subgroups into the mainstream economy, and low-skilled jobs were viewed as good opportunities for women and ethnic minorities. However, these notions merely echo stereotyped sexist and racist ideologies and reinforce the social stratification systems present (de Kadt 1979). They also create overt gender and ethnic divisions of labor within the tourism industry (Britton 1991).

Reinforcement of the gender divisions of labor are not always interpreted pessimistically, however. In Greece, host to large numbers of migrants from neighboring former communist countries, women have gained wage-earning opportunities through the development of tourism cooperatives (Castelberg-Koulma 1991). The work has enabled women to gain more independence and move their traditional domestic labor into the public domain. In such cases, changing gender relations are evident as women work and earn publicly and gain an element of financial autonomy. This is so despite the fact that the nature of the work does not appear to threaten prevailing gender roles and can be accommodated within the prevailing sexual division of labor.

Such attractions for Western investors as access to trained labor, relatively low wages, minimum regulatory powers, and encouragement from official agencies are variable across the region. The best-trained labor and most sophisticated market tastes can be found in Central Europe, where there is often intense competition for qualified labor, a situation appropriately educated and trained women can turn to their advantage. Regulatory controls may be least effective in the Balkans and the Commonwealth of Independent States (CIS), where lower levels of disposable income, economic and infrastructural development, and continuing political uncertainty have not inspired confidence in potential investors and visitors. In such labor markets, which may anyway suffer most explicitly from traditional male attitudes, women are likely to have fewer opportunities to command good positions and salaries.

Focus on Rural Tourism

Rural tourism is a potential major growth area in CEE, offering opportunities for both employment and self-determination among the region's rural women, whether it be in the provision of bed-and-breakfast accommodation, farm-based attractions, or setting up new small and medium enterprises (SMEs). The issue of employment provision for rural women in general has only recently begun to be addressed in any systematic way across the region (Petrin 1996; Kulcsar and Verbole 1997). Women make up the majority of the region's rural population and represent the oldest age groups, but the situation and status of farm women varies across the region. For example, Slovenian agricultural extension officers have identified two distinct groups of farm women: "independent" and "traditional" (Verbole and Mele-Petric 1996). The former enjoy equal status with men (their fathers, husbands, brothers, or sons), or have a slightly privileged status. In terms of property, these women live on smaller farms that are engaged in such supplementary activities as tourism. Male family members are usually employed outside the farm (if no other sources of income are available). Women are employed at home and have their own regular or occasional income. These women make their own decisions or actively participate in making all decisions concerning the farm and its enterprises, the family, and the home. They organize their own work, such as agrotourism, and enjoy more free time than traditional farm women.

Traditional farm women do not enjoy equal status with their male relatives in the household nor on the farm. In this group, the men usually work exclusively on the farm and outside employment is rare. The women usually make decisions that concern the household and children. Because of their economic dependence on husbands or other male relatives, they are often perceived as a source of labor that may or may not be appreciated within the family. The women from this group are limited or even restrained from decision making regarding the issues related to the farm and any additional activity, such as tourism. Husbands usually even reserve the right to manage the household funds, and also manage their wives' free time and their social and other activities.

Problems of rural women in CEE connected to social and political change have been related to structural levers on independence and autonomy (Siiskonen 1996). In many CEE countries the rural social infrastructure was connected with the communist agricultural production system; giving up the state and cooperative farms led to the loss of social services such as kindergarten, as well as health and maternity care provided by state and cooperative farms. Cultural activities similarly connected with the state and cooperative farms have also been lost. There has been a reinforcement of the male-dominated decision-making culture at both the local and national levels, and the role of rural women in public life is weak. This is reinforced in the Catholic countries, where women are not able to be elected to church organizations, which may act as a major foundation of rural social life and control. Levels of education in rural areas tends to be low. There is a need for rural women to be trained in new technologies and business development. There are often problems with communication, as there is a lack of telephones in rural areas and distances are long.

Development programs for rural women have increased in recent years. The Estonian Farmers' Union has a special training program for rural women; in Poland the Village Housewives' Training Organization provides a number of opportunities for rural women, while the Foundation for the Development of Polish Agriculture (FDPA) has a Women in Rural Enterprise Development Program (WRED). In Slovakia there are Food and Agriculture Organization (FAO) projects on management, while in Slovenia (Trebnje) the FAO and the European Commission on Agriculture have had a training project on rural entrepreneurship and, most recently, projects organized by the Action Plan for Coordination Aid to Poland and Hungary (PHARE) (Siiskonen 1996). All have implicitly supported diversification into tourism, although only recently has this been viewed as an appropriate vehicle for rural women's economic development.

Such areas as Romania's Danube Delta, one of Europe's most important wildlife habitats (now subject to conservation and protection) have required considerable effort to involve the local population in processes of sustainable development and planning. Employment and income-generating processes such as the recruitment of park wardens and the encouragement of hosting bed-and-breakfast type accommodations have been pursued, particularly in an attempt to prevent local communities from feeling that their livelihoods are threatened by conservation designations (Hall 1993). Women have been an important catalyst in this process, both as agents of development training and encouragement and as the target for education programs, although political impediments have been significant.

In Albania women have been targeted, through the employment of participatory rural appraisal (PRA) in small-scale "community-based sustainable" rural tourism projects sponsored by the United Kingdom, the Dutch (Pelgrom 1997), and foreign organizations in conjunction with local NGOs. Such schemes have aimed to reduce the danger of villages becoming impoverished in the backwash of large-scale coastal tourism development by strengthening local economic and social structures and encouraging financial institutions to support small, rural "self-help" schemes (Fisher 1996). Encouragement of the local ownership of accommodation for small numbers of implicitly high-value, low-impact rural tourists has been pursued, but community involvement and ownership of development schemes is inhibited by the legacy of almost half a century of centralized, top-down civil administration, which has afforded local people minimal experience of bottom-up development or of genuine opportunities to participate in meaningful local decision making. This has been superimposed upon a tradition of male dominance, thereby doubly subjugating women in decision-making processes.

The pursuit of such projects raises important questions concerning social sustainability in small developing countries. In "ecotourism" projects, for example, the promoters emphasize that the lack of local infrastructure offers a pristine, uncommercialized environment that appeals to niche rural tourists. Yet residents, and especially women, participating in such projects may offer their support on the assumption that tourism will help improve their local infrastructures and services (such as clean water supply, piped-sewage disposal facilities, electricity, an access road, and telecommunications), and thereby reduce their daily burden.

WOMEN AS CONSUMERS OF TOURISM

Women with families rarely have a holiday, even as tourists (Deem 1986). The domestic, unpaid working role continues and is exacerbated when self-catering, unserviced accommodation modes are used, as is the case with much CEE domestic and international tourism. Women are likely to be less influential in decisions over the nature, location, and timing of a holiday if men consider themselves to be the wage earner paying for it. Thus, not only is women's domestic work unwaged, but by the very nature of that financial nonrecognition it is also demoted, with significant power implications for household decisions, including those determining tourism experiences. Increasing private ownership of motor vehicles in CEE may further emphasize gender-role polarization in tourism consumption, whereby men drive and are thus in control, while women undertake the repetitive domestic chores of looking after the children, preparing food, and cleaning. When male "control" is undermined, as when confronted by an unfamiliar culture or language, having to cope with a challenging waiter, or getting lost, domestic tensions rapidly intensify, and women often carry the burden of diplomatic resolution. Although rarely documented, there is a rich vein of empirical material waiting to be tapped in the region on the impacts of "transition" on such relationships and experiences.

As a symbol of post-socialist "freedoms" opening up the potential for travel both within and out of the countries of the region, the pursuit of tourism by the region's inhabitants has, of course, been constrained by financial circumstances. For access to domestic tourism, ability to pay has become the major criterion, further influenced by national and local inflation, loss of subsidies, and the imposition of often high rates of value added tax (VAT). Privatization and subsidy removal for domestic tourism accommodation and transport has reduced the level of formal domestic tourism in a number of countries, although this structural change in supply has been counterbalanced by the easier availability of private transport mobility and removal of administrative constraints on internal movement, substantially modifying domestic patterns of demand.

Although a wide range of niche tourism activities have been developed and promoted for both international and domestic markets, there is relatively little evidence to suggest the specific targeting of women as consumers. For example, Hungary, Slovenia, and Poland (Marciszewska and Wyznikiewicz-Nawracala 1996) provide equestrian holidays that tend to be more popular with women and girls, yet overall there appears to have been little explicit development of gender targeting and segmentation of gender-related niche markets in the promotion of the region's specialist tourism products.

With an increase in crime in the region, relating to a range of changing socioeconomic and political circumstances (Alejziak 1996), women tourists would appear to be more likely potential targets than either local women or male tourists for crimes against the person, ranging from petty theft to rape. But again, little analysis appears to have taken place to indicate if such a hypothesis can be sustained, or, if it can, what measures have been undertaken to address it (e.g., Bach 1996, 288).

In terms of outbound travel and tourism, the "Iron Curtain" has been replaced by a "Dollar Curtain" lowered by Western host countries in fear of a flood of Eastern migrants. Although the need to secure exit visas from home countries normally no longer exists, hard currency entry visas, often costing more than a month's income, are still required by some Western governments for citizens of several of the region's countries. Two trends have been evident in outbound travel from the region: (1) a considerable reduction of the "euphoric" mobility of the early post-communist months, and (2) a nonetheless strong continuing growth in outbound travel from some of the more developed Central European states, suggesting a "rejuvenation" of the mass-tourism product cycle.

Indeed, an early characteristic of post-communist restructuring and privatization processes within the tourism industry of the more advanced CEE countries was the rapid growth of travel agents and holiday companies, both responding to Western niche segmentation, but more particularly providing Mediterranean coast packages for the region's consumers (Hall 1998b). For example, some 10,000 Czech tourists took charter flights out of Prague in the summer of 1994 to Croatian coast resorts. With a long-term consolidation of CEE's economic stability and standards of living, increasing numbers of households will raise their levels of mobility and access to international travel, a process that, nonetheless, will be both socially and spatially uneven. Indeed, by the mid-1990s outbound travel rates for Central European countries ranged between four-fifths and four-and-a-half times the equivalent of the countries' own population sizes, but the rates for Bulgaria and Romania in Southeastern Europe, were just under half the population size equivalent (World Tourism Organization 1996; Hall 1998a).

For Bulgarians at least, with shopping and visiting friends and relatives (VFRs) the most important elements, a "neighborhood" pattern, involving short-distance cross-border travel, has been recognized (Bachvarov 1997). Certainly, this factor is also significant across a number of "traditional" borders, such as Russia–Poland, and those of a more recent political nature, such as the Czech–Slovak division. Substantial cross-border shopping and petty trading activity is carried on as a result of differences in national or local laws, taxes, prices, and goods availability, or in national attitudes and customs, although this was a trend initiated before the fall of communism.

CONCLUSION

This chapter has indicated that although conflicting interpretations exist, a wide range of evidence indicates that women in post-communist CEE appear to be variously disadvantaged in their tourism-producer roles and access to those roles, compared to men. But national, local, cultural, educational, and status differences place some women at greater disadvantage than others. Most status equality and social-welfare provisions that existed to support women in employment under communism has been largely removed, and the international ownership of the tourism industry appears to have little regard for the social welfare of its employees of either gender.

The position of women as consumers relates perhaps much more closely to domestic (family) relationships. Although domestic tourism and recreation has been marketized and opportunities of access to the formerly subsidized services have decreased for many, theoretical improvements in opportunities for travel have increased access to international tourism. In terms of their domestic family relations and responsibilities, when on holiday women's positions are unlikely to have improved. Indeed, with the greater likelihood of opting for self-catering, unserviced types of accommodation because of cost considerations, many CEE women's positions of access to "leisure" while on holiday are likely to have deteriorated.

Several measures are required to ameliorate women's employment status in the region if CEE's economic and social potential, notwithstanding human rights issues, are to be realized. These embrace women as both producers and potential consumers of tourism (Weiner 1997, 497): (1) improved collection of data and information pertaining to women, (2) attention by employment-service providers to the specific needs of women, (3) design of training and retraining programs with due consideration of the constraints and incentives for women, (4) government provision of nonprofit child-care facilities or the subsidization of private child-care facilities, (5) specialized training and access to credit in order to encourage women's entrepreneurial activity (6) assertiveness and leadership training, particularly for women managers and entrepreneurs, (7) labor union advocacy for equity in male and female work wages, (8) organization of political parties and groups that advocate for legislation and policy reform relevant to women's issues, and (9) empowerment through networking among women, nationally and internationally. The pivotal role of tourism in this process places considerable responsibility on the industry's managers.

REFERENCES

Alejziak, W. (1996). Tourism and the crime rate in Poland. In *Tourism in Central and Eastern Europe: Educating for Quality*, edited by G. Richards. Tilburg, The Netherlands: Tilburg University Press.

Aslanbeigui, N., S. Pressman, and G. Summerfield. (1994). Women and economic transformation. In *Women in the Age of Economic Transformation: Gender Impact of Reforms in Post-Socialist and Developing Countries*, edited by N. Aslanbeigui, S. Pressman, and G. Summerfield. London: Routledge.

Bach, S. A. (1996). Tourist-related crime and the hotel industry: A review of the literature and related materials. In *Tourism, Crime and International Security Issues*, edited by A. Pizam and Y. Mansfeld. Chichester: Wiley.

Bachvarov, M. (1997). End of the model? Tourism in post-communist Bulgaria. *Tourism Management* 18 (1): 43–50.

Bacon, W. M., and L. G. Pol. (1994). The economic status of women in Romania. In *Women in the Age of Economic Transformation: Gender Impact of Reforms in Post-Socialist and Developing Countries*, edited by N. Aslanbeigui, S. Pressman, and G. Summerfield. London: Routledge.

Beneria, L., and S. Feldman, eds. (1992). *Unequal Burden: Economic Crises, Persistent Poverty and Women's Work*. Boulder, Colo.: Westview Press.

Britton, S. (1991). Tourism, capital and place: Towards a critical geography. *Environment and Planning* D9: 451–478.

Buckley, M., ed. (1997). *Post-Soviet Women: From the Baltic to Central Asia*. Cambridge: Cambridge University Press.

Castelberg-Koulma, M. (1991). Greek women and tourism: Women's cooperatives as an alternative form of organisation. In *Working Women*, edited by N. Redclift and M. T. Sinclair. London: Routledge.

Coppock, V., D. Haydon, and I. Richter. (1995). *The Illusions of "Post-Feminism": New Women, Old Myths*. London: Taylor and Francis.

Corrin, C., ed. (1992). *Super Women and the Double Burden*. London: Scarlet Press.

Debbage, K. G., and P. Daniels. (1998). The tourist industry and economic geography: Missed opportunities. In *The Economic Geography of the Tourist Industry*, edited by D. Ioannides and K. G. Debbage. London: Routledge.

de Kadt, E., ed. (1979). *Tourism—Passport to Development?: Perspectives on the Social and Cultural Effects of Tourism in Developing Countries*. New York: Oxford University Press.

Deem, R. (1986). *All Work and No Play? A Study of Women and Leisure*. Milton Keynes, England: Open University Press.

Edmundson, L., ed. (1992). *Women and Society in Russia and the Soviet Union*. Cambridge: Cambridge University Press.

Einhorn, B. (1991). Where have all the women gone? Women and the Women's Movement in East Central Europe. *Feminist Review* 39: 16–37.

Einhorn, B. (1993). *Cinderella Goes to Market: Citizenship, Gender and Women's Movements in East Central Europe*. New York: Verso.

Fischer, G., and G. Standing, eds. (1993). *Structural Change in Central and Eastern Europe: Labour Market and Social Policy Implications*. Paris: Organization for Economic Cooperation and Development.

Fisher, D. (1996). Sustainable tourism in southern Albania. *Albanian Life* 59: 27–29.

Fodor, E. (1997). Gender in transition: Unemployment in Hungary, Poland and Slovakia. *East European Politics and Society* 11: 470–500.

Fong, M., and G. Paull. (1993). Women's economic status in the restructuring of Eastern Europe. In *Democratic Reform and the Position of Women in Transitional Economies*, edited by V. M. Moghadam. Oxford: Clarendon Press.

Graham, A., and J. Regulska. (1997). Expanding political space for women in Poland. *Communist and Post-Communist Studies* 30 (1): 65–82.

Hall, D. R. (1984). Foreign tourism under socialism: The Albanian "Stalinist" model. *Annals of Tourism Research* 11: 539–555.

Hall, D. R. (1993). Ecotourism in the Danube Delta. *Tourist Review* 3: 11–13.

Hall, D. R. (1998a). Central and Eastern Europe. In *Tourism and Economic Development in Europe*, edited by A. M. Williams and G. Shaw. Chichester: Wiley.

Hall, D. R. (1998b). Tourism development and sustainability issues in Central and South-Eastern Europe. *Tourism Management* 19 (5): 423–431.

Hall, D. R., ed. (1991). *Tourism and Economic Development in Eastern Europe and the Soviet Union*. London: Belhaven Press; New York: Halsted Press.

Holmes, L. (1997). *Post-Communism*. Cambridge: Polity Press.

Johnson, M. (1997). Hungary's hotel industry in transition, 1960–1996. *Tourism Management* 18 (7): 441–452.

Kinnaird, V. H., and D. R. Hall. (1996). Understanding tourism processes: A gender-aware framework. *Tourism Management* 17 (2): 95–102.

Kinnaird, V. H., and D. R. Hall, eds. (1994). *Tourism: A Gender Analysis*. Chichester: Wiley.

Kotowska, I. E. (1995). Discrimination against women in the labor market in Poland during the transition to a market economy. *Social Politics* 2: 76–90.

Kulcsar, L., and A. Verbole. (1997). *National Action Plans for the Integration of Rural Women in Development: Case Studies in Hungary and Slovenia.* Rome: Food and Agriculture Organization of the United Nations.

Lakhova, Y. (1998). Transition—a mixed blessing for women. *Transition* (26 February): 25–26.

Marciszewska, B., and A. Wyznikiewicz-Nawracala. (1996). The relationship between tourism products and demand: The example of equestrian tourism. In *Tourism in Central and Eastern Europe: Educating for Quality,* edited by G. Richards. Tilburg, The Netherlands: Tilburg University Press.

Medvedev, K. (1998, February 26). A review of women's emancipation in Hungary: Limited successes offer some hope. *Transition* (26 February).

Ners, K. (1992). *Moving Beyond Assistance: Final Report of the IEWS Task Force on Western Assistance to Transition in the Czech and Slovak Federal Republics, Hungary and Poland.* Boulder, Colo.: Westview Press.

Pearson, R. (1991). Questioning perestroika: A socialist-feminist interrogation. *Feminist Review* 39 (Fall): 91–96.

Pelgrom, H. (1997). *SNV: At Home in the South.* The Hague: SNV Netherlands Development Organisation.

Petrin, T. (1996). *Basic Facts on Rural Women in Selected Central European Countries.* Rome: Food and Agriculture Organization of the United Nations.

Rees, G., and S. Fielder. (1992). The services economy, subcontracting and the new employment relations: Contract catering and cleaning. *Employment and Society* 6: 347–368.

Rudolph, H., E. Appelbaum, and F. Maier. (1994). Beyond socialism: The uncertain prospects for East German women in a unified Germany. In *Women in the Age of Economic Transformation: Gender Impact of Reforms in Post-Socialist and Developing Countries,* edited by N. Aslanbeigui, S. Pressman, and G. Summerfield. London: Routledge.

Siiskonen, P. (1996). *Overview of the Socio-Economic Position of Rural Women in Selected Central and Eastern European Countries.* Rome: Food and Agriculture Organization of the United Nations.

Siklova, J. (1994). *The Gender Consequence of Political and Economic Reform.* Warsaw: Social Science Research Council, Social Bases of Liberalization.

Standing, G. (1989). Global feminization through flexible labor. *World Development* 17: 1077–1095.

Stratigaki, M., and D. Vaiou. (1994). Women's work and informal activities in southern Europe. *Environment and Planning* A26 (8): 1221–1234.

Swain, M. B., ed. (1995). Gender in tourism. *Annals of Tourism Research* 22 (2).

Szalai, J. (1991). Some aspects of the changing situation of women in Hungary. *Journal of Women in Culture and Society* 1991: 152–170.

United Nations. (1992). *The Impact of Economic and Political Reform on the Status of Women in Eastern Europe.* Vienna: Proceedings of a United Nations Regional Seminar.

Verbole, A., and M. Mele-Petric. (1996). *National Action Plan for Integration of Farm and Rural Women in Development: a Case Study of Slovenia.* Wageningen: Food and Agriculture Organization Workshop.

Weiner, E. (1997). Assessing the implications of political and economic reform in the post-socialist era: The case of Czech and Slovak women. *East European Quarterly* 31: 473–502.

Weyr, T. (1992). Women's economic hardship in Albania. *Albanian Life* 2: 24.

Williamson, A. (1992). Bringing down the other iron curtain. *The European*, 4 June, 12.

World Tourism Organization. (1996). *Compendium of Tourism Statistics 1990–1994*. 16th ed. Madrid: Author.

World Travel and Tourism Council/Wharton Econometric Forecasting Associates. (1997). *Travel and Tourism—Jobs for the Millennium*. London: Author.

Part IV

WOMEN AND TOURISM:
NEW DIRECTIONS

10

Women and Mountain Tourism: Redefining the Boundaries of Policy and Practice

Scott Walker, Georgia Valaoras,
Dibya Gurung, and Pam Godde

Over the past century and continuing in the present, global tourism has been changing in such a way to include the participation of women. From the World Tourism Organization's Global Code of Ethics for Tourism, which supports the "equality of men and women" (World Tourism Organization 1998) in tourism activities, to the founding of women-only tourism organizations, women are increasingly finding it easier to partake in tourism activities as both consumers and producers. Worldwide, women are forging the opportunities and means to expand their destinations of travel to include developing countries and regions, a phenomenon not so long ago considered rare and, in many regions, once impossible. Further, involvement in the production of tourism is expanding to include women in developing regions, most notably women restricted from social interaction by cultural norms. With current tourism trends beginning to favor small-scale infrastructure and nature- and culture-based activities, women in developing regions, who generally have lower education and literacy levels, are able to participate in tourism production. As such, women from around the world and across varying socioeconomic niches are coming into contact with one another. Such interchange is particularly important for the advancement of women in developing regions, as it can change the attitudes and lives of women, and by extension, societal attitudes toward women.

Regionally speaking, mountains constitute a significant portion of the developing places in the world. They also provide resources essential to human existence both upstream and downstream, including water, timber, and medicinal plants. Despite these resources, communities in mountain regions tend to lack the same levels of health, education, and information that lowland communities have, simply due to their isolation. Limited access to mountain regions has allowed villages to generally maintain certain cultural norms throughout time, but has also restricted development. As such, mountain regions are becoming the destination of choice among many tourists, including women. This in part has come about through the belief that travel, including adventure travel in mountain regions, allows women to face challenges and enhance their confidence and self-esteem (e.g., Mindspring Enterprise 1998, 11). All-women's travel organizations (such as Adventure Women Inc., which arranges mountain trips specifically for women) and gender-sensitive travel organizations (such as the Chhetri Sisters Guest House in Pokhara, Nepal, which links female trekkers with female porters) lend to the attraction of women traveling in mountain areas.

Undoubtedly, women from the industrialized world constitute the majority of guests in mountain regions; however, in some cases even women from developing mountain regions are gaining the ability to travel. For example, in Makalu-Barun, Nepal, a national nongovernment organization facilitates study tours for villagers involved in tourism enterprises. Women who travel on such tours learn about tourism production from other women (Banskota in Godde 1999). While this is but a single case, and it is based on study tourism through the intervention of external organizations as opposed to adventure tourism, it is significant in its demonstration of the potential that tourism has for broadening women's experiences and confidence.

A shift in global attitudes toward the advancement of women is also helping to bring about active participation from women in the production of mountain tourism. Women in mountain villages have long been engaged in tourism in ways that overlap with their domestic responsibilities; they provide home-cooked meals and hospitality for guests staying in their homes, and during seasons when men migrate from villages for work or military duty, women are largely responsible for the care of tourists. However, not until the latter years of the second millenium have increasing numbers of women been gaining the knowledge, skill, and confidence to create enterprises across mountain regions and to transform domestic production into public earning. This has in part been facilitated by national and international

NGOs that provide training to women, and by funding agencies that allocate funds to women's causes. It has also been facilitated by recent qualitative research on women and tourism, which has led to a greater understanding of the effects tourism can have on the lives of women and the contributions women make through tourism. Our present understanding of the situation, however, has only recently come about and remains limited. The delay in this understanding may partially be related to the present emphasis on alternative forms of tourism, for as Kinnaird, Kothari, and Hall (1994, 2) acknowledged, the emphasis on special-interest tourism, ecotourism, and alternative tourism leads to a risk of overlooking other dimensions of tourism, such as gender divisions and family relations. Publications and policy reports that address the importance of women in mountain tourism in less developed mountain regions of the world, specifically in community-based mountain tourism and ecotourism (e.g., Gurung 1995; Rao 1998; Godde 1999; Lama 1999), reveal much about the current situation of women's work and women's status when tourism is introduced into a mountain region. However, they also reveal a greater need to continue research and advocacy in this area. This is especially true when considered alongside Byers and Sainju's (1994) acknowledgment that despite the growing awareness of women's environmental concerns, "Women have become poorer and have progressively lost control over even a bare subsistence base of resources" (p. 214).

Considering that tourism is one of the fastest growing industries in the world, it becomes clear that women directly and indirectly generate a significant portion of the world's economy through their production and consumption of tourism-based enterprises. The rise of new economies in mountain regions, including tourism, is largely dependent on the participation of women. Yet the value of women as contributors or as essential players in the production and consumption of mountain-based economies, including tourism, is often overlooked. Similarly, the changes tourism brings to the lives of women who consume and produce tourism, and by extension the entire community, are seldom taken into consideration in mountain policy or planning.

Policies and programs aimed at improving the situation need to be gender sensitive to bring about greater participation, and in some cultures, empowerment. As Lama (1999) notes in her study of participatory appreciative approaches to village tourism planning among women of Langtang National Park in Nepal, the understanding and awareness of women's roles in mountain socioeconomic structures, including specific forms of environmental management, household management, and tourism-based enterprises, can lead to greater gender sensitivity in policy and programs and, by extension, close the gender gaps in participation.

While it is important to understand the role women play in consuming tourism, for the purpose of advancing women in developing mountain regions we must begin by understanding how women produce tourism. For this reason, this chapter looks primarily at women as producers of mountain tourism, and it does so through the lens of three case studies. It locates the various challenges to the advancement of women in mountain regions through tourism enterprise opportunities. Most specifically, it argues that policy objectives need to refocus on the role women play in tourism enterprise opportunities. Such policy objectives further need to consider the gender relations predominant in a region, changes in these relations that are likely to occur with new policy implementation, and the effects these changes may have on the existing social infrastructure.

WOMEN AND TOURISM ENTERPRISE

The following three stories from the field explore the various ways in which mountain women produce tourism and how men and women mediate their gendered roles and relations when tourism enterprises are brought into a society. They show that while women balance their traditional domestic roles with public enterprises and while they adjust the traditional divisions of labor, mountain women are still often restricted by social boundaries common in rural mountain regions. However, these stories also show the potential that tourism production offers women in crossing these boundaries.

The research described in this chapter is based upon extensive long-term fieldwork, with a variety of methods including participant observation, interviews, and questionnaires. The areas for study were selected to reflect the diversity of rural tourism and gender roles in economically disadvantaged mountain areas throughout the world. While Greece is not a developing country, the rural mountain regions therein are economically less advantaged than their lowland counterparts, suffering from lack of facilities and lower educational levels. For this reason, it is included in the study.

Women and the Production of Mountain Tourism

Annapurna, Nepal

The region of Annapurna, named after an Indian harvest goddess, has been a major agricultural area throughout time, providing a subsistence-based economy to the many villages at the foot of the Annapurna range. Women in these villages have long grown up with domestic responsibilities that remain with them throughout life. Securing food, water, fuel, and clothing all play a part in the daily life of village women. During periods when men temporarily migrate for military service, these responsibilities increase. Women then must take full responsibility for the care of family.

Traditionally, clear gender roles and division of labor dictate day-to-day life. Women are responsible for managing the household activities, including cooking, cleaning, and child care, with occasional assistance from men. Both men and women are involved in activities outside the home, such as farming and fuel-wood and fodder collection, but only men are involved in plowing the fields. Nonetheless, most of these outdoor activities are carried out by the men and women from the occupational caste.[1]

Household decisions rest primarily with the men, yet women are given some say in domestic matters. Due to poverty, lower-caste women often accompany the men in their work or take jobs outside their homes to supplement family income, increasing their physical mobility throughout the village and, thus, their status within the family. Gurung, Thakali, Manangi, and Mustangi women are also given some voice in domestic matters, yet while mobility outside the home is curtailed, these women do not share the same status within the domestic realm as their lower-caste counterparts. At the community level, however, women from most castes and ethnic groups have little or no role in decision making, and their participation in community activities is very low. Ironically, however, the majority of the economically active and permanent residents are women.

Since the 1960s and particularly the 1970s, when tourism to the Annapurna region became a more prominent phenomenon, women from most castes and ethnic groups have been given opportunities to expand their work experience, from the Sherpanis who work as porters for trekkers and mountain climbers (Blum 1980, 30) to the women of upper castes who run lodges and teashops. Initially, the more affluent families were not involved in tourism, as they considered the job to be degrading, especially as it entailed washing foreigners' dishes and letting them stay in their houses. But as the tourism industry has become attractive in terms of the money and free time it can bring, the affluent families have become involved. With the increased influx of tourism, women have become more heavily involved and have slowly started shifting away from agricultural work to tourism. Their involvement also has increased from cooking and cleaning to general management responsibilities, which has led to greater interaction with tourists. Today, about 60 percent of the total trekkers visiting Nepal come to the Annapurna region, with its roughly 480 lodges (Nepal 1990) and teashops. The lodges and teashops form the main enterprises, with some diversification through other types of enterprises, such as handicrafts (carpet weaving and nettle-fiber products), vegetable farming, alcohol brewing, food processing, and petty trade. Women manage the majority of these enterprises and there are a growing number of women owners. However, with restricted control over a family's income, women face limitations in starting enterprises independently.

With the introduction of trekking tourism in the Nepali hills and mountains, along with development and conservation initiatives initiated by the government, local committees, and nongovernmental and international organizations, the lives of the people in the local communities, particularly women, have undergone tremendous changes in the past few decades. It has been convenient for women to enter the trekking tourism business, as the majority of the enterprises are lodges and teahouses, which are seen as extensions of their traditional roles (cooking, cleaning, and managing the household). In addition, the out-migration of most of the economically active male members has further provided opportunities for women to be involved in tourism-related activities. In general, trekking tourism has brought some positive changes, especially in the economic context. Nevertheless, the impact has been different for each woman in the community, depending upon her ethnicity, economic status, and geographical location within a village.

The economic opportunities provided by trekking tourism can be broadly divided into direct tourism-related activities (represented by lodges, teahouses, petty trade, and handicrafts), and indirect tourism-related activities (consisting of horticulture, fuel-wood selling, alcohol brewing, and livestock and poultry farming). Between both the direct and indirect tourism-related activities in Annapurna, lodge ownership generates the highest revenue, followed by teashops. Since lodges require a substantial capital outlay, most are owned by the community's affluent sector, who are usually the families of Gurkha soldiers, wealthy farmers, or families of men working overseas. Only very few people from the occupational caste and lower-income groups own or manage lodges.[2] On the other hand, men and women from lower-income groups, occupational castes, and the off-trekking routes are mainly involved in teashops, petty trade, alcohol brewing, horticulture, and handicrafts businesses. In comparison to the lodges and teashops, other enterprises are not well developed and, thus, women who work in these enterprises are not able to fully participate in and benefit from trekking tourism. While the work of NGOs, such as the King Mahendra Trust for Nature Conservation (through such projects as the Annapurna Conservation Area Project), has facilitated the building of community-based local institutions in which women are given a voice (Sharma in Godde 1999), the disparity between various groups of women as well as between men and women in general remains clear.

Alta Cima, Mexico

The area surrounding the mountain community of Alta Cima, Mexico, had been an ecotourism destination long before the word "ecotourism" was coined. Alta Cima sits in Mexico's northernmost cloud forest, a primary destination for loggers in the state of Tamaulipas until the mid-1980s. In 1985 the state government declared 144,530 hectares (356,442 acres) of mountainous forest El Cielo Biosphere Reserve, a state-operated reserve, protecting it from destruction by commercial logging ventures. This declaration brought logging as well as jobs and economic opportunities in the area to a halt. Sergio Medellín Morales, president of Terra Nostra, a local social and environmental NGO, wrote, "The Reserve was looked upon with sore eyes by the community" (Medellín Morales and González Romo 1999, 3). This was despite the fact that the United Nations Education, Scientific, and Cultural Organization (UNESCO) designated the reserve a Man and the Biosphere (MAB) reserve.

In a 1995 study the overall unemployment rate in cash-producing jobs in the *ejido*, or autonomous community, of Alta Cima was 70 percent (Walker 1996). Men and women alike had little opportunity for employment. The seasonal work for men consisted primarily of harvesting wild *palmilla* (Chamaedorea radicalis), a plant used in floral arrangements (Medellín Morales and Contreras 1994). Women, on the other hand, traditionally tended to household tasks. An average family income was $17 per month. During the winter months, when *palmilla* is not as suitable for harvest, the men rented their burros as pack animals for tourists, leading to roughly $10 per month income per household directly resulting from tourism. By contrast, women in this rural mountain region had no involvement in the cash economy.

However, during this same period the situation was changing. In 1993 Terra Nostra implemented a community-development program in the *ejido*. The program began with a series of facilitated workshops directed toward establishing the community's demography and history, charting their work (growing season, harvest time, and so on), and mapping out their problems and proposing potential solutions to their plight. From this series of problem and solution exercises they developed project proposals designed to both enhance the quality of life in Alta Cima and to conserve the natural resources that attracted tourists (Medellín Morales and Contreras 1994). The first project to be realized was the Ecotienda La Fé (the Faith Eco Store), developed and operated by a newly formed cooperative of twelve women in the community with funding from international grantors. The original idea was to capture business of local tourists by selling sodas and handmade items such as tablecloths, embroidered t-shirts, fruit preserves, and natural wines. Shortly thereafter the women built a simple kitchen and began offering meals in a *palapa*, a large dirt-floored, tin-roofed shed with no sides. With no other place for tourists to escape downpours or to eat or drink, the project was a great success and has since become a gathering point for tourists.

Today, the restaurant and *ecotienda* have improved facilities; the *palapa* is now a screened-in, concrete-floored restaurant with a greatly expanded kitchen. Previously the kitchen had one chimneyless wood-burning stove. Smoke filled the lantern-lit room and soot collected on the walls and assuredly in the lungs of the women and their children who stay with them during the day. Now the women have a healthier four-burner gas stove. They have fluorescent light powered by photovoltaic cells and the nearby outhouses are no longer used, as they've been replaced by separate men's and women's toilets with running water. Twelve women from the approximately twenty-five households in Alta Cima are employed in the cooperative. Their ages range from fifteen to sixty-three years, with most of them in the thirty-one to forty-year-old age range. Ten of the women are married and one is a single mother of two daughters, one of whom has a severe mental handicap.

Resulting from the ideas and capacity-building workshops that began in 1993, the cooperative, *El Grupo de Mujeres de Alta Cima*, has created a series of successful projects. These projects include the Restaurant Natura, the Ecotienda La Fé, the management of a captive population of threatened avifuana, a nursery growing and selling native ornamental plants, and environmental interpretation programs.

The co-op has encouraged the development of other working groups of men and women in El Cielo (Medellín Morales and González Romo 1999). The women of the co-op now work directly with other women within the reserve to organize and implement collaborative development projects beyond the reach of most tourists' travel. Moreover, the women reflect their leadership abilities by serving on regional organizing and resource-management committees, an unheard-of proposition only a few years ago in a male-dominated society. The confidence and self-esteem brought out by their successful programs has allowed this group of women to break the rural "glass ceiling" in Mexico with confidence.

Upland Greece

Over the last 100 years Greece has experienced profound demographic changes that especially affected the role of women. For thousands of years Greeks lived on mountainous terrain, which covers over 75 percent of the country's territory (Ministry of the Environment 1995), in villages that based their survival on subsistence agriculture and receipts from trade and emigration (Valaoras 1976). Women in these traditional societies were mostly illiterate, with large families and with much of the responsibility for managing the food, water, clothing, fuel wood, and other necessities required for survival. In the villages, as men emigrated abroad or spent many months of the year as merchants and traders in the Balkans and the rest of Europe, the women were in effect the heads of households and caretakers of the extended families that lived together in mountain hamlets (Sfikas 1991).

Wars, emigration, and urbanization emptied the mountain villages of their population. Between 1961 and 1971 the rate of decline was as high as 2 percent per year. Young people moved to the cities and towns, leaving only the aging population (Valaoras 1980). A drop in the birthrates accompanied the dramatic decline in the rural population as women entered the workforce in urban areas and lost the support system necessary for raising large families (Valaoras 1980).

In the 1980s progressive legislation for women removed, at least on paper, the remaining relics of discrimination against women, a heritage of the long history of rural mountain life. The dowry was abolished and women had the right to own their inheritance as opposed to signing it over to their husbands. Salaries, pensions, and health benefits were raised to the level of their male counterparts. Despite these measures, many rural women continued to work long and hard hours as farm laborers, food preparers, small shopkeepers, and many other occupations in the context of family-owned enterprises, without fair compensation or benefits (Papagaroufali 1986).

Rural illiteracy rates for women in the postwar period were nearly five times higher than those for urban dwellers. These dropped dramatically after the 1950s from nearly 14 percent to less than 2 percent in 1975 (Valaoras 1980). However, it was still customary for women to end their formal education with secondary school at best. Training for any occupation beyond motherhood was not an option for women still living in the countryside.

In the mid-1980s the Greek state once again sought to address the plight of low wages and underemployment (in the sense of regularly paid salaries and benefits) of rural women by establishing and supporting women's cooperatives. Starting in 1983, five women's cooperatives were founded in the mountain villages of Prespa, Chios, Arachova, and Ambelakia, and the coastal town of Petra on the island of Lesvos. These were linked to an emerging form of tourism called agrotourism. Women of the cooperatives supplemented their farm income by hosting tourists in their homes and providing the opportunity to visitors to participate in agricultural activities, such as harvesting and preparing food and other agricultural products (Papagaroufali 1986; Tsartas and Thanopoulou 1994).

In the 1990s another form of women's cooperative played a significant role near protected natural areas with high biodiversity. Two such areas are Prespa National Park and Ramsar site in northwestern Greece and the Dadia–Soufli Forest Reserve in northeastern Greece, on the border of the River Evros. A characteristic of both sites is the relatively low level of development compared to other areas of Greece and the lack of basic services, such as hospitals, schools, or commercial activities.

On both sites, conservation bodies were founded by investments in public awareness, education, and basic conservation activities. Under joint partnership with local authorities and private nongovernmental organizations, these protected areas acquired the basic infrastructure to host ecotourism. Information centers, guided tours, scientific meetings, and volunteer activities were initiated, based on the support of the local people for food, lodging, and local transportation. Many of these services have been provided by women's cooperatives.

Women of all ages have since become involved in supporting and developing ecotourism. Older women assist in cleaning and preparing rooms, cooking, preparing and serving traditional meals, and reviving traditional handicrafts or food products such as jams, honey, herbs, or spices. These can be sold to visitors through the information centers or the guesthouses that host ecotourists, further supplementing their family incomes. Younger women have become trained as ecoguides and have organized volunteer groups, developed environmental-education programs for schoolchildren, and handled the administration and merchandising of local products.

Changes in the Lives of Women from Tourism Production

The production of tourism in the three mountain regions studied, along with external intervention from NGOs, has played a significant role in improving women's lives and empowering them. Though the level of impacts, especially in the context of providing economic opportunities to women, has been different for different social groups, the overall impact has been seemingly positive, most notably in the areas of (1) heightened self-esteem and status within family and community, (2) decrease or shift in workloads, (3) increased awareness of family health and education issues, (4) strengthening of women's groups and conservation efforts, and (5) greater input on policies and decision making.

Heightened Self-Esteem and Status within Family and Community

Tourism production in all three communities has led to women earning cash who traditionally had little or no dealing with a cash economy. This direct benefit of tourism production, while important to the economic security and stabilization of family incomes in communities relying on seasonal activities, has perhaps its most important benefit in the increase of women's self-esteem and status. This has come about largely through women's ability to transform the private, domestic economy into public earning, and, in some cases, through breaking down the traditional division of labor.

With regard to the women of Alta Cima, local biologist Claudia Guadálupe Romo (1999) states that in this rural setting the projects the women have successfully developed allow the "women's value to go up as men value the work the women have done," thus confirming Eusubia Berrones Benitez's (1999) assertion that the women's group "increases the women's confidence and benefits everyone in the community." And again, Sergio Medellín Morales reflected this theme when he wrote, "The women take higher levels of self-esteem and empowerment to the local and regional level" (Medellín Morales and González Romo 1999).

The brothers and husbands of the Alta Cima women support their wives and sisters working outside the home and outside of the traditional parameters of rural Mexican communities. According to Adelfio Serrano Garay (1999), husband of a co-op member, his wife "helps contribute money to the family to buy food and clothes," while both control the money. Where the average monthly household income was $17 in 1995 (Walker 1996), women now report monthly contributions to their families of up to $27 per month, increasing monthly household incomes to $44. This is over and above their husband's incomes, with the co-op member reporting average earnings of $16 per month.

The increase of value in women's work is also apparent among families of women in the Annapurna region who are actively involved in tourism enterprises. For the first time women's work has been accountable and given value, and more men are seen to be supporting and sharing household work, which to date has been exclusively "women's work." Because of the value added to women's production of tourism in Annapurna, women's status within the family and community has improved, although not as significantly as in the case of Alta Cima. Though the women of Annapurna are fully involved in the tourism enterprises, they still do not have full control over their income. While they control smaller investments in food, clothing, and household supplies, men still make the decisions regarding major investments, which is one reason women are handicapped in starting their own enterprises.

In the mountains of Greece the additional income generated by women's tourism production, which to some extent provides compensation to local people for certain restrictions in grazing, woodcutting, fishing, or other traditional activities, has transformed the attitudes of the local people toward the value of women's work. This is in part due to the fact that their villages have experienced a local reversal of the social, economic, and demographic decline character-istic of most rural areas, and instead have become poles of attraction for visitors from all over Greece. Yet the attitudes of men toward the newly acquired activities of women have been slow in changing. In the beginning women faced mistrust and disapproval from the men in their families and communities; namely fathers, husbands, or com-munity leaders who were approached for the necessary paperwork to allow the cooperatives to operate. The traditional role of women as wives and mothers remained the dominant model for women, and traditions die hard in rural areas. As women were able to organize themselves effectively with scarcely any support and began to apply for and receive training for skills related to visitor activities, the num-bers of visitors increased. As family incomes were supplemented with newly generated funds, men gradually acknowledged the benefits of women working part time outside the home, and began to actively support their involvement (Valaoras, Pistola, and Pistola 1999).

Shift in Workloads

Among other things, tourism production in the local rural settings of these three mountain regions has brought about a shift in the workloads and free time of women, largely dependent on the tradi-tional gender roles and division of labor within the culture of the com-munities. In the case of Annapurna, where women traditionally work the fields as well as tend to the family, women now feel that their workloads have decreased despite their work hours in tourism pro-duction. Women have expressed that with their involvement with the tourism-related activities they have been relieved from the drudgery of farm work. Also, the introduction of time-saving devices and the improvement in the basic infrastructure of the area brought about by tourism have contributed to extra time. Drinking-water facilities ei-ther in or close to homes, improved trails, and alternative sources of energy (kerosene stoves, improved cook stoves, gas ovens, electric cookers, solar water heaters), all of which comprise basic but essential tourism infrastructure, are some of the devices that have contributed considerably to decreasing workloads. On the other hand, the seasonal nature of the tourist season and the patterns of tourist arrival have also provided women with more free time for other activities.

Nevertheless, the shift in workload patterns brought about by tour-ism is not always for the better. For example, the case of Alta Cima suggests that in rural mountain regions where women's traditional roles tend to be in the domestic economy, the production of tourism services adds to their workload, as they are expected to maintain their traditional roles at the same time as they are managing cooperative enterprises. Two women were obligated to drop out of the cooperative in the early stages in Alta Cima due to workload increases, thus robbing these women of self-esteem benefits and the sociable nature of working with other women in a productive environment.

Increase in Awareness of Family Health and Education Issues

The exposure to training, the interaction with tourists, and the income earned have empowered the women in the three mountain regions and have made them aware about various issues, both at the household and community levels. In Annapurna women are found to give more emphasis to their family's and the community's health and sanitation, children's education, and other community-development activities. About 90 percent of the households in the trekking areas now have their own toilets and regular village clean-up campaigns (Annapurna Conservation Area Project 1995). Extra income has allowed children to be relieved from farm or domestic work and to attend nearby schools. Furthermore, the extra training received by external intervention has encouraged women to pursue further enterprise-building activities.

Education is an outstanding change in the overall aspect of women's roles in Alta Cima, particularly with regard to the ability to send children—especially female children—to secondary school full time (Saucedo 1999; Reyes 1999). Without a secondary school in Alta Cima, children must attend the nearest school several hours walk down the mountain in another town, if their parents can afford it. Parents must pay for tuition and uniforms for their children to attend these schools. Often parents must also pay for their children to live in the other town during the week while school is in session. Secondary-school-age girls especially benefit from the activities of their mothers. The new-found ability to send children to school through the earnings that tourism brings strengthens the chances that women of future generations will have more control over their lives.

Strengthening of Women's Groups and Conservation Efforts

The link between conservation and women's participation in tourism increasingly has become recognized at the national and international policy levels, and to a lesser extent at the level of practice. Through the case studies it becomes clear that women hold the ability to steward mountain biomes indirectly through their participation in mountain-based enterprises related to tourism, most notably ecotourism.

The arrival of tourism in the isolated mountain communities of Greece has sparked women's interest in conservation efforts. The women of Dadia and Prespa have involved themselves as ecoguides and environmental educators for visiting school children. Younger women have sought additional training in forestry or similar fields in order to contribute more substantially to the conservation of the protected areas.

In Annapurna and Alta Cima the traditional women's groups have allowed women to mobilize and motivate the community to carry out various development activities, including those related to conservation. Clean-up campaigns and tree-plantation programs are some of the examples of conservation efforts. In Alta Cima women grow a variety of native ornamental plants in a small nursery next to the restaurant. The nursery, in such close proximity to the tourist hub of the reserve, encourages tourists to purchase plants for a small fee rather than illegally gather them from the surrounding forest. Likewise, the women tend to the feeding and care of two threatened bird species found in the reserve. They charge tourists a fee to photograph the birds, which in turn leads to the perpetuation of a program to reproduce the species.

Input on Policies and Decision Making

A solid indicator of the degree of success a gender-based project has on a community is the extent to which women provide input on policies and engage in decision-making activities. In many mountain regions around the world this remains the goal (Byers and Sainju 1994), while in others it is slowly becoming a reality. The women in Alta Cima, for example, not only meet tourists face to face because of their projects, they also have input on more overarching policies that govern the actions of tourists in the reserve. Several women represented residents of El Cielo Biosphere Reserve in a facilitated ecotourism management workshop in 1997. The goal of the workshop was to give residents the opportunity to develop guidelines for tourism use and access in the reserve. In another policy-setting situation, a woman represents the women's co-op in the Campesino Development Association of El Cielo Biosphere Reserve. This group works cooperatively to develop action strategies among the geographically disparate communities within the reserve.

By contrast, however, while the women's groups in Annapurna have been very successful in mobilizing the community in clean-up campaigns and plantation programs, they have not been able to fully participate in the community's main decision-making processes, which are still very male dominated. There are a few isolated examples in which women from affluent families have been able to do so.

Constraints and Opportunities for Integrating Women in Mountain Tourism Production

The constraints and opportunities for integrating women into projects promoting tourism production are varied and dependent on the local context and priorities of each region. In general, however, these constraints and opportunities correspond to those listed by Byers and Sainju (1994); namely, access to information, resources, and decision making; gender awareness and institutional support; and availability of trained or professional women. From the case studies cited, four related constraints and/or opportunities seem present in determining the involvement of women in tourism production: (1) preexisting socioeconomic, cultural, and caste structures present in society; (2) the degree of family and spouse involvement in community activities; (3) the degree of isolation of community; and (4) the degree of external intervention.

Preexisting Socioeconomic, Cultural, and Caste Structures in Society

The degree to which women across a mountain region (as in the cases of Annapurna and Greece) or within a single mountain community (as in the case of Alta Cima) are involved in tourism production is highly dependent on the various cultures of the regions, on the socioeconomic class of each woman involved, and, where applicable, on the caste structure present. In the case of Annapurna, the benefits of tourism have been greater for the women from affluent families and higher castes, who are able to run or even own lodges. However, tourism has created more choices and economic opportunities for women from the lower castes, from those who work as porters to the few who own lodges and teashops. Further, these women are in a better position to negotiate better working conditions with their employers. Yet for many women, especially those of lower castes, the problems of low demand for local products among the tourists, quality control, irregular supply, marketing, and lack of seed money to start enterprises restrict full participation in trekking tourism. It becomes apparent, then, that women in mountain regions, while characterized as a subgroup of society, are not a homogenous entity, a consideration essential for effective policy development and project planning.

It might be noted, however, that while there is disparity within the same gender groups in the Annapurna region, some lower-caste individuals have become owners of lodges and teashops. With the ability to run tourism enterprises and with training received from external intervention, lower-caste women are given greater respect than usual from the higher castes. This suggests that tourism could be a vehicle for bringing women of different castes onto similar planes.

Degree of Family Involvement in Community Activities

From the case of women tourism producers in Alta Cima, it is suggested that the degree to which men are involved in tourism or in community activities may affect the extent to which women are able or willing to participate in tourism activities. As previously mentioned, two women from the Alta Cima cooperative experienced difficulties maintaining their households to their husbands' standards and were subsequently no longer able to participate. The husbands of these two women were not participants in the local men's cooperative or active participants in community-development activities, unlike the husbands of most of the women in the co-op, who were active in their community. This suggests a potential correlation between the success of the individual woman in cooperative settings with the success of their husbands in similar settings. This potential relationship is something to be considered in the replication of such cooperative endeavors in other locations. That is, it may be the case that the women succeeded in part due to the recognition by their male counterparts that they were making a contribution to the family by working outside of the home. Women's and men's cooperatives should be thought of as two parts of a whole in any community-development activity.

Degree of Isolation of Community

As previously mentioned, mountain communities are characterized in part by their isolation from urban centers and hence from information and ideas that might catalyze change. As such, the degree to which the lives of women have been transformed through ecotourism may depend on how isolated the mountain communities are. The cases of two protected areas, Prespa and Dadia, illustrate the range of response that can be observed in a relatively short number of years. Both areas have established and operated women's cooperatives that have become models for the wider region. In Prespa, the first women's cooperative in the village of Aghios Germanos was followed by another in the village of Psarades, and new cooperatives are being established in two other remote mountain villages within the national park boundaries. As this is one of the most isolated areas of Greece, at the borders of Albania and the former Yugoslavia in the northwest, the participation of local women has not fundamentally changed gendered roles in families and communities, with the exception of the respective directors of the first two women's cooperatives. In both cases, these women were single, independent women, divorced with children, and relatively self-sufficient. This is not the case with most of the other women who participate in the cooperatives, who see their employment only as a means to add income for the family, income that is still for the most part handled exclusively by the men in the family (Malakou 1999). By contrast, in Dadia, a village close to the important urban center of Alexandroupolis and other municipal administrative centers such as the town of Soufli, the traditional roles of women are changing rapidly. Galvanized by the expanding social, intellectual, and commercial activities that have become available through the promotion and implementation of ecotourist activities, younger women are seeking further education and training in professions that can be applied in the local area. Some are even delaying marriage and child rearing, following the pattern of urban women in Greece (Pistolas 1999).

Degree of External Intervention

A fourth factor determining the success of women's participation in tourism production is the external aid given by outside agencies, most notably NGOs. The involvement of various NGOs in Annapurna, Prespa, Dadia, and Alta Cima has allowed the women in these rural mountain regions to receive the training and education necessary for their involvement and subsequent rise in self-esteem and, in some cases, status.

The one-week integrated lodge-management training organized annually by the Annapurna Conservation Area Project (ACAP) for lodge and teashop owners of the area is a case in point. ACAP has allowed women to receive training in the use of local materials for food preparation, waste disposal, first aid, and the use of alternative energy, as well as education in English and hospitality. Due to this training, the women of the region now separate garbage into biodegradable and nonbiodegradable pits, a system that motivates them to conserve natural resources and, by extension, helps attract conservation-minded tourists to their lodges.

In Alta Cima, the NGO Terra Nostra initiated a communitywide rural assessment program funded by various international entities. This program resulted in an action plan based on a series of workshops in which women had substantial representation and input. This plan outlined local problems and achievable solutions. It also outlined general projects, quality-of-life programs, conservation proposals, and potential funding sources to serve as solutions to the problems identified. To date, most of the projects and programs have been implemented. Though this intervention was community based and not specifically women oriented, women significantly benefitted.

In both Prespa and Dadia the nascent ecotourism activities could not have taken hold without external aid. First of all, conservation NGOs such as the World Wildlife Fund provided funding during crucial periods between European Union programs to support ecoguides or wardens for the protected areas. Later, state development funds actively supported women's cooperatives by providing training sessions, linking local cooperatives with other areas of Greece, and by supporting the expansion of infrastructure, such as guest houses and information centers.

RECOMMENDATIONS FOR POLICY, PRACTICE, AND RESEARCH REGARDING WOMEN AND MOUNTAIN TOURISM

With regard to the development of mountain-tourism enterprises, women must be brought in from the periphery and fully included in policy, decision making, and project design and implementation. This is especially true where tourism is linked to conservation in mountain regions, as women are often the primary keepers of mountain environmental knowledge (Byers and Sainju 1994). From the case studies presented in this chapter, it becomes clear that the following areas need increasing attention in policy, practice, and research related to mountain tourism.

Recommendations for Policy and Practice

Support of Alternative Rural Occupations

Support of alternative rural occupations at local, regional, and national levels, including mountain-tourism enterprise development and women's participation therein, is of tremendous importance for the advancement of women in rural mountain areas. With alternative occupations comes a break from traditional labor roles and hence the possibility to break free from cultural norms that can keep women from exerting greater control over their lives.

Greek government policy, as well as overall EU regional-development trends, are beginning to favor the support of alternative rural occupations, hence increasing the capacity of women to step outside of traditional roles and, in certain situations, increasing their chances of improving their quality of living. This is justified, on the one hand, to relieve the overwhelming concentration in urban centers, which has rendered the two major Greek cities, Athens and Thessaloniki, difficult to live in; on the other hand, it rejuvenates the rural population by providing occupations other than agriculture and stock raising. Products from these traditional agricultural activities are considered as surplus within the EU and subsidies are steadily declining. Thus, mountain tourism, agrotourism, and ecotourism have been identified as growing sectors to be funded by the EU in strategic plans produced by government services (Ministry of the Environment 1999).

National and regional policies are therefore working in tandem with local women's initiatives in rural mountain areas of Greece having already shown success, such as Dadia and Prespa. These serve as models for other rural women all over the country as a means to provide viable, part-time occupations to women without abandoning their traditional roles in their homes and families.

Development of Credit Programs

Working hand in hand with the support of rural occupations is the development of credit programs that might allow women to obtain capital for start-up projects and enterprises. According to Jacobson (1992), credit, along with education, training, and land ownership, may be key to giving women greater control over their lives. Credit programs have given the women of Alta Cima a financial resource used for capital improvement, as well as operations and maintenance. While Mexico does not have special assistance programs designed specifically to aid rural women in developing ecotourism-oriented projects, they do have limited credit programs for women in general, and the state of Tamaulipas, within which the reserve lies, has a women's solidarity-grant program and a rural women's program.

Credit programs need not always provide extensive capital to be effective. Small amounts of credit can lead to new opportunities. For example, a government-credit program to fund purchases of simple photovoltaic power systems allowed the restaurant in Alta Cima to extend hours past dark during winter months. The small power system provides light for the kitchen, too, making it a safer working environment for women. A citizen's band radio also runs off of the power, providing communication to the health clinic in the valley below the community.

Credit programs must be appropriate for women in remote mountain regions, though, in order to provide opportunity. Micro-credit programs in general in India have been reported to charge interest rates of up to 30 percent to individual borrowers despite the 95 percent repayment rate (Indian Economy Overview 1997).

Increased Training for Women

Women in rural mountain regions generally lack training or experience serving the public, much less trying to communicate with unsympathetic tourists. Often, one of the missing aspects to the development of the services that women provide tourists is training in service-oriented job skills. Skill-based training has been noted to be essential to the success of tourism in mountain regions (Banskota in Godde 1999), and to the advancement of women in particular (Lama 1999).

Coupled with training in service skills is the need for basic management and business-operation skills. Business tasks (such as developing and keeping simple financial records or financial planning and forecasting for seasonal fluctuations, often found in ecotourism) must be part of an enterprise-development program from the outset. Although women can often manage without service-oriented and business-skills training, their enterprises would flourish and growth pains could be minimized if such training were available. Moreover, the success rate of such projects would likely increase.

A secondary training issue is that of natural-resource management and interpretation. Many women-operated projects (such as restaurants, stores, and teahouses) become informal, yet important, local clearinghouses for mountain travelers. If the women operating these businesses can knowledgeably interpret environmental issues and/or regulations with a sense of authority, they serve as spokeswomen for conservation and preservation. Thus, they bring women as ecotourism producers closer to sustainable conservation efforts that they can model for their communities and tourists alike. A case in point is the women's cooperative in Alta Cima, Mexico. The Ecotienda La Fé is a natural gathering point for tourists. When the women can efficiently and effectively interpret environmental issues, they can also lead visitors to information on the field interpretation and guide services of the men's cooperative. In a sense, the women's knowledge of environmental issues and their ability to speak with the public on these issues leads to an informal promotion of the interpretation, guide, and pack-animal business the men operate. This promotion leads to revenue for the men, and thus greater welfare for the entire community. When women have such knowledge and skills, they have power to direct visitors to certain activities, thus increasing local profits. This power establishes the women as respected community participants, if not leaders.

Holistic Community Capacity Building to
Promote the Condition of Women

Anecdotal evidence from the mountain regions discussed in this chapter, as well as other mountain regions (e.g., see Godde 1999; Lama 1999), suggests the success of women's participation in mountain tourism has been due in part to communitywide capacity-building efforts that recognize the potential of women in the early stages. When entire mountain communities, or the primary "spark plugs" in communities, become involved in capacity building, women are given the opportunity to take on leadership roles. Quantitative questions remain as to how much influence communitywide efforts have on women's success in developing ecotourism-oriented enterprises. Are women more successful when spearheading efforts alone, or should ecotourism capacity-building programs focus on the momentum that women can provide for communitywide endeavors?

Recommendations for Research

Analysis of Women Producer–Consumer Relations

Contributing the introductory article to the special edition of *Annals of Tourism Research*, Swain (1995) tackles a number of questions and issues related to gender. In her critique of an earlier book on gender and tourism by Kinnaird, Kothari, and Hall (1994), she acknowledges that their five-point map for future research has significant validity. This "map" is laid out as (1) how tourism development interacts with the socioeconomic, political, environmental, and cultural aspects of a society, creating pluralism instead of dualisms; (2) how societies construct the "environment"; (3) how men and women construct power within their gendered realms; (4) how gender relations change for both hosts and guests through tourism; and (5) how these change in relation to the different types of tourism. While the stories from the field presented in this chapter lead to an understanding of the first and, at least partially, fourth areas of study with regard to mountain regions, there is still a greater need to understand how men and women consume mountain tourism, and how this consumption effects female hosts in mountain regions. There is also a need to understand the relation between women as consumers of tourism in mountain regions and as producers, and particularly the levels of influence each plays upon the other. As suggested, women who play opposing roles can influence each other's thoughts and actions once they recognize their connection through "femaleness."

Inclusion of Symbolic Analysis

From the preceding, it becomes clear that, fundamentally, there is a need to understand how different people construct the world in which they live, including both the natural environment and power relations. Hence, and in line with Byers and Sainju's (1994) recommendation that facilitating women's participation in projects requires an understanding of the local context, there is a greater need to adopt approaches of study that allow for the understanding of the symbolic world of a society (Swain 1995). The spheres in which women move through tourism in their country need to be further studied to understand how newly achieved spheres of activity are valued within the context of their geographical location and unique cultures.

CONCLUSION

At a time when mountain environments are becoming ever more popular for travelers and when women's betterment worldwide is a growing concern, it becomes essential to examine the extent to which and in what manner women produce and consume mountain tourism. The case studies in this chapter were selected to examine the effect that the production of mountain tourism has on the lives of women. While mountain-tourism production is specific in terms of the geological constraints therein, it may well be representative of tourism in other developing regions, as the characteristics of limited access to information and education are often shared. As such, the concern with integrating women in tourism production may not be limited to mountain regions, but instead may extend to many developing regions throughout the world.

That tourism production potentially can enhance the lives of women seems clear, particularly through improved self-esteem, status, workloads, family health, education, conservation efforts, and participation in decision making. In addition, although the degree to which women in mountain regions, and perhaps in developing regions generally, are empowered by tourism is difficult to discern from an objective viewpoint, tourism production can provide women with a means to realize some of their strengths and gain a voice in their communities. As women come to manage tourism enterprises, they gain a sense of self that is otherwise difficult to achieve within rural constraints. This typically extends to the well-being of the family, the community, and the natural environment as well. The same appears to be equally true of women who consume mountain tourism. Metaphors that equate climbing a mountain to achieving a goal may also be understood literally, as women who trek, kayak, or climb in mountain regions may achieve personal goals as well as heightened self-confidence and esteem. The sense of vast space and time that comes with visiting mountain areas can also strengthen reflection and provide meditation, a component of healthy living that many women lack. In general, however, it is clear that further research on women as producers and consumers of mountain tourism and on the interaction and influence between women from each group is necessary for the purpose of improving the quality of women's lives globally.

As both consumers and producers in a world economy and their own mountain economies, women form a significant force that requires heightened consideration in policy and practice in mountain tourism. Only through gender-sensitive policies and practices can the full potential of mountain tourism be reached and women given greater control over their lives.

NOTES

1. Members of the occupational castes in the Hindu caste system are blacksmiths, tailors, or shoemakers. With the stigma attached to these occupations and the easy and cheap availability of ready-made goods, these groups are abandoning their traditional occupations and today form the main workforce (outdoor) of the area.

2. Lower-income groups are mainly the families whose men are not in the army or working overseas. In the context of the Annapurna region, they are usually the Brahimins and Chettris, who are from the higher caste and form minority groups. They are usually well-educated and work as teachers or are employed in other government services.

REFERENCES

Annapurna Conservation Area Project. (1995). *Annual Progress Report.* Kathmandu, Nepal: Author.

Benitez, E. B. (1999). Personal communication with author.

Blum, A. (1980). *Annapurna, a Woman's Place.* San Francisco: Sierra Club Books.

Byers, E., and M. Sainju. (1994). Mountain ecosystems and women: Opportunities for sustainable development and conservation. *Mountain Research and Development* 14 (3): 213–228.

Garay, A. S. (1999). Personal communication with author.

Godde, P. M. (Ed.). (1999). Community-based mountain tourism; practices for linking conservation with enterprise. Summary report of the Mountain Forum e-conference, April–May 1998, the Mountain Institute, Franklin, West Virginia.

Gurung, D. (1995). *Tourism and Gender: Impacts and Implications of Tourism on Nepalese Women.* Discussion Paper Series no. MEI 95/3. Kathmandu, Nepal: International Centre for Integrated Mountain Development.

Indian Economy Overview. (1997). Microcredit: Band-aid or wound? Accessed 26 October 1999. Available <http://www.ieo.org/kav001.html>.

Jacobson, J. L. (1992). *Gender Bias: Roadblock to Sustainable Development.* Special ed. Washington, D.C.: Worldwatch Institute.

Kinnaird, V., U. Kothari, and D. Hall. (1994). Tourism: Gender perspectives. In *Tourism: A Gender Analysis,* edited by V. Kinnaird and D. Hall. Chichester: Wiley.

Lama, W. B. (1999). Community-based tourism for conservation and women's development. In *Tourism and Development in Mountain Regions,* edited by P. Godde, M. Price, and F. Zimmermann. Wallingford: CAB International.

Malakou, M. (1999). Personal communication with author.

Medellín Morales, S., and A. Contreras. (1994). *Plan comunitario de manejo de recursos naturales del ejido Alta Cimas [Alta Cimas community natural re-*

source management plan]. Proyecto ¡Organizate! Ciudad Victoria: Instituto de Ecologia, A.C. and Terra Nostra, A.C.

Medellín Morales, S., and C. E. González Romo. (1999). Microempresa rural y desarrollo sustentable desde la perspectiva etnobiologica en la reserva de la Biosfera El Cielo, Tamaulipas [Rural microenterprise and sustainable development from the ethnobiological perspective in El Cielo Biosphere Reserve, Tamaulipas]. Paper presented at the XXII Congreso Annual de la Society of Ethnobiology, Oaxaca, Oaxaca, Mexico.

Mindspring Enterprise. (1998). Adventures for women: A Web hosting success story. *Spring Times Newsletter* 1 (3): 11.

Ministry of the Environment. (1995). *Greece: Ecological and Cultural Resources. Facts, Actions and Programmes for the Protection of the Environment.* Athens: Author.

Ministry of the Environment. (1999). *Community Support Program 1994–1999: Subprogram 3, Management and Protection of the Natural Environment.* Athens: Author.

Nepal, S. (1990). Tourism induced environmental change in the Nepalese Himalaya. Ph.D. diss., Center for Development and Environment, Institute of Geography, University of Bern, Switzerland.

Papagaroufali, E. (1986). *The Woman Farmer and Women's Cooperatives.* Athens: Mediterranean Women's Studies Institute.

Pistolas, K. (1999). Personal communication with author.

Rao, N. (1998). India's mountain women kept in the background. In *Sustainability in Mountain Tourism*, edited by P. East, K. Luger, and K. Inmann. Innsbruck, New Delhi, and Studienverlag: Book Faith India.

Reyes, M. (1999). Personal communication with author.

Romo, C. G. (1999). Personal communication with author.

Saucado, S. (1999). Personal communication with author.

Sfikas, G. (1991). *Epirus.* Athens: Kedros.

Swain, M. B. (1995). Gender in tourism. *Annals of Tourism Research* 22: 247–266.

Tsartas, P., and M. Thanopoulou. (1994). *Women's Cooperatives in Greece: An Evaluation of their Operation.* Athens: Mediterranean Women's Studies Institute.

Valaoras, G., N. A. Pistola, and A. K. Pistola. (1999). The role of women in the conservation and development of the Dadia Forest Reserve. In *Gender and Tourism, Women's Employment and Participation in Tourism*, edited by M. Hemmati. London: United Nations Commission on Sustainable Development/UNED-UK.

Valaoras, V. G. (1976). The Greek village (its history, contribution and decline). *Nea Estia* 100: 925–929.

Valaoras, V. G. (1980). *The Population of Greece in the Second Half of the 20th Century.* Athens: Methodological Studies, National Statistical Service of Greece.

Walker, S. (1996). Ecotourism impact awareness. *Annals of Tourism Research* 23: 944–945.

World Tourism Organization. (1998). *Global Code of Ethics for Tourism.* Article 2, Point 2. Available <http://www.world-tourism.org>.

11

Gender Relations in Tourism: Revisiting Patriarchy and Underdevelopment

Dallen J. Timothy

Today the world is experiencing unparalleled levels of economic and political transformation. Borders that once restricted the flow of goods and people are becoming obsolete, and the functions of many have shifted from military defense and economic protectionism to lines of friendship and cooperation. These changes, coupled with people's improved standard of living and rapid advances in technology, have created a smaller world where few places remain unaffected by global changes in politics, economics, and tourism. Recent advances in transportation technology have enabled throngs of people to travel to exotic places that for many years were only within the grasp of a few individuals. As a result, few places exist in the world today that have not been influenced in some way by tourism. This, coupled with the fact that many of the most spectacular remnants of ancient civilization, natural endowments, cultural traditions, and beaches are located in developing countries, has created conditions of rampant tourism growth in the less developed world during the past thirty years. Increasingly, developing countries are turning to tourism as a way of earning much needed foreign currency and increasing employment levels.

Despite rapid globalization, which can be defined as the processes by which the world becomes a single place (Robertson 1990), an obvious division still exists between the developed and developing world. Within the developing world, the chasm is growing between the rich and the poor in economic terms as the rich get richer, and the gender partition in economic and social terms is still wide. These differences are most obvious in the roles that women play as producers of tourism. While women's domain traditionally has been domestic in nature, the growth of tourism (although not tourism alone) has provided increasingly more opportunities for women to become employed outside the home, although there is a clear gender bias toward males in the workforce. Also, although increasingly more women in the developed world are traveling for business and pleasure, this prospect for women in developing countries is still rather low.

This concluding chapter attempts to highlight some of the prominent concepts and issues that were introduced in the previous ten chapters. The first section briefly reexamines the primary themes. The second part attempts to draw out additional themes that were alluded to either implicitly or explicitly by the authors and raises important concerns that might be answered through additional research.

WOMEN AND TOURISM IN DEVELOPING REGIONS

The contributors to this text have made it abundantly clear that the role of women in tourism in developing countries is a complex phenomenon that encompasses multitudinous perspectives on gender, tradition, economic development, culture, politics, and choice. These issues influence the role of women as both producers and consumers of tourism. In concert with the overall framework of the book, this section treats women as producers and consumers of tourism separately.

Women as Producers of Tourism

The most prevalent theme in the production of tourism is women and employment. Millions of women in the less developed world are employed either directly or indirectly in tourism. In most cases, however, men prevail in the workforce, which is a reflection of the traditional socioeconomic patriarchy in communities worldwide. While male dominion in the labor force and in most decision-making capacities is the norm in the developing world, it is also very much the case in developed regions (e.g., North America and Western Europe), where gender equity goals are only now beginning to be realized.

Men and women play different parts in the production of tourism. Where women are employed in the industry, they tend to be concentrated in positions that mirror their traditional domestic roles: cooks, cleaners, caregivers, and entertainers. While there are some exceptions (e.g., the British Virgin Islands example in this volume), men commonly earn more and are valued more in their decision-making capacities and social standing in less developed nations, another reflection of the male-centered managerial domain that exists in much of the world.

In the developing world, much of the female economic province outside the home takes place in the informal sector (Aspaas 1998). Likewise, in tourism most working women are employed in the informal sector, where their efforts are often trivialized through a lack of official recognition. Men, on the other hand, are more often employed in the formal sector, which is recognized, encouraged, and supported by public agencies. This situation, along with the fact that informal-sector ventures are illegal in some places (Timothy and Wall 1997), further marginalizes the status of womanhood and contributes to the pervasive view that female employees are more superfluous than men and therefore stand little chance of making it to the top managerial ranks.

Very often, development indicators such as education level and fertility rate determine the extent to which women can work outside the home. While men usually have better access to training and education in developing regions, women are sometimes required to be more educated than men to do the same job, which can act as a gender-filter mechanism, particularly since women are not as encouraged to seek formal education. Even when women have higher levels of education, they are usually paid less than men for doing the same work (Cukier and Wall 1995). In regions with high birthrates, it becomes difficult for women who have several children to consider working outside the home. If such opportunities do exist, they are likely to be, as mentioned previously, in the informal sector, with little job security and miniscule wages. Formal-sector jobs may be less accessible, since some managers might prefer to hire childless women.

Outside commentators and destination residents alike often equate women's employment in tourism with empowerment. This is partially a faulty assumption, for participation in the benefits of tourism rarely assures participation in decision making and policy formulation, as some of the cases in this book have demonstrated. The type of empowerment created by tourism employment is on a personal level, where more independence and financial autonomy are the common result. Bras and Dahles (1998) found that many women in Bali prefer involvement with tourism to activities in agriculture or domestic trade because they earn more money. In this sense, tourism does provide new possibilities for formerly disadvantaged women, but little has yet been accomplished to the advantage of women in the realm of policy making.

In some cultures women must be chaperoned when in the company of men, and women are encouraged (or compelled) not to drive or venture far from home. These traditions restrict the types of employment that can be undertaken. A woman would be hard pressed to find work as a guide or driver under these conditions. Work as vendors or guest-house employees may be much easier to find. Similarly, it is often the women's place to keep the closest ties with extended family, home, and village life. As a result, they are more likely than men to return to their villages for important religious and family occasions. This undoubtedly affects their capacity to work in certain occupations. In this way, traditional gender roles determine what types of employment are most suitable or even possible for women (Cukier and Wall 1995; Feldman 1992).

Another example of the role of cultural traditions in determining women's work in tourism is that in some cultures a woman's social stature and familial value increase when she is employed in tourism. In other cultures it is frowned upon and women are viewed as unfeminine and of lesser value. This is dangerous, for whenever a material or financial value is placed on gender in any context repellent practices may follow (e.g., female infanticide and clitoridectomy).

Clearly the underlying reason for these issues of inequity is the traditional patriarchal order of social dominance, decision making, and culture that exists in much of the developing world (and is still common in much of the developed world). Views of power concentration are still very strong in traditional societies, and they continue to influence local political structures and social standards. These conventions accept that control rests in the hands of a central social figure or a privileged few (Anderson 1972; Brown 1994; Harrison 1992) who, out of concern for the potential loss of control, are reluctant to submit to efforts that might redistribute power (Reed 1997). In most cases the central figures of power are men who dictate their own roles and those of women. Resistance by a woman (or her male sympathizers) rarely surface because rebellion against the norm would insult the central power and bring dishonor to her family (Anderson 1972).

Another prominent theme in this text is the portrayal of women as consumable product. Appealing to sexual desire is one of the advertising industry's most prominent approaches to selling products today. This tactic has been utilized in the promotion of tourism just as much as in any other industry, and perhaps even more. In terms of promotional campaigns and their accompanying literature, the image created is clearly gender biased. According to Pritchard and Morgan (2000), "The language and imagery of promotion privilege the male, heterosexual gaze above all others" (p. 885). They also argue that travel has traditionally been characterized in terms of masculine ideas of pleasure, exoticness, and adventure, "while femininity has been defined in opposition to independent experience, revolving instead around notions of domesticity" (p. 886). Promotional literature often uses "body shots" (photographs of beautiful young women) to promote the sensual nature of exotic destinations and to highlight the potential "rewards" of visiting (Heatwole 1989).

Much of the travel literature from developing countries continues to reinforce traditional images of women as dutiful and submissive companions for men. A study by Sirakaya and Sönmez (2000) supports the discussions in this book by concluding that "women are portrayed unrealistically—even if with little conscious intent—in printed tourism advertising" (p. 361). They found women to be portrayed disproportionately more in traditional stereotypical poses (i.e., submissive, overly subordinate, dependent on men) than men. This, Sirakaya and Sönmez contend, is a clear visual manifestation of power relations in the context of gender relations.

These traditions and practices, commentators argue, are rooted in the masculine desire to possess and control, where women become objects of dominion, remain submissive to the male tourist, and in effect are consumed by men in destination areas. As a result, gendered tourism spaces are created, where women must behave differently from men and where the product being offered to men is different from the one offered to women. For example, Pritchard and Morgan (2000) conclude that destinations all throughout the world cater primarily to men. The northern destinations, they argue, present an unmistakable male slant in advertising, being more in tune with the adventurous outdoors(man), while the southern and eastern exotic destinations are explicitly gendered (male oriented) in their appeal, featuring women as the product.

Another example of gendered space is the tourist districts in Mexican cities along the U.S. border. Here, prostitution developed rapidly during the U.S. prohibition era (1918–1933), and continued to grow far into the twentieth century, particularly during World War II, when dozens of U.S. military installations were established near the border (Timothy 2001). These Mexican frontier towns developed as "convenient yet foreign playgrounds, tantalizingly near but beyond the prevailing morality and rule of law north of the border" (Curtis and Arreola 1991, 340). By the 1970s this gendered tourist space had so developed that guides were even published to assist American men in finding hot spots all along the border where their every fantasy could be realized. Of Nuevo Loredo's red light district, one publication suggested,

The one entrance and exit is carefully supervised by Nuevo Loredo's finest. Girls come from all over Mexico to work in the four or five nicest places. This is the best on the border. . . . Most unique and pleasing structurally, both in building and clientele, is the *Tamyko,* a huge Japanese pagoda with outside patio and fishponds spanned by arched bridges, surrounded on two levels by bedrooms. The girls are almost all between 14 and 18 years old. (West 1973, 73)

Prostitution is perhaps the most powerful example of gendered space and women as producers of tourism, and many developing destinations, like the Mexican example, have become notorious for it. In the early 1990s, despite the AIDS scare, males comprised over 65 percent of foreign tourists entering Thailand, and over 85 percent of Western, Middle Eastern, and Asian male tourists came for the expressly declared purpose of "holidays," which were most likely sex oriented (Askew 1998). Some NGOs estimate that upward of 1 million women are involved in the Thai sex trade (Askew 1998). The predominance of prostitution tourism has been so strong that much of the urban milieu of Bangkok, for example, has been transformed into red-light districts for the pleasure of men.

Women as Consumers of Tourism

Much less is known or written about women as consumers of tourism, although evidence demonstrates that women traveling for business comprise one of the industry's fastest-growing market segments. Women experience travel, whether for business or pleasure, in the context of a male-dominated industry; therefore women must go out of their way to create their own space and be recognized as equal consumers of a similar product but with individual needs. For example, Westwood, Pritchard, and Morgan (2000) found several differences in male and female perceptions of airline services and marketing. Their research also suggests that male and female travelers' needs are different. However, most airlines (and probably other service suppliers) adopt a gender-neutral approach in service provision, which ultimately favors the needs of men over women. Other studies, however, show that while gender differences may determine preferences of adults, among young tourists gender has little to do with activity and destination choice (Carr 1999).

Similarly, male and female roles as tourists are often different, particularly when children are involved. For instance, when women travel, especially with children, their tasks often become an extension of their roles at home: caregiver, cleaner, and cook. Thus, their holidays rarely resemble a leisure pursuit, while men's holiday time is more notably leisured.

The subject of women from developing countries as tourists is notably lacking in the tourism literature, although some of the authors here examined it in some detail. Economics and culture tend to be the two primary constraints on women traveling from and within the developing world. In most traditional societies, aside from trade and visiting relatives, travel is alien to indigenous practices: people in less-developed regions, women in particular, tend not to be leisure minded. For them it would be ridiculous to travel for pleasure when their primary concern is basic survival. Excess funds are a rarity and would be used for something more important, like education and clothing for their families. In any case, there is always too much to do around the house or at their place of employment. Furthermore, even if they could afford to travel domestically, they often lack interest in the types of attractions that typically appeal to tourists.

Likewise, as discussed earlier, in many traditional societies being feminine means staying close to home. In these societies women's travel is discouraged and becomes difficult in light of the fact that they are not permitted to drive or travel unescorted by a chaperone.

Women in developing countries are, however, receiving more opportunities to travel, with the exception of those in the lowest socioeconomic classes. Globalization processes, economic improvements, and recent shifts to more service-based, high-tech economies have brought about the growth of a sizable middle class and a more widespread distribution of wealth in many developing regions. This has resulted in more women being able to travel for pleasure. It has also resulted in women gaining employment in higher-paying jobs with more leadership responsibilities. For example, although still limited by masculine traditions, more women are becoming employed in lower-order leadership positions in Indonesia. In my interviews with women at one province's department of tourism, I learned that more women who previously had never been abroad were seeing opportunities to travel on business trips at least. One woman who had never traveled outside Indonesia was given an opportunity to visit Singapore. For her this was the experience of a lifetime.

REDEFINING GENDER ROLES IN TOURISM: A FUTURE AGENDA

The aim of this section is to discuss issues and concepts that were alluded to throughout the text or seem to flow naturally from the previous discussion, and which are in need of additional research attention.

In Chapter 2, Gibson highlights some important questions about women as consumers of tourism, but little else is known about women travelers, their use of space, their interests and desires, and how these differ from those of men. The needs, motivations, and impacts of female business and leisure travelers, whether with other women, as individual travelers, or with men, have all but been ignored (Johns 1997; Westwood, Pritchard, and Morgan 2000). This is clearly an area in desperate need of additional examination.

While there has been increased interest in recent years surrounding the issue of gender and tourism, the perspective of sexuality remains virtually unexplored (Hughes 1997). Issues of sexual orientation have significant implications for personal identity and can result in distinct travel behavior. For example, owing to social taboos that are strong in both developing and developed countries, homosexuals often are able to express their sexuality only in places that are beyond their normal realms of experience (Hughes 1997). Thus, homosexual leisure spaces are created, which allow gays and lesbians to explore their sexual identities without fear of mistreatment. This has recently been manifest in the development of homosexual resorts, gay and lesbian cruises, and travel agencies that focus on the travel needs of this growing market niche.

Sex tourism has long been viewed as a shameful trend that is cruel to women and diminishes their social value, particularly in the developing world. Thus, the exploited fate of female sex workers is usually bemoaned in the gender literature, where men are the predators and women the prey. Jeffreys (1999), for instance, declares that all forms of men's prostitution behavior toward women are sexual violence. She also adamantly argues that "women's 'choice' of prostitution is socially and politically constructed out of poverty, child sexual abuse, homelessness, family obligation" (p. 180). This argument is flawed, of course, and would likely anger many of the female prostitutes in both developed and developing countries who were never abused as children, who are not poverty stricken or homeless, and who have few family obligations to fulfill. Many of the women interviewed by Ryan and Hall (2001) in New Zealand claim to have legitimately "chosen" their occupation, and prostitution unions have been formed to protect the rights of these women. They claim to enjoy their chosen occupation and the lifestyle that goes with it and assert that they find it every bit as intellectually and socially satisfying as they imagine they would find any managerial or academic pursuit (Ryan and Hall 2001). Another study (Askew 1998) found similarities among the sex workers in Thailand, and concluded that "women, at the level of their own life courses, in their work environments and with their customers, are agents, not victims, despite their position in a socio-economic formation which disadvantages them" (p. 146). Askew's comments are telling, because "at the level of their own life courses, in their work environments" reminds us of the context in which these women's choices are made. There are various levels of free choice, and when someone claims to have chosen prostitution, it is important to remember the context of that choice. If, as demonstrated in the rest of this book, many women are constrained in various ways (education, transportation, or even a male-defined concept of self) that significantly impact their occupational choices, to what extent does it make sense to say that they had choices? Clearly, in some subjective sense (their own) they did, but in another, objective sense (the outsider's view, which may be more or less reliable than their own) they did not. This is a complex area, in which philosophical positions may be fruitfully brought to bear upon new research.

Unlike male visitors seeking encounters with local women, which is usually termed sex tourism or prostitution, women tourists' pursuit of sexual encounters with resident men is nearly always referred to in gentler terms, such as "romance tourism," as if to suggest that it is somehow less harmful and motivated by different needs and desires. This attitude, Pritchard and Morgan (2000) indicate, "provides a significant commentary on gender and power relationships in tourism and society, since the terminology implies that when women pay for sexual encounters these are not described in terms which place their male partners in a less powerful position, that is, as prostitution" (p. 889).

These matters beg answers to questions, such as, is it only male prostitutes and tourists who truly have a choice in their occupational pursuits and leisure behavior? What about the plight of homosexual prostitutes? While the growth and continuation of sex tourism would undoubtedly diminish if men would cease participating, the female counterpart would still continue, albeit on a much smaller scale (Dahles 1997). In our academic rhetoric we need to answer questions such as these, but we must take on a more balanced approach to examining sex and tourism and accept the concept of accountability for both genders.

A discussion of sex and tourism, particularly in the context of the less developed world, would not be complete without at least a brief mention of health. That both men and women travel in search of sexual encounters, or happen upon them if conditions are right, has a great deal to do with health. Recent media estimates place the number of AIDS cases in Africa and Asia, for example, in the hundreds of millions. While most of the spread of diseases like AIDS is not tourism related, tourism is assuredly involved. It is generally accepted that people have a tendency to let down their guard when traveling away from home (Mathieson and Wall 1982). This has the potential to contribute to the spread of diseases, particularly from sexual encounters that are unexpected or spontaneous and in which protection is not used. This may be more common among youth, but additional research is needed to confirm this. As long as sex continues to be produced and consumed in tourist destinations, either between hosts and guests or between guests and guests, health should be an important concern for tourism scholars.

Another important concept in the burgeoning gender and tourism arena ought to be how the role of men is changing as women are becoming ever more involved in the production and consumption of tourism. Men are, even in some developing areas, having to take on tasks that have traditionally been regarded as "women's work," such as assisting in household chores, child care, and tending the garden. Without a doubt, for many men this is a threatening prospect. It remains to be seen how traditional gender divisions will evolve as more women become involved in the production of tourism. It is clear from this volume that so far little has changed, and by working outside the home women simply double their workloads, for they are still responsible for completing their daily household tasks. Likewise, the role of children in all of this has been ignored by tourism and gender scholars and ought to be studied as part of the overall changes occurring within the customary family structure.

The research attention now being devoted to the worthy and long-ignored place of gender issues in tourism is remarkable and exciting. Nonetheless, many other traditionally disadvantaged social groups have yet to receive scholarly attention commensurate with their importance. People with disabilities, for instance, comprise an ever-growing cohort of global travelers who have unique needs, expectations, and experiences that must be addressed. Ethnic and racial issues are also important, for tourism in the past has been dominated overwhelmingly by ethnic and racial groups that have controlled political and economic environments since the days of colonialism. Only a small number of racial and ethnic minorities have had equal access to travel. Another point is race and ethnic issues in the production of tourism. How do these genetic characteristics affect accessibility to the economic benefits of tourism and dictate the nature of backward and forward economic linkages? It is the racial and ethnic minorities, along with women, who have traditionally been relegated to the economic and social periphery of tourism. This raises many uncertainties regarding migration and the meaning of nationality.

Likewise, enveloped deeply within the gender debate are additional perspectives on class, race, and nationality that need to be addressed. The division of women's labor into even more biased categories further marginalizes many women based on their ancestral heritage. Thus, even greater divides exist between classes of women. It is not unusual for immigrants or women of an indigenous minority to be consigned to occupations that are considered unsuitable or undesirable for local women (Scott 1995). Sometimes the gaps in employment terms be-

tween classes in these circumstances are even wider than those between men and women.

Much of the gender rhetoric in recent tourism inquiry has focused
on women in the workforce and the feminization of tourist landscapes.
Future discussions need to go beyond this to include additional areas
that can be improved upon to strengthen the lot of women and improve their quality of life. For example, one theme touched upon in
this book is policy and planning. The political rights of women and
their entitlement to participate in tourism planning and decision making are ill-defined in tourism policy. If women, particularly those in
the informal sector, are not heard, their positions become even more
tangential, for with every new regulation their work becomes progressively peripheral (Bras and Dahles 1998). Women must be given a
louder voice in policy making on regional and national levels if the
goals of sustainability (e.g., equity, harmony, balance, cultural and ecological integrity) are to be realized.

Attention also needs to be directed to women who are not employed
in tourism. Although more developing-area women are in the workforce than ever before, the majority of women's work "cannot be adequately understood by looking exclusively at employment categories
of economic and statistical surveys. These relegate to 'nonwork' many
forms of women's labour in society" (Stratigaki and Vaiou 1994, 1221).
Thus, it would be wrong to ignore the work of women who either
choose or are bound by tradition to stay at home. They too, in some
senses, are a part of the tourism product. For these women, and those
who labor in family-run businesses where the work is often unpaid
and without job security, "their difficulties are of a different order but
no less important" (Stratigaki and Vaiou 1994, 1230).

Having said this, while all of these gender issues are vital to consider, and it is important to find ways in which the lives of women
everywhere can be improved, we as scholars must be careful not to
allow our Western, Eurocentric biases alone to dictate our actions in
the developing world. As foreign researchers we often find the gender
divide irresistible and inexcusable, but there is danger in blindly im-
posing our developed-world standards, ideals, and paradigms on traditional societies. Concepts like equity and power distribution are
essentially Western notions that might be met with resistance on the
part of both men and women if not carefully addressed in a culturally
sensitive manner. From a development perspective, therefore, it is critical for tourism developers and scholars to consider local sociocultural
conditions in decision making. As Smith (1985) argues, the social and
political cleavages are great in the developing world, and the policies
devised by elitist players (including foreigners) may be inappropriate

for local circumstances. Empowerment processes are long and tiresome, which is evident from the recent political changes in Eastern Europe. Despite any argument to the contrary, to force Western views upon women (and men) in developing regions in essence decreases their free agency even further and is reminiscent of the dependency and neo-colonialist relationships that have long existed between less developed areas and metropolitan powers (cf. Timothy and Ioannides 2001).

Nonetheless, scholars must also recognize that cultural relativism can only go so far in helping us understand and improve the situation of any segment of a given society that experiences discrimination, harassment, or worse on a systemic basis. There is, after all, a gray area in which some Western "notions" bleed into universally recognized human rights issues. This gray area is growing, as more and more countries sign on to U.N.–sponsored declarations of human rights principles. There are many cultural practices that affect women only, including clitoridectomy and suttee, that are considered by many Westerners to be abhorrent violations of human rights. But when individuals, whether men or women, in the societies that practice these things come to view them as human rights violations, a paradigm shift occurs that cannot be explained solely in terms of the triumph of Western notions. Regardless of whether prostitution ever attains that sort of status, and it is doubtful that it would, many other cultural practices and conditions that affect women's freedom of choice of occupation fall well within the purview of this debate.

CONCLUSION

Gender differences are obvious in the production of tourism in developing countries. Women's work in tourism usually resembles the types of work they have traditionally done in the domestic setting. Women are commonly relegated to positions in the informal sector, earn less than their male counterparts, and are usually underrepresented in policy formulation and decision making for planning. Far less is known about women as consumers of tourism, although evidence suggests that female travelers have different needs and expectations than men have. Travel by female residents of the developing world is virtually nonexistent, for leisure travel is usually an alien concept and funds are scarce. Similarly, since relatively few women ever manage to access top executive positions, business travel is also uncommon.

The term "gender" in contemporary tourism scholarship appears exclusively to mean women. Perhaps this is evidence of a recent escape from the male-dominated subject areas that have driven tourism inquiries in the past. Despite this past, as this review has demonstrated, maleness and changes that have occurred within male identity are also gender issues that should not be ignored. As this volume and others (e.g., Kinnaird and Hall 1994) have stressed, distinct differences and similarities do indeed exist between men and women in the context of tourism. This unbalanced history naturally leads into other as yet unexplored topics, such as race, disability, nationality, sexuality, and socioeconomic class, that particularly within the realm of women's studies makes our research task all the more complex.

Much of what has been written about gender issues and tourism has been descriptive in nature. It is critical for researchers to delve deeper into the symbolic meanings and values ascribed by traditional societies (Pearce, Moscardo, and Ross 1996; Swain 1995) to understand the sociocultural underpinnings and power relations that have created gender disparities. Such relationships have always existed, and developed regions themselves are just now beginning to resolve them. This research genre is important, for gender equity and involvement in tourism is much more than the employment of women in the industry and women as an undifferentiated consumer cohort. Scholars must begin viewing women as key players in an enormous multidimensional system of dependency, empowerment, production, and consumption. This volume represents a step in this direction, but there is more work to be done.

REFERENCES

Anderson, B. (1972). The idea of power in Javanese culture. In *Culture and Politics in Indonesia,* edited by C. Holt. Ithaca, N.Y.: Cornell University Press.

Askew, M. (1998). City of women, city of foreign men: Working spaces and reworking identities among female sex workers in Bangkok's tourist zone. *Singapore Journal of Tropical Geography* 19 (2): 130–150.

Aspaas, H. R. (1998). Heading households and heading businesses: Rural Kenyan women in the informal sector. *Professional Geographer* 50 (2): 192–204.

Bras, K., and H. Dahles. (1998). Women entrepreneurs and beach tourism in Sanur, Bali: Gender, employment opportunities, and government policy. *Pacific Tourism Review* 1: 243–256.

Brown, D. (1994). *The State and Ethnic Politics in Southeast Asia.* London: Routledge.

Carr, N. (1999). A study of gender differences: Young tourist behaviour in a UK coastal resort. *Tourism Management* 20 (2): 223–228.

Cukier, J., and G. Wall. (1995). Tourism employment in Bali: A gender analysis. *Tourism Economics* 1 (4): 389–401.

Curtis, J. R., and D. D. Arreola. (1991). Zonas de tolerancia on the northern Mexican border. *Geographical Review* 81 (3): 333–346.

Dahles, H. (1997). The new gigolo: Globalization, tourism and changing gender identities. *Focaal, Tijdschrift voor Antropologie* 30: 121–137.

Feldman, S. (1992). Crises, poverty and gender inequality. In *Unequal Burden: Economic Crises, Persistent Poverty and Women's Work*, edited by L. Beneria and S. Feldman. Boulder, Colo.: Westview Press.

Harrison, D. (1992). Tradition, modernity and tourism in Swaziland. In *Tourism and the Less Developed Countries*, edited by D. Harrison. London: Belhaven.

Heatwole, C. A. (1989). Body shots: Women in tourism-related advertisements. *Focus* 39 (4): 7–11.

Hughes, H. (1997). Holidays and homosexual identity. *Tourism Management* 18 (1): 3–7.

Jeffreys, S. (1999). Globalizing sexual exploitation: Sex tourism and the traffic in women. *Leisure Studies* 18: 179–196.

Johns, B. H. (1997). Stress-free, safe travel for women. *Delta Kappa Gamma Bulletin* 64 (1): 40–43.

Kinnaird, V., and D. Hall, eds. (1994). *Tourism: A Gender Analysis*. Chichester: Wiley.

Mathieson, A., and G. Wall. (1982). *Tourism: Economic, Physical and Social Impacts*. London: Longman.

Pearce, P. L., G. Moscardo, and G. F. Ross. (1996). *Tourism Community Relationships*. Oxford: Pergamon.

Pritchard, A., and N. J. Morgan. (2000). Privileging the male gaze: Gendered tourism landscapes. *Annals of Tourism Research* 27: 884–905.

Reed, M. G. (1997). Power relations and community-based tourism planning. *Annals of Tourism Research* 24: 566–591.

Robertson, R. (1990). Mapping the global condition: Globalization as the central concept. In *Global Culture: Nationalism, Globalization and Modernity*, edited by M. Featherstone. London: Sage.

Ryan, C., and C. M. Hall. (2001). *Sex Tourism: Liminalities and Marginal People*. London: Routledge.

Scott, J. (1995). Sexual and national boundaries in tourism. *Annals of Tourism Research* 24: 385–403.

Sirakaya, E., and S. Sönmez. (2000). Gender images in state tourism brochures: An overlooked area in socially responsible tourism marketing. *Journal of Travel Research* 38 (4): 353–362.

Smith, T. B. (1985). Evaluating development policies and programmes in the Third World. *Public Administration and Development* 5 (2): 129–144.

Stratigaki, M., and D. Vaiou. (1994). Women's work and informal activities in Southern Europe. *Environment and Planning* A 26: 1221–1234.

Swain, M. B. (1995). Gender in tourism. *Annals of Tourism Research* 22: 247–266.

Timothy, D. J. (2001). *Tourism and Political Boundaries*. London: Routledge.

Timothy, D. J., and D. Ioannides. (2001). Tour operator hegemony: Dependency, oligopoly and sustainability in insular destinations. In *Island Tourism and Sustainable Development: Caribbean, Pacific and Mediterranean Experiences*, edited by Y. Apostolopolous and D. Gayle. Westport, Conn.: Praeger.

Timothy, D. J., and G. Wall. (1997). Selling to tourists: Indonesian street vendors. *Annals of Tourism Research* 24: 322–340.

West, R. (1973). Border towns: What to do and where to do it. *Texas Monthly* 1: 62–73.

Westwood, S., A. Pritchard, and N. J. Morgan. (2000). Gender-blind marketing: Businesswomen's perceptions of airline services. *Tourism Management* 21 (4): 353–362.

Index

About the Editors and Contributors

Yorghos Apostolopoulos is a Research Associate Professor of Sociology, Arizona State University, Tempe, Arizona.

Tracy Berno is a Professor of Tourism Studies, University of the South Pacific, Suva, Fiji.

Antònia Casellas is a Research Associate, Center for Urban Policy Research, Rutgers University, New Brunswick, New Jersey.

Colleen Ballerino Cohen is a Professor of Anthropology and Women's Studies, Vassar College, Poughkeepsie, New York. She is also Chair of the Department of Anthropology at Vassar.

Peter U. C. Dieke is a Senior Lecturer of Tourism, the Scottish Hotel School, University of Strathclyde, Glasgow, Scotland, United Kingdom.

Heather J. Gibson is an Assistant Professor of Recreation, Parks, and Tourism, University of Florida, Gainesville, Florida.

Pam Godde is a Research Associate at the Mountain Institute, a non-profit scientific and educational organization based in Franklin, West

Virginia, committed to the preservation of mountain environments and advancement of mountain cultures around the world.

Dibya Gurung is a Ph.D. candidate at the School of Tourism and Hotel Management at Griffith University, Australia.

Derek R. Hall is a Professor of Regional Development, Head of the Department of Leisure and Tourism Management, the Scottish Agricultural College, Auchincruive, Ayr, Scotland, United Kingdom.

Briavel Holcomb is a Professor, Department of Urban Studies and Community Health, Bloustein School of Planning and Public Policy, Rutgers University, New Brunswick, New Jersey.

Trudy Jones is a Tourism Development Consultant in Christchurch, New Zealand.

Sara Kindon is a Lecturer of Human Geography and Development Studies, Victoria University of Wellington, Wellington, New Zealand.

Sevil Sönmez is an Assistant Professor of Tourism Management, Arizona State University, Tempe, Arizona.

Dallen J. Timothy is an Assistant Professor of Tourism Studies, Arizona State University, Tempe, Arizona.

Georgia Valaoras is an Adjunct Professor, Department of Science and Mathematics, University of La Verne, Athens, Greece.

Scott Walker is a Visiting Professor, Our Lady of the Lake University, San Antonio, Texas.